Open access edition supported by the National Endowment for the Humanities / Andrew W. Mellon Foundation Humanities Open Book Program.

© 2019 Johns Hopkins University Press
Published 2019

Johns Hopkins University Press
2715 North Charles Street
Baltimore, Maryland 21218-4363
www.press.jhu.edu

The text of this book is licensed under a Creative Commons Attribution-NonCommercial-NoDerivatives 4.0 International License: https://creativecommons.org/licenses/by-nc-nd/4.0/.
CC BY-NC-ND

ISBN-13: 978-1-4214-3031-7 (open access)
ISBN-10: 1-4214-3031-2 (open access)

ISBN-13: 978-1-4214-3145-1 (pbk. : alk. paper)
ISBN-10: 1-4214-3145-9 (pbk. : alk. paper)

ISBN-13: 978-1-4214-3146-8 (electronic)
ISBN-10: 1-4214-3146-7 (electronic)

This page supersedes the copyright page included in the original publication of this work.

Patricians and *Popolani*

FOR MY GRANDPARENTS
Arthur and Elizabeth Graf
Lorenzo and Virginia Romano

❧ What is the city, but the People?
True, the people are the city.
— *Coriolanus,* act 3, scene 1

Patricians and Popolani

The Social Foundations of the Venetian Renaissance State

DENNIS ROMANO

THE JOHNS HOPKINS UNIVERSITY PRESS
BALTIMORE AND LONDON

Frontispiece: *Veneration of the Body of Saint Mark.*
Paolo Veneziano and Sons. Cover of the Pala d'oro,
San Marco. Photo: Osvaldo Böhm.

© 1987 The Johns Hopkins University Press
All rights reserved

The Johns Hopkins University Press,
701 West 40th Street, Baltimore, Maryland 21211
The Johns Hopkins Press Ltd., London

This book has been brought to publication with the
generous assistance of the Delmas Foundation.

The paper used in this publication meets the minimum requirements
of American National Standard for Information Sciences—Permanence
of Paper for Printed Library Materials, ANSI Z39.48-1984.

LIBRARY OF CONGRESS CATALOGING-IN-PUBLICATION DATA
Romano, Dennis, 1951–
   Patricians and popolani.
  Bibliography: p.
  Includes index.
  1. Social classes—Italy—Venice—History.
2. Social structure—Italy—Venice—History.
3. Community organization—Italy—Venice—History.
4. Venice (Italy)—History—697-1508. I. Title.
HN490.S6R63 1987   305.5′0945′31   87-2826
ISBN 0-8018-3513-5 (alk. paper)

Contents

List of Illustrations xi

Acknowledgments xiii

ONE Community and Conflict in Early Renaissance Venice 1

TWO Urban Form and Social Stratification: The *Civitas Venetiarum* 12
    The Evolution of the Early Renaissance City 12
    Patricians, *Popolo Grande*, and *Popolo Minuto* 27

THREE Family Structure and Marriage Ties 39
    The Patrician Family 41
    The *Popolano Grande* Family 50
    The *Popolano Minuto* Family 56

FOUR The World of Work: Guild Structure and Artisan Networks 65
    Production Techniques and Guild Structure 66
    The Social World of Venetian Artisans 77

FIVE The Parochial Clergy and Communities of the Sacred 91
    The Parish Clergy as Social Intermediaries 91
    Communities of the Sacred 102

SIX *Vicinanza* and *Amicizia:* Neighborhoods and Patronage in Early Renaissance Venice 119

        Male Patronage: The Development of State-Centered Ties 120

        Neighbors and Friends: Female Patronage 131

SEVEN From Community to Hierarchy: The Transformation of Venetian Social Ties 141

        Venetian Society in the Early Renaissance 142

        From Community to Hierarchy 152

Notes 159

Bibliography 199

Index 215

Illustrations

Figures

3.1 The Badoers 43
3.2 The Dalle Boccole 47
3.3 The Bedolotos 52
3.4 The Reglas 53

Tables

2.1 Breakdown of Wealth in the *Estimo* of 1379 34
2.2 Distribution of Dowry Wealth, 1309–1419 35
3.1 Selection of Fiduciaries among Artisans 58
4.1 Residential Patterns of Furriers 81
5.1 Occupational Composition of *Scuole* 108
5.2 Geographic Distribution of *Scuole* Members 109
7.1 Distribution of Charitable Bequests 153

Plates

1 *Mark's Relics Transferred into Church* 3
2 A Master Furrier and a Worker 37
3 Gentile Bellini, *Procession in Piazza San Marco* 132
4 *Venice as Justice* 158

Maps

1 Venice (1677) 16
2 Site of Vair Furrier Associations 82
3 Distribution of San Giacomo dall'Orio Burial Sites 116
4 Distribution of Santa Trinità Burial Sites 117

Acknowledgments

It is a special pleasure to thank those who have provided assistance with this work. I would like to thank the Fulbright-Hays Commission and the Gladys Krieble Delmas Foundation for their support of my dissertation research, from which this study later grew. During 1981–82, a Charles Phelps Taft Postdoctoral Fellowship at the University of Cincinnati allowed me to expand and broaden that research. Additional trips to Venice during the summers of 1983, 1985, and 1986 were made possible through the generous assistance of a Grant-in-Aid from the American Council of Learned Societies, a Summer Stipend from the National Endowment for the Humanities, and grants from the Delmas Foundation, the Graduate School of the University of Mississippi, and the University of Mississippi Department of History Special Research Fund. I would also like to thank the editors of the *Journal of Medieval and Renaissance Studies* for permission to reprint parts of my study "*Quod sibi fiat gratia:* Adjustment of Penalties and the Exercise of Influence in Early Renaissance Venice," *Journal of Medieval and Renaissance Studies* 13, no. 2: 251–68. Copyright 1983 by Duke University Press. My alma mater, Wake Forest University, deserves special gratitude for allowing me to be a guest at its Venetian residence, Casa Artom. I want especially to acknowledge the kind reception given me by Bianca Artom.

This study would not have been possible without the patient and able assistance offered me by the staffs of the Archivio di Stato di Venezia and the Biblioteca Nazionale Marciana. A very special note of thanks is owed to Dottoresse Michela Dal Borgo and Alessandra Sambo, who helped guide me through the riches of the archives and made it fun in the process. The Interlibrary Loan staff of the John D. Williams Library at the University of Mississippi also provided crucial support.

Along the way I have accumulated many debts to colleagues and friends. I want especially to acknowledge the help of Judith Brown,

Linda Carroll, Tracy Cooper, Sharon Farmer, Joanne Ferraro, Laura Gianetti, Kees Gispen, Robert Haws, Pamela Long, Donald Queller, Kris Ruggiero, Ronald Weissman, and Roberto Zago. Four friends, who read and commented on earlier versions of this study, deserve special recognition. John Martin has been a good friend since we both arrived in Venice in the autumn of 1979 intent on exploring Renaissance Venetian society. The influence of our conversations can be felt in every page of this study. Edward Muir has offered good advice and careful readings of my work. I owe a great debt to Guido Ruggiero, who has been unusually generous with his time, his knowledge of the Venetian archives, and his sense of humor. And in Stanley Chojnacki I had the good fortune to find both an advisor and a friend. For ten years now he has offered me sound advice, encouragement, and support. To all these friends and others unnamed I am deeply grateful.

Finally, I want to thank my parents, who have been supportive in so many ways for so many years. I would like, in turn, to dedicate this study to their parents.

Patricians and *Popolani*

ONE

Community and Conflict in Early Renaissance Venice

A powerful message greeted the fourteenth-century visitor to the piazza San Marco. On the façade of the basilica in the lunettes above the portals was a series of mosaics depicting the translation of the relics of Saint Mark from Alexandria to Venice in 828/29. Completed in the 1260s, the mosaics portrayed the smuggling of the relics past Moslem guards, their journey by ship from Alexandria to Venice, their veneration by the doge and people, and their entry into the church.[1]

Why of the many decorative schemes available did the Venetians choose this particular motif for the façade? Partly they did so in order to impress foreign visitors, both pilgrims and diplomats. The mosaics reminded pilgrims, embarking for the Holy Land, that they could begin their journey in the proper spirit by visiting in Venice itself the relics of one of the four evangelists. The basilica housed a treasure trove of relics. Representatives of foreign governments were reminded that Venice had a powerful patron. They would find the Venetians under the patronage of Mark either faithful friends or potent adversaries.

The mosaics also carried a message to the Venetians themselves. During the Middle Ages translations were regarded as occasions when God showed special favor to a city. This was especially true in cases of *furta sacra*, sacred thefts, like the translation of Mark. Contemporaries viewed sacred thefts as signs that saints wished to be moved from one place to another and therefore allowed the "thefts" to take place. The arrival of a saint's relics in a city was a sure sign of God's favor.[2]

According to Peter Brown, translations also were interpreted as "an unambiguous token of God's enduring capacity to forgive the inhabitants of the ... city." The arrival of relics was an indication of God's mercy. Citizens responded to this amnesty with contrition.

Squabbles and quarrels subsided; vendettas ceased. The translation was a time for peacemaking and civic concord.³

It was this special moment that Venetians sought to memorialize on the façade of the basilica. By depicting the translation of Mark's relics, Venetians reminded themselves of a time when God showed them special favor; and they responded by coming together as a true community. This message was particularly strong in the decorations of the fourth doorway (to the left of the central porch). The mosaic depicted the reception of the relics by the doge, the clergy, and the people. The inscription above the lunette left no room for misunderstanding of the mosaic's meaning:

> Corpore suscepto gaudent modulamine recto;
> Et Ducis, et Cleri, populi processio meri.
> Ad Theatrum cantuque plausuque ferunt sibi sanctum
> Currentes latum venerantur honore locatum.⁴

The inscription emphasized that the entire community (Ducis, et Cleri, populi) received the saint. By visually reenacting the translation, the mosaics reminded Venetians of the social harmony that accompanied that event (Plate 1).

The mosaics of San Marco were not the only place where Venetians gave expression to the ideal of concord. The theme resonated through their public laws and private acts. In the prologue to his redaction of Venetian legislation, Doge Giovanni Dandolo referred to justice as the universal virtue leading to "peace and concord." The *giudici del piovego*, Venice's building commissioners, spoke of the need to promote "love and fruitful happiness between . . . good neighbors and dear friends." The members of the confraternity of San Giovanni Evangelista, acting "in one single spirit," sought salvation "through love of brotherhood and with aid of prayer." The stonecutters of Venice worked for the "good and welfare of all in the . . . guild and the fruitfulness of the same." Arbiters in a dispute between brothers tried to promote "peace and concord in perpetuity between them." And a Venetian father wished his sons "would find accord" when dividing the patrimony.⁵

Chroniclers echoed the theme as well. Martino da Canal's chronicle, *Les Estoires de Venise*, written about the time the mosaics were created, emphasized the role that nobles and commoners alike played in Venice's greatness. For da Canal, Venice was a place where "neither Patarenes nor Cathars, neither usurers nor assassins, neither robbers nor thieves" dared live.⁶ Those who spread heresy, those who profited unfairly from the plight of others, those who robbed cit-

PLATE 1 *Mark's Relics Transferred into Church.* This mosaic is the only one of the thirteenth-century translation mosaics extant. Photo: Osvaldo Böhm.

izens of their lives and goods were the enemies of community and therefore not welcome in Venice.

At heart was the idea that as neighbors, as ritual brothers, as workers, as kinsmen, and ultimately as citizens Venetians were (or ought to be) a people of community. It was through communal action, by working together, that Venetians would find prosperity in this world and salvation in the next. The Christian virtue *caritas* became a political virtue as well. It is therefore not surprising that the caritative meal, the love feast, stood at the center of many guild, confraternal, and parochial ceremonies.[7]

This emphasis on concord contributed powerfully to the myth of Venice—to the idea, propagated and fostered by the Venetians themselves, that their city was free of the civil strife that plagued other cities. Many foreigners took up this theme. The thirteenth-century chronicler Rolandino of Padua spoke of Venice as a place where the people "have the common interest so much at heart that the name of Venice is held as divine!" In the mid-fourteenth century, Petrarch expressed a similar opinion. He described Venice as "solidly built on marble but standing more solid on a foundation of civil concord." And in the fifteenth century Saint Bernardino preached that in Venice, "All pull together for the common good."[8] To the troubled peoples of north Italy, Venice seemed the exemplar of civic concord.

The situation, however, was rather more complex. One has only to scratch the surface of documents from the early Renaissance to realize that Venetian society was rife with conflict, strife, and clashing interests. The 1260s, the decade in which the translation mosaics were executed, was one of the most tumultuous in the city's long history. The *popolo* (people) were in a state of agitation; they rioted in 1265. To counter the threat of popular unrest, a provision was written into guild statutes prohibiting unauthorized assemblies. The *Serrata*, or closing, of the Great Council in 1297, which defined the city's political elite, led to discontent among those who were excluded. In 1300 a shadowy conspiracy led by Marino Boccono was uncovered. And the regime faced a very serious threat when, in 1310, two members of venerable patrician families, Baiamonte Tiepolo and Marco Querini, sought to overthrow the regime.[9]

The attempted coup d'état by Doge Marino Falier in 1355 showed just how precarious the regime was. Falier was an old man with no male heirs; nonetheless, the lure of signorial rule was so strong that he instigated a conspiracy that would have made him *signore* (lord) of Venice.[10] More ominous was the fact that the conspirators were able to play on class tensions latent in Venetian society. According to one anonymous fourteenth-century chronicler, the Falier conspirators planned to "rob all the houses of the nobles, kill those who opposed them, and rape all their womenfolk."[11] Another chronicler, Lorenzo de Monacis, writing in the early fifteenth century, records that the conspirators planned to arouse the ire of the popolo against the nobles through a ruse. According to de Monacis, in the dark of night, the conspirators planned to disperse throughout the city and proceed to the homes of leading commoners (popolani). Pretending to be nobles, they intended to pound on the doors of the houses and shout insults against the men's wives and daughters. Believing the rioters below to be nobles, the popolo would be aroused "contra universam nobilitatem."[12] Even if these two chroniclers do not faithfully record the actual plans of the conspirators, they give a sense of what contemporaries thought were the sources of tension in Venetian society. The wealth of the patricians and their sexual violence grated on the popolo. The chroniclers believed that the popolo would respond by robbing patrician houses and shaming their wives.

Conflict was not confined to politics. It went to the heart of economic, social, and familial relations as well. Guilds struggled with it. In 1337 (1336 Venetian style) Bertuccio Stevano, a judge (iudex) in the furriers' guild was expelled from office when he advised the gastaldus (prior of the guild) to "throw out" the guild statutes.[13] Three years earlier, the furriers discovered that five members had made a mockery of guild ideals by drawing up an illegal price-fixing scheme among themselves. The government fined the men for making an agreement "damaging and prejudicial to the men of the said guild and to the entire community (comunança) of the city."[14]

The city's religious confraternities faced similar problems. The scuola piccola (confraternity) of Santa Maria della Celestia had to write into its statutes special instructions for cases of disagreement (discordia) between brothers. According to the capitulary, discord among brothers was the equivalent of sin. It was an unchristian act that only could occur "per instigacion del demonio."[15] Heresy too threatened the Christian community, which once had played the role of mediator between emperor and pope.[16]

Relations between and within families also revealed stresses. Families squabbled with their neighbors over the ownership of canals, streets, and bridges and sought to load the expense of improvements onto others' shoulders. Brothers resorted to the appointment of official arbiters when they were unable to settle their differences privately. And parents filled their wills with incentives for their children and widowed spouses to live together in harmony as if they realized that the prospects for such were dim.[17] Enmity often went to the heart of familial relations.[18]

Viewed in this light, Venice seems less serene but more real. Venetians of the early Renaissance were not the demigods of myth with the answers to successful civic life; instead they were ordinary mortals who struggled constantly with the tension between the caritative act, which would promote harmony, and the selfish act, which would lead to conflict. Nonetheless, historians agree that Venice, especially when compared to other north Italian city-states, did show a remarkable degree of political and social stability. Although factionalism and class conflict were clearly present, as the Querini-Tiepolo and Falier conspiracies demonstrate, these forces were not powerful enough to topple or alter the regime, as occurred in Venice's maritime rival Genoa and its fellow republic Florence. Venetian patricians maintained a considerable degree of internal cohesion, and the popolani either failed or did not attempt to bring down the regime. Understanding the sources of that stability has been a primary concern of historians interested in the history of Venice.[19]

Generally, modern explanations of Venetian stability can be grouped into three categories. A number of historians have examined what might be termed structural factors, including Venice's geographic location and topography and its economic base. They believe that the city's location in the lagoons of the north Adriatic had important social consequences, for in the early centuries of its development, the Venetian ruling class did not have to contend with a disruptive feudal nobility. Confined to the lagoons, the *grandi* families of medieval Venice, unlike their Genoese counterparts, did not maintain independent feudal power bases in the countryside. This made them less troublesome. Similarly, the absence of a *contado* freed the Venetian community from many of the problems and preoccupations that engaged the governments of other medieval communes. The Venetians concentrated instead on securing their position as the staple port of the Adriatic.[20]

The city's topography also contributed to its stability. Secured by vast stretches of water separating it from the *terraferma* and by shoals making navigation difficult for all except the most experienced natives, Venetians did not have to expend vast sums on the erection of city walls. The watery environs contributed to a sense of security and stability.[21] Within the city itself, the canals served a double purpose: both uniting and separating Venetians from one another. The sixteenth-century writer Giovanni Botero saw in the canals a partial explanation for the city's internal stability. According to Botero, the canals prevented the rapid assembly of crowds and so hindered mass demonstrations of discontent with the regime.[22] The difficulties that the Querini-Tiepolo conspirators encountered trying to coordinate their efforts and move through the streets seem to support Botero's contention.[23]

The nature of the Venetian economy also affected the city's internal history. Venice was the busiest port city of the Latin West. Strategically located near the intersection of Mediterranean sea routes and Alpine passes, Venetians were the intermediaries for increasingly wealthy northern Europeans who wanted to purchase silks and spices from the East. Deprived of land as a source of wealth, Venetians turned naturally to the sea and to commerce. As a consequence, there was no social stigma associated with trade. The ruling class in Venice was a class of rich merchants, and the government made it a point to protect the interests of those merchants.

Historians suggest that the identity of the ruling class with the merchant class spared Venice the social disruptions that occurred in other cities when new men, who made their fortunes in trade, began to contend for power with the old semifeudal class of magnates. As Gino Luzzatto and Frederic Lane note, no guild of merchants developed as a focus of merchant aspirations in Venice because the government itself played that role.[24] Furthermore, during the twelfth and thirteenth centuries the ruling class remained open and accessible to new men—to men who recently had made their fortunes in the volatile world of international trade. The acceptance of these *novi cives* by the ruling aristocracy relieved the pressure that the pent-up frustrations of new men seeking power created in other Italian cities. Lauro Martines suggests that when the closing of the Venetian ruling class did come, in the early fourteenth century, it coincided nicely with a general contraction of the economy. The Venetian nobility closed ranks at the very moment when the volume of new men making their fortunes and seeking power declined.[25]

While historians have looked to structural factors in order to understand the cohesion of the city's ruling elite, they have looked to various institutions in order to understand the quiescence of the laboring classes. In his work *Rich and Poor in Renaissance Venice*, Brian Pullan has called attention to the role played by the six powerful and well-endowed religious confraternities known as the *scuole grandi*. Offices in the confraternities were reserved for *cittadini*, a hereditarily defined caste of men below the nobility. Pullan suggests that the scuole grandi provided an outlet for the political ambitions of the cittadini who were deprived of political offices. In addition,

Pullan notes that the charitable activities undertaken by the scuole, including burial of poor members, provision of dowries, and distribution of alms, relieved tensions not only by redistributing a portion of the wealth in Venetian society but also by creating feelings of goodwill among members.[26] Cittadini were also tied to the regime through their monopoly of posts in the chancery. A recent study of the career of *cittadino* Zaccaria de' Freschi illustrates how these men served the state.[27]

The organization of a large portion of the Venetian populace into guilds was another factor contributing to stability. By the middle of the fourteenth century there were more than fifty guilds, which, on the surface at least, would seem to have presented an ideal focus for the popolo's political aspirations. Yet Giovanni Monticolo argues that the patricians' strict supervision of the guilds through the office of the *giustizieri vecchi* effectively extinguished any opportunities for the guilds to become a focus of discontent.[28] Richard Rapp, in his study of the guilds in the seventeenth century, believes a sense of cooperation developed between the government and the guilds.[29] And Richard Mackenney suggests that the very proliferation of guilds contributed to stability. The establishment of so many guilds (a much greater number than in Florence, which had twenty-one) served not only to fragment the Venetian artisan community, but also to create a good-sized class of *boteghieri* (shopkeepers) who were essentially satisfied with the regime.[30]

Neighborhoods, parishes in particular, are a third institution to which historians attach special significance. In his work *Venice: A Maritime Republic*, Lane, following Lewis Mumford, argues that Venetian neighborhood life contributed to social harmony. Socially heterogeneous parishes were a meeting place of rich and poor. Lane and others believe that the intimate ties created between patricians and popolani at the parochial level served to mitigate class tensions on the civic level.[31]

A third category of explanations is government policy. Historians argue that the patricians consciously pursued policies designed either to placate or subdue the popolo. Lane, for instance, argues that the government was careful to maintain adequate food supplies in the city in order to prevent bread riots, a common form of political protest.[32] Stanley Chojnacki suggests that government attempts to render justice equitably won the loyalty of the popolo to the regime.[33] And Edward Muir in his study of civic ritual sets forth the view that the patrician government consciously adapted potentially disruptive popular rituals and integrated them into formal civic rituals, thereby rendering them inoffensive to the government.[34]

These interpretations form part of what John Najemy calls the Anglo-American "consensus school" of Italian communal politics. Najemy notes that historians of Florence, Siena, Venice, and other Italian republics tend to regard politics in terms of the formulation of policy by the elites and its reception by the nonelites. As long as the elites meet the basic needs of the popolo, the argument goes, they are secure. Only when an elite loses touch with its subjects does it become vulnerable to revolt.[35]

Other historians suggest that the patricians pursued policies that cowed the popolo into obedience. In his studies of violence and criminality, Guido Ruggiero demonstrates that, by the early years of the fourteenth century, the government had a police force and judicial apparatus capable of meeting any challenge. With one policeman for every two hundred fifty inhabitants and a series of courts culminating in the ruthlessly efficient Council of Ten, the patricians were able to quell brawls that might ignite into popular uprisings and to seek out and dispose of noble opponents plotting revolt.[36] In a sweeping overview of Venice in this period, Giorgio Cracco argues that, during the fourteenth century, the Venetian state became the preserve of plutocrats who pursued policies beneficial only to themselves. In Cracco's memorable phrase, the popolo were reduced to a "corpo morto."[37] Alberto Tenenti and Roberto Cessi present similarly unflattering views of the popolo.[38]

By analyzing the structure of the Venetian economy, the prevailing social institutions of Venetian life, and government policies, historians have presented a complex, multifaceted picture that goes a long way toward explaining the celebrated (though fragile) stability of Venetian society. What is missing from this picture, however, is an analysis of how individual Venetians, torn between the caritative and the selfish act, reacted to and interacted with one another within this matrix of structures, institutions, and policies. In this picture of Venetian society, the Venetians themselves are obscured. The present study tries to expand our understanding of Venetian stability by analyzing the private lives of early Renaissance Venetians. It seeks in the personal associations of Venetians a key to their public actions and attitudes, their perceptions both of themselves and of the regime. The underlying premise of this work is the one voiced in *Coriolanus*, that "the people are the city." Only by examining the lives of the people themselves can we understand the tenor and therefore the history of the city.

In keeping with this premise, the vision presented in this study is of the city as a "network of networks."³⁹ Individuals move in networks of association that either link them to or isolate them from individuals moving in other networks. This study analyzes kinship, artisan, religious, and patron-client associations in order to see where the tensions and solidarities in Venetian society lay. This approach lets all Venetians, not just patricians, speak for themselves through their deeds. The result is not history from the top down nor history from the bottom up. Instead, it is a vision that tries to capture the complexity of the Venetian social experience.

What this study will suggest is that the contrasting impulses toward community and conflict at the heart of all social interactions led Venetians of the early Renaissance to group themselves in a myriad of intersecting networks that did not follow narrow class or factional lines. Associations were not determined by any one factor such as wealth or legal status. Instead they tended to be freewheeling. The ties between patricians and popolani and among popolani were complex and multifaceted, and this militated against an easy division of society into nobles and commoners. Indeed, this study will show that the greatest tension in early Renaissance Venetian society was not between patricians and popolani but rather between wealthy popolani who, through a variety of personal ties, associated with patricians and the *popolo minuto*, little people, who were isolated from the mainstream institutions of Venetian life and who therefore had to create their own social worlds.

The period under scrutiny is the early Renaissance—the period from 1297 to 1423. This is a particularly appropriate period for exploring Venetian stability, for it was precisely this period in which Italian communes were most susceptible to political turmoil and in which Venice itself experienced its worst political crises.[40] In 1297, after a century of effort bent on refining their government system, the Venetians turned to the task of defining their political elite. The Serrata of the Great Council in 1297 defined that elite. The inclusion of a select number of families in the elite and the prospect of permanent exclusion for everyone else seemed to sow the seeds of dissent. Compounding the problem was the exclusion of the guilds from a voice in political affairs. Venice's fellow republic Florence saw its electoral system vacillate between two views of the constitution— one based on consensus, the other on corporatism.[41] In Venice the consensus view triumphed in the Serrata, leaving the popolo without a viable constitutional position.

A series of crises throughout the period heightened the tension. Notable were the Black Death in 1348, the revolt of Crete in 1364, and two wars with Genoa. The second of these wars, the War of Chioggia (1378–81), brought Venice to the brink of disaster. Any of these crises might have ushered in a new regime. The Black Death caused serious disruption to the Sienese regime, and Florence's war with Lucca from 1429 to 1433 helped the Medici come to power. Yet in each instance of crisis, the Venetian patrician regime weathered the storm.[42]

The period from the War of Chioggia to 1423 was a period of consolidation. With its Mediterranean rival Genoa defeated, Venice turned increasingly to Italian affairs. In the first decade of the fifteenth century Venice acquired Padua, Vicenza, and Verona. Before long Venice's interests were as firmly rooted in Italian politics as they were in the eastern Mediterranean. With its interests and regime firmly entrenched, Venice in 1423 entered its century of grandeur. The election of the young and westward-looking Francesco Foscari as doge marked the beginning of this new era.[43]

This study will also show that over the course of the early Renaissance a transformation took place in Venetian social relations. From the time of the Serrata on, but with increasing intensity in the years following the War of Chioggia, patricians began to identify their own well-being with that of the state. As the bureaucracy grew, patrician families looked increasingly to public offices for income and sought to increase their honor and prestige through the bestowal of public, state-sponsored favors known as *grazie*. Traditional attachments, such as those to neighborhoods, loosened as patrician and popolano men adopted a state-centered and civic as opposed to a private and parochial orientation.

A new status-consciousness that is most easily documented among the patricians accompanied this shift. The last decades of the fourteenth century and the early years of the fifteenth century witnessed an increasing sense of exclusivity on the part of patricians as they scurried to get their genealogical houses in order and to tighten the lines of noble status. This new sense of status affected personal associations and the formation of networks. During these years exclusivity and hierarchy replaced older, freewheeling tendencies. In guilds, scuole, even in family life, a more hierarchical, status-conscious ordering of Venetian society overwhelmed the more open associations of the trecento. Venice remained politically stable in its century of grandeur because the ideal of community and concord that had allowed it to overcome the crises of the early Renaissance was replaced by a new sense of hierarchy.

TWO

Urban Form and Social Stratification: The *Civitas Venetiarum*

People do not associate with one another in arbitrary ways. Kinship ties, common work experiences, shared values, and physical proximity are among the factors that shape and affect their associations. Venetians of the early Renaissance were no different in this regard. The marriages they contracted, the confraternities they joined, the friends they made, and the patrons they cultivated all were influenced by a myriad of factors. Among these were locality and social status. Venice's unusual topography, its watery environs, heightened the residents' awareness of urban space. The lagoon clearly demarcated the city's boundaries, and the canals that sliced through the city served both to divide the city into neighborhoods and to link the neighborhoods together. Similarly, the division of Venetians into legally defined status groups divided the populace by awarding privileges to some and burdens to others, while implicitly recognizing that the parts constituted a social whole. As a prelude to examining the social networks of early Renaissance Venetians, let us first consider the evolution of Venice as an urban complex and the stratification of Venetians into status groups, for these factors to some degree influenced their associative tendencies.[1]

The Evolution of the Early Renaissance City

Fourteenth-century Venice did not find among its native sons a chronicler like Florence's Giovanni Villani. In his chronicle, Villani described with great pride his native city, enumerating its banking firms and notaries, boasting of its consumption of victuals, praising its woolen industry and schools. Venetian chroniclers were less given to enumerating the blessings of their city, yet they could feel that God, through his intermediary Saint Mark, had smiled on them. On the eve of the Black Death, Venice had a population nearing 120,000, seventy parish churches, numerous monasteries and convents, and hundreds of workshops. The city's Arsenal, which Dante vividly described (*Inferno*, 7.21), was probably the largest industrial complex in western Europe; and the glassmakers of Murano produced fine glass products for export to sites around the Mediterranean basin. Venetian merchants carried merchandise from the Black Sea to the North Sea, while Venetian artisans worked furs from Russia, soda ash from Syria (for glassmaking), and cotton from Egypt.[2]

Rising as it did from the sandbars of the lagoon, Venice presented an extraordinary spectacle to visitors arriving from the terraferma. They would disembark at Rialto, where a great wooden bridge that was locked at night linked the two halves of the city. Rialto was the city's mercantile center, site of banks, workshops, public scales, and massive buildings. One of the most impressive buildings was the Fondaco dei Tedeschi, the residence and warehouse of German merchants. A myriad of tongues could be heard at Rialto—testimony to the reach of Venetian trade.

Not far from Rialto stood the Franciscan church Santa Maria Assunta or Santa Maria Gloriosa. Its huge nave and gigantic bell tower dominated the western half of the city just as the Dominican church—Santi Giovanni e Paolo or San Zanipolo as the Venetians called it—did the eastern. The two churches stood as sentries and rivals, facing each other across the city. A third point in this sacred triangle was the island of San Giorgio Maggiore, where the Benedictines had their appropriately claustral headquarters. Venice's bishop, who was subordinate to the city's secular authorities, had his remote seat at Castello in the swampy eastern reaches of the city beyond the Arsenal. The city center was the piazza San Marco, site of the doge's palace and the basilica of Saint Mark. The church, with its Greek cruciform plan, cupolas, and glittering mosaics, recalled the city's Byzantine past, while the moralizing sculptures of the ducal palace bespoke its republican present. Adjoining these buildings was the massive campanile whose bells and torches called craftsmen to work, noblemen to council, and seamen home through the shoals and tides of the north Adriatic. At piazza San Marco Venetians found their spiritual and social center. Petrarch had little doubt that it was the greatest square in the world.[3]

The city that greeted the fourteenth-century visitor already had a venerable past. Its foundation can be dated to the sixth century, when people from the Paduan plain fled the Lombards and settled in the lagoon. A number of sites vied for preeminence within the Byzantine province. Torcello, Jesolo, and Grado were important urban centers; Heraclea and Malamocco each served for a time as the ducal capital. After their defeat at the hands of Charlemagne's son Pepin in 810, the Venetians decided to move their capital from Malamocco on the Lido to a more secure spot within the lagoon itself. The site they chose was Rivoalto.[4]

When the ducal seat was transferred to Rivoalto, or Rialto, in 810, there were already a number of settlements in the area. Islands with names such as Luprio, Gemini, and Spinalunga had been settled earlier and contained small communities.[5] The most important of these settlements was Olivolo (Castello) located near the mouth of the river (*flumen*) whose course was eventually to form the Grand Canal. Olivolo was a major settlement; it contained a fortress (*castrum*), and in the year 774 became the episcopal seat of the Rialtine settlements. With the transfer of the ducal capital to Rialto in 810, the site gained political as well as religious prestige over other settlements. This increased the flow of immigrants from other parts of the lagoon so that during the ninth century, the area around San Marco grew into a thriving community. The parishes forming the core of this area (San Bartolomeo, San Zulian, San Canciano, Santa Sofia, Santa Fosca, San Marcuola, San Geremia, San Paternian, San Moisè, and San Procolo) were all founded between the late eighth and ninth centuries.[6]

During the tenth century, the Rialtine settlement expanded beyond this central core. According to traditional foundation dates, twenty-five new parishes were created during the tenth century. Most of the parishes were located in two zones east and west of the flumen. The effect of their settlement was to give definition to the course of the Grand Canal. The creation of seven parishes between San Bartolomeo and San Marco (San Benedetto, San Vitale, Sant'Angelo, San Samuele, San Fantin, Santa Maria Zobenigo) defined the left side of the canal. The establishment of ten parishes across the waterway (San Cassian, Santa Maria Mater Domini, San Stae, San Simeon Grande, San Giovanni Evangelista, San Stin, Sant'Agostin, San Giovanni Elemosinario, San Giacomo dall'Orio, San Giovanni Degolà) shaped the canal's right side. As a consequence of these settlements, the canal received its characteristic U-shaped bends. Other foundations of the tenth century (San Vio, San Tomà, San Felice, Santa Maria Nova, Santa Chiara, Sant'Andrea) gave indications of the zones into which later development would turn. By the tenth century, settlement in the central core was already quite dense. A fire in 976 destroyed three hundred houses between San Marco and Santa Maria Zobenigo.[7] The process of internal settlement continued during the course of the eleventh century so that by 1100 Venice had nearly achieved the geographic contours that it maintains to this day. By 1100 almost all of the city's seventy parishes had been established (Map 1).

Although the contours of the city were already apparent by 1100, the patterns of settlement themselves differed noticeably from those of the later city. In this period each parish was a distinct island community separated by water from its neighbors, and people traveled between communities by boat. Consequently, churches and homes of the wealthy were built directly on the water for easy access. Vestiges of this period are apparent today along the canal (rio) that winds its way from the Grand Canal into the heart of the settlement creating the first U-shaped bend. The four churches along this canal (San Giovanni Degolà, San Giacomo dall'Orio, Sant'Agostin, and San Polo) are situated so that they virtually abut the canal. These churches were designed to be viewed from and approached by the water, thereby accentuating their autonomous character.[8]

The orientation of these parishes mirrored their social significance. Although little documentation exists for this period, it appears that one or two powerful families dominated each of these island communities. The Participazi family had its headquarters in the Rialtine settlement, in the latter-day parish of Santi Apostoli. Agnello Participazi was the first doge to make his capital at Rialto.[9] As controllers of the territory and in most instances founders of the parish churches, great families enjoyed proprietary rights over the area, including patronage rights known as *iuspatronatus*.[10] Grouped around the houses of the powerful were dwellings of their clients and retainers who provided support, gardens and vineyards that stocked their tables, and fish ponds and salt beds that yielded revenues. In their earliest form then, these island communities resembled small feudal estates, and the powerful families that controlled them vied with one another for control of the dogeship.[11]

One such island community was the parish of San Giovanni Elemosinario, or, as it is more commonly known, San Giovanni de Rialto. The Orio and Gradenigo families dominated the territory. They owned adjoining properties bordering the Grand Canal and resided in the parish. Their residences, however, were not very impressive. As late as the mid-thirteenth century, the property of the Gradenigos was built partly of stone and partly of wood; and much of the surrounding land was unoccupied. In addition to the dwellings of retainers, the island housed butcher shops. In 1097 Pietro and Tiso Orio bequeathed their property in San Giovanni to the doge and people

MAP I The Canals and Parishes of Venice (1677)

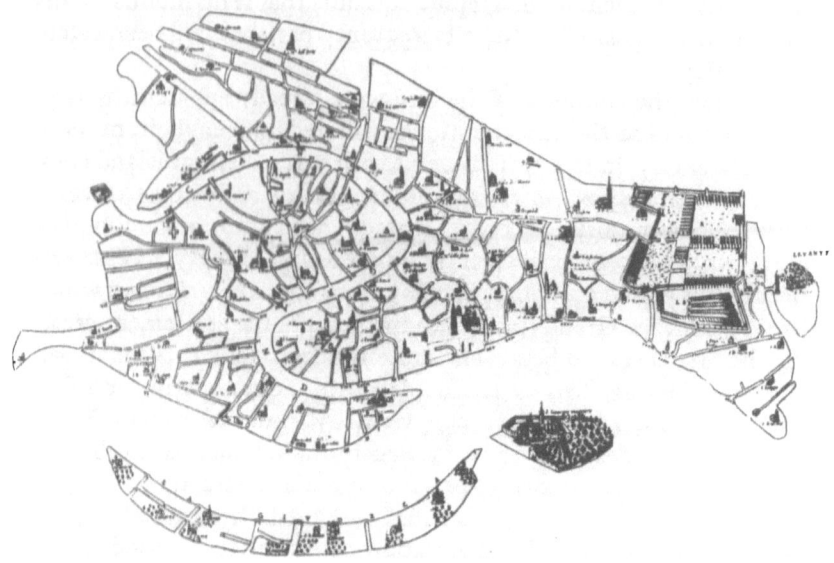

Photo: Museo Civico Correr.

(Dominicali, et cuncto populo Venetiae) for the creation of a public market. From these beginnings grew the great market of Rialto. As the character of the area changed from residential to commercial, the Gradenigos abandoned their residence there and sought domicile elsewhere in the city.[12]

The twelfth century marked a new stage in the city's development both internationally and domestically. During the course of the twelfth century Venice became an international trade center. Whereas the city's early growth had depended on the transportation of products such as salt, fish, and timber to and from the growing towns of Lombardy, in the twelfth century the city's merchants turned increasingly to the eastern Mediterranean where great profits could be made in the shipment of luxury items. Men such as Sebastiano and Pietro Ziani and Romano Mairano made huge fortunes in the eastern trade.[13]

Venice underwent a political transformation as well. Until this time the dogeship was quasimonarchical and semihereditary, with a few families such as the Michiel controlling the dogeship election after election. But during the early years of the twelfth century the doge's powers began to be hemmed in by his councillors, and in 1172 an important change occurred with the appointment of a special nominating committee. Thereafter the power of the doge diminished, and he became simply the chief official in the Venetian commune.[14]

Transformations occurred in the city's urban development as well. The island communities from which Venice emerged began to lose their autonomous character. As the population of the settlements grew, expansion at the city's periphery gave way to development within the settled areas. Canals and fish ponds were filled, the course of other canals was regularized, and the building of the bridges began. The construction of bridges was especially significant for it provided an alternative to water transportation. A rudimentary system of streets (*calli*) evolved, which linked the city together. Although builders had to account for many peculiarities of topography, generally speaking streets were laid out to run parallel to canals; and buildings were situated so they had access both to the canal and the street. Two major pedestrian thoroughfares developed running parallel to the two sides of the Grand Canal. The parishes of San Giovanni de Rialto and San Bartolomeo served as the hubs from which these thoroughfares fanned out into other parts of the city, and they became the city's central commercial nexus. In 1255 the parishes were linked by a permanent wooden bridge. It apparently replaced a pontoon bridge constructed at the end of the twelfth century.[15]

As the mercantile, political, and physical character of the city changed, the social structure underwent a transformation as well. By the late eleventh century, any feudal characteristics the island communities had were disappearing as the parishes ceased to resemble private family estates. Like the Gradenigos of San Giovanni de Rialto, great families began the process of physical dispersal that characterized Venetian patrician families throughout the city's history. The ties of direct dependency that may have linked noble families and their fellow parishioners disappeared as well.[16]

The explanation for this transformation lies in the changing commercial and political character of the city. In the early centuries, when powerful families vied for control of the ducal throne, necessity dictated the maintenance of fortified island enclaves and armed retainers. But the need for fortresses and retainers diminished as other officials hemmed in the power of the doge. Furthermore, Venice's commercial character necessitated flexible, changeable ties between persons, like those between the *tractator* (traveling partner) and the *stans* (investor) in the business contract known as the *commenda*. Rigid social ties did not suit a mercantile people. The fortuitous nature of livelihoods earned from trade further affected social bonds. The practice of using property as collateral for loans meant there was rapid turnover of property, making it difficult for families to maintain control of territory.[17]

The changes that occurred in the city, especially the welding of the island communities into an urban complex, created a variety of problems requiring an effective, efficient system of urban administration. Up to this point, responsibility for keeping canals, streets, and other facilities in good repair had lain with the parishes and especially with the leading parochial families. But as the parishes lost their autonomous character and the involvement of great families with particular communities declined, questions of jurisdiction, responsibility, and ownership arose.[18]

In order to resolve these and similar questions, the government intervened. It divided the city for purposes of administration into a number of geographically defined units and assigned officials to them. The government was then able to treat these units as corporate bodies and assign them responsibility for maintenance of public facilities. The system of urban administration that evolved in the twelfth century remained more or less intact throughout the early Renaissance.

The basic unit of urban administration was the *contrata* (parish). At some point, probably in the late eleventh century, the government systematized the island settlements and designated each of the parish churches and its territory as a contrata. In so doing, the government superimposed a regularized system of secular administration on the pre-existing ecclesiastically based parochial system. Administrative responsibilities were given to officials known as the *capi di contrate*, two of whom were assigned to each parish.[19]

The responsibilities assigned to these parish-based officials involved fairly routine administrative tasks. The thirteenth-century *Capitulary Concerning the Bridges and Streets of Venice* assigned the capi the task of keeping streets and bridges in good repair and gave them power to assess parishioners for their share of maintenance costs. In addition, the capi had to distribute grain to parishioners on the basis of need.[20] On other occasions the capi served as census takers. In November 1296, the Great Council ordered the capi to survey all monasteries, churches, and members of the clergy in order to determine whether or not they had paid their share of loans to the government. And in August 1319, the Council of Ten ordered the capi to make a census of foreigners living in their parishes. This may indicate that the government was expecting trouble from its foreign population—a group known for its violence.[21]

Parishes and their officials also played a role in the military organization of the city. Until the sixteenth century, members of the city's reserve fleet were recruited according to a parish-based "dozens" system. Men between the ages of twenty and sixty were grouped in units of twelve. A militia based on units of twelve men was also organized at the parish level and was under the jurisdiction of the capi di contrate. Nobles and commoners served separately. The capi were supposed to see that all members were properly armed and that they put in archery practice each week.[22]

The central government also used the parishes as centers for the dissemination of information. In an attempt to find the murderers of nobleman Rayniero Zeno, the Great Council in 1283 ordered the capi di contrate to call the men of their parishes together to announce the offer of a reward. When the government wanted information diffused, it ordered public criers to make announcements in the piazzetta at San Marco, at Rialto, and "in all the parishes of Venice."[23]

Parishes were also responsible for one of the major festivals of the city, the festival of the *Marie* (Marys). According to legend, in 944 pirates seized a group of Venetian girls who had gathered at the cathedral of San Pietro di Castello for the feast of the Transfer of Saint Mark. The doge, Pietro Candiano III, pursued the pirates and recovered the girls on the feast of the Purification of the Virgin. Thereafter, in commemoration of the event, an eight-day festival was held in which the parishes played a major role. Each year two parishes were responsible for selecting and sponsoring twelve girls or figures of girls known as the Marys. Banquets were held in the homes of nobles in the sponsoring parishes; and on the final day of the festival an elaborate procession of boats made a circuit from the cathedral at San Pietro to San Marco, up the Grand Canal as far as the Fondaco dei Tedeschi, and then to the church of Santa Maria Formosa. As this parish-based festival grew in elaborateness and expense, it came under increased government control. During the War of Chioggia, the festival was suspended and never revived.[24]

The parishes were subsumed by six districts known as *sestieri*, which were created in 1171 for purposes of administering government loans.[25] It seems likely that some effort was made to balance the two halves of the city, since each side of the Grand Canal was accorded three sestieri: on the San Marco side, the sestieri of San Marco, Castello, and Cannaregio; on the opposite side, San Polo, Santa Croce, and Dorsoduro. Like the gonfalons of Florence and the *terzi* of Siena, the sestieri encompassed several parishes. The original division into sestieri may have had some topographical basis, but very quickly the changing morphology of the city made it impossible to distinguish one sestiere from another. Indeed, the physical integrity of the sestieri was of minor importance. The sestiere of Santa Croce included the parish of Santa Lucia on the opposite side of the Grand Canal. The division, which originally may have had some internal logic, quickly became purely administrative and formal.[26]

Two groups of officials had special ties to the sestieri. The first of these were the *capi di sestieri*. An act of the Council of Ten dated 1319 stated that the Ten were to choose "six good and honest noblemen to be the capi di sestieri, namely one capo for each sestiere." Among the responsibilities assigned to the capi in the legislation was the appointment of the capi di contrate and supervision of taverns and inns. The capi, who had to be at least thirty years of age, got help from four aides who had to be at least twenty-five years of age. The number of capi and their assistants increased over time.[27]

The *signori di notte*, Venice's Lords of the Nightwatch, also had ties to the sestieri. Like the capi di sestieri, there were six signori di notte; and each was assigned to a particular sestiere. Each signore was allotted sixteen assistants, or *custodes*, who were supposed to patrol the city heavily armed.[28] The law required that the custodes be Venetians or foreigners with ten years' residence in the city and that they be residents of the sestiere in which they served; but during the later thirteenth century concessions were made allowing the signore di notte of Cannaregio to choose custodes from other sestieri, "if he cannot find custodes from his sestiere."[29] Unlike the capi di contrate, whose primary responsibility was the welfare of the inhabitants, the capi di sestieri and signori di notte were primarily responsible to the city. These officials had as their task the maintenance of peace and order within the city.

The Grand Canal created the largest geographic division within the city. With its single bridge at Rialto, the canal was a formidable barrier; and the division of the city into halves seems to have engendered some feelings of loyalty (and rivalry) between the two. As we have seen, the government was careful to maintain equity between the sides by according three sestieri to each. The cobblers' and jacket-makers' guilds showed similar concern when they required that guild offices alternate between residents of the San Marco and Rialto sides of the city.[30] Rivalries, ritualized into fistfights between the *Nicolotti*, fishermen from the right side of the canal in the parish of San Nicolò dei Mendicoli, and the *Castellani*, arsenal workers and others from the left side of the canal, further bespeak this loyalty.[31]

It was therefore quite natural for the Venetian government to adapt this topographical division to its administrative framework. The most notable example involved the procurators of San Marco, the officials responsible for the basilica and the executors for many Venetians. In order to meet an increasing work load, the government decided in 1319 to increase the number of procurators from four to six and to assign them specific duties. Two, known as the *procuratori de supra*, were placed in charge of the basilica itself; two more, the *procuratori de citra*, were in charge of all estates left in their care by persons living on the San Marco side of the Grand Canal; and the final two, the *procuratori de ultra*, were responsible for estates on the opposite side. Since the San Marco side of the canal was more densely populated, the procuratori de ultra got the additional task of assisting the procuratori de citra with estates in the sestiere of Cannaregio. The two sides of the Grand Canal provided a convenient and logical way for the government to divide responsibilities and authority among some of its officials.[32]

The government's elaboration of a system of urban administration during the twelfth and thirteenth centuries is a clear indication that Venice had reached a new stage in its urban development. Certain problems superseded the interests of local residents and called for city-wide action. The Rialtine settlement had indeed grown into a *civitas*, a city.

The processes that began in the twelfth century continued unabated throughout the early Renaissance. More canals were filled, more bridges were constructed, and more vacant sites were developed into houses and shops. Construction flourished during the fourteenth and first half of the fifteenth centuries. Indeed, the core of Venice's urban tissue was constructed during this period, giving the city its present mazelike quality. Yet even in the sixteenth century parts of the city, especially those on the periphery in Cannaregio, Castello, and Dorsoduro, retained their medieval aspect with gardens, orchards, and ponds. Titian's house near the Gesuiti had many of the characteristics of a country villa.[33]

This points to another aspect of Venice's urban development. Increasingly, various zones within the city (and the lagoon) began to take on special characteristics and to be differentiated from one another.[34] From the time of Venice's foundation, certain areas of the city had been associated with particular functions. Castello and San Marco had long traditions as the religious and political centers, Rialto served as the commercial center, and the secluded islands housed monasteries. But as the economy grew and occupations multiplied, specialization accelerated. The far eastern end of the city, the area closest to the Adriatic, became the center of shipbuilding; the western end, the area closest to the terraferma, became an industrial center. The port areas included the basin of San Marco, the shores of the Grand Canal, and the shores of the canal separating Venice from its neighbor island, the Giudecca.[35] Most of this specialization was a response to natural conditions, but some was instituted by design. Fear of fires led the government to prohibit glassmaking within the city. Furnaces had to be transferred to Murano, where they have remained to this day. Similarly, concern for safety of the water supply led the government to restrict tanning to the Giudecca.[36]

As Venice evolved from a series of isolated island settlements into a great urban center, an urban ideology emerged as well. In the early centuries when Venice was still a congeries of isolated settlements, the notion of Venice as a city and as a community was inchoate. Private interests prevailed over public authority. For instance, when the Orio brothers left their property in San Giovanni de Rialto for the creation of a public market, they stated that they were leaving the property "Dominicali, et cuncto populo Venetiae"—to the doge and all the people of Venice. They used the term *patria* to describe the city, a term lacking in communal connotations.

During the twelfth century, Venetians began to use the term *comune Venetiarum* to describe the city. The term, layered with political and social meanings, emphasized the common interests of the inhabitants and indicates that just as the island communities had been forged into a unit, so *cuncto populo Venetiae* had become a *comune*, a community. Whereas in earlier centuries private interests had been paramount, now public concerns, the interests of the commune, began to take precedence.[37]

The subordination of private interests to the common good is evident in the establishment of the giudici del piovego, the officials who were in charge of the city's public facilities. The office of the piovego (a corruption of the Latin *super publicis*) was created in the first half of the thirteenth century. The giudici resembled to some extent modern-day building commissioners, for changes in buildings, repair of streets, and maintenance of canals all required their approval; yet like many Venetian magistracies, the piovego also had jurisdiction in other matters, in this instance in cases of usury. In 1282 the Great Council enjoined the piovego to inquire into the encroachment onto public land and waters by private individuals and groups. Most of the cases preserved from this period (in the *Codex Publicorum*) concern disputed ownership. The rulings provide clues to official assumptions about the city.[38]

A case from 1305 involving a piece of property in the parish of San Maurizio was fairly typical and provides a good example of the special problems posed by Venice's unusual topography.[39] The dispute concerned a vacant lot (*terra vacua*) where once there had been a pond (*piscina*). The residents and property owners in the parish claimed that the land was publicly owned, whereas the parochial clergy claimed that it was church property. The property in question happened to abut the church. To support their claim, the parishioners submitted charters dating as far back as the late eleventh century, which in their opinion proved that the property was public. The main point emphasized by these charters was that the pond adjoined on one end a public street (a *via comune*). Apparently, the parishioners wished to suggest that the pond (and now the lot) was a continuation of the public thoroughfare. Marco Dorabona, parish priest of San Maurizio, contested the claim and produced charters from 1278 in which the parish chapter granted to the Viadro brothers the right to construct a building on the site. The charters specifically stated that the property belonged "de iure et pertinenciis" to San Maurizio.

Having heard the arguments and examined the charters, the giudici had a crier announce the case in the parish, demanding that anyone with additional information come forward. None did. So, having examined the evidence, the giudici ruled that the lot was "a public and common street which is to be perpetually open and unoccupied to the glory and profit of the church of San Maurizio and the entire commune of Venice and all surrounding that vacant lot . . . and that it ought to be and remain open for all wishing to come and go, by day and by night."[40] The giudici ruled that the steps or landing at the edge of the property were for communal use as well.

Judging solely from the evidence of the charters (which are transcribed in the codex), it appears that the chapter of San Maurizio had a better claim to the property than did the parishioners; yet the giudici ruled that the property was publicly owned. Why? Apparently, what swayed the giudici was the common need to have the street open. They were careful to note in their ruling that the land was to be open both day and night and that the landing (where goods could be unloaded) was publicly owned as well.

A case from the year 1314 involved a dispute over a piece of property (again a former pond) in the parish of San Zulian next to ca' Pasqualigo.⁴¹ The *vicini* (property owners) claimed that the land was public and produced in support of their claim testimony from the piovego's own records. It seems that three years earlier the giudici had investigated the site and interrogated eleven old men about it. They had asked the old men what they recalled about the site when it was a pond and especially had asked them to try to recall its dimensions. One witness had testified that he had seen boats use the pond; others had testified that they had swum there. All had tried to describe its size. The parishioners' opponent was nobleman Andrea Donato who, acting on the power of attorney given him by his brother-in-law Nicolò Vitturi of San Zulian, claimed that the property belonged to the Vitturi family. He produced a number of Vitturi family charters that seemed to illustrate that the land was theirs.

As in the previous case, the giudici had the case announced in the parish; at which point, Elena Querini, widow of nobleman Romeo Querini, came forward to claim that the property was hers. She produced as evidence a charter from 1253 made by the Vitturi that granted her late husband access to the property and the right to construct a footbridge. Having heard the evidence, the giudici ruled as they had in the previous case, that the property was "public and common and ought to remain so perpetually."⁴²

In this case, the claims of the Vitturi and of Elena Querini were less clear than those of the chapter of San Maurizio in the first case. Yet again, what seems to have concerned the giudici was the fact that when the land was a pond, it was open to maritime traffic. The wording of the parishioners' complaint is also significant (in fact it is the same wording used by the parishioners in the previous case). In presenting their case, they asked the giudici to declare the land public, "for the public good (publicam utilitatem) for all wishing to come and go, by day and night."⁴³ Again, the exigencies of commerce and urban life appear to have overcome private interests.

A third case from 1328 involved a dispute between nobleman Raffaele Ghezzo of San Pantalon and the chapter of San Basilio.⁴⁴ It concerned a street that ran between the church of San Basilio and its campanile. The chapter claimed that the street was private property, asserting that the church's foundations lay under it. Ghezzo claimed that the street, bordering property that his family had acquired from the Pino family, was public. Both produced charters in support of their claims; and in the end, the giudici ruled as they had in other cases that the street was public.

What is significant about this case is that in issuing their ruling, the giudici tried to establish a general principle for future cases.

URBAN FORM AND SOCIAL STRATIFICATION 25

They stated that "all canals, streams, ponds, alleys, streets, pools, courts, sandbars, and land are public and common and ought to be preserved and maintained publicly and communally unless public documents or legitimate claims to the contrary are made."[45] This statement from 1328 marks a significant change from Rialtine days when ownership of facilities was assumed to belong to private families.[46] In 1328, the government was asserting that all land was publicly owned unless a legitimate claim to the contrary could be made. The burden of proof rested on those who claimed that a particular piece of property was privately owned, and as the preceding cases illustrate, it was sometimes difficult to convince the giudici del piovego of such a claim.

What these cases reveal is an evolving notion of the public good and an evolving sense of Venice as a city. The giudici no longer viewed Venice as a series of autonomous communities in which private and patronal rights were paramount. Instead they believed that the city was a unit and that there was a greater good—the public good—that it was their duty to protect.

Furthermore, it appears that when the giudici spoke of the public good they had something quite specific in mind. They equated the public good with the unimpeded flow of people and goods on the streets and canals of the city. They believed that these thoroughfares ought to be open to friends and foes alike, at all times of the day and night. This was the reason the giudici were so concerned whether or not ships had once used the pond in San Zulian and were so interested in asserting that the landing in San Maurizio was a public landing. For the giudici del piovego, the good of Venice lay in the free movement of goods and people; any private impediments to that movement had to be removed. The problem was a recurring one. In 1356 (1355 Venetian style) the Great Council encouraged the giudici del piovego to redouble their efforts in recovering public lands and waters usurped by private individuals. The council even offered financial rewards to the giudici and their functionaries as an incentive.[47]

The new consciousness of Venice as a city is also apparent in the growing concern with public sanitation. During the course of the fourteenth and early fifteenth centuries, the Great Council passed a series of laws specifically designed to safeguard the health of the city's inhabitants. In 1321, for instance, the council asked the signori di notte to determine which canals were in need of dredging. Canals were becoming clogged with silt, and the government feared contagion from the fetid waters. In May 1333 the council decided that canals ought to be dredged in order to maintain "the health and well-being of the city." And in September 1413, while an epidemic was raging in the city, the council banned dyeing of cloth in waters, "in corpore civitatis nostre." Instead, dyeing was to be confined to the periphery of the city where there was access to open waters.[48] The intent of these rulings was to protect the health of the inhabitants and thereby the strength and power of the city. In 1407 the Great Council made an explicit equation of population with power in a law that relaxed the requirements for citizenship. The preamble stated, "cities are rich and powerful when they are copiously populated."[49]

Civic pride was another justification for government action. In 1339 the Great Council voted to make improvements at San Marco, "since it is an honor to ornament the city." The council voted in 1368 to allow the monastery of San Cristoforo to build a bridge. The giudici del piovego recommended the improvement, arguing that it would be "a thing of great beauty and beneficial to all wishing to make the crossing." And the decision made in 1422 to rebuild the west wing of the Ducal Palace was justified on the grounds that it befit the peaceful times God had brought to the city.[50]

The rulings of the giudici del piovego and the laws passed by the Great Council show that by the fourteenth century the government had a clear sense of Venice as a civic community—a place in which the common good was paramount. The piovego's use of the term *publicam utilitatem* has clear resonances of Roman law and the classical *res publica*. As the actions of the piovego and laws of the Great Council reveal, the notion of the common good became increasingly associated with the government. The common good could only be protected by state action.[51]

Yet old patterns die hard, and it is important to note that even in the fourteenth century the government continued to view the city in some respects as a congeries of communities. The numerous responsibilities assigned to parishes and their officials reveal that the government viewed parishes as communities of interest with responsibilities to a larger community—the city itself.

A decision reached in 1342 concerning payment for widening the street running from San Bartolomeo to San Giovanni Grisostomo reveals this thinking. The street was one stretch of the main thoroughfare running along the left side of the Grand Canal—the thoroughfare linking Santa Lucia (the site of today's railway station) to San Marco. This section of the street was especially important since it bordered the Fondaco dei Tedeschi and opened into the mercantile center at San Bartolomeo. In order to widen the street, several houses had to be altered and the campanile of San Giovanni Grisostomo destroyed. Commissioners were appointed to apportion the costs of the improvements.

Their decision is revealing. Since the benefits of the improvements extended to all residents of the sestiere of Cannaregio by improving their link to Rialto and San Marco, the commissioners decided to assess residents of all parishes between San Giovanni Grisostomo and Santa Lucia. Yet the payment schedule was calculated in such a way that those who benefited the most bore the greatest cost. Residents between San Giovanni Grisostomo and Santa Sofia were assessed at a rate of 2 *soldi, 6 denarii* for every 1,000 lire of property value; from San Marcuola to San Felice the rate was 1 soldo, 6 denarii; and for people living between San Leonardo and Santa Lucia the rate was 1 soldo. San Bartolomeo was exempt. The decision illustrates the sense of the city as a group of communities corresponding to parishes. Yet the interests of any particular community were subordinate to the larger, common good.[52]

The official designation of parishes and sestieri as entities with responsibilities to a larger entity, the city, became an inescapable aspect of life for the residents of early Renaissance Venice and would affect to some extent their associations. A final measure of the distance traversed between the ninth and the fourteenth centuries can be taken in the way Venetians identified themselves. In the early centuries they used a physical site or a topographical feature to distinguish themselves from others with similar names. They used terms such as *de rivo* and *de capite*. By the eleventh century they began to identify themselves by parish. Their legal identity derived in part from their place of residence as designated by the government. The city became inescapably a part of a person's public identity. The Rialtine settlement had become the *civitas Venetiarum*.[53]

Patricians, *Popolo Grande*, and *Popolo Minuto*

The phrase *comune Venetiarum* emphasized the communal aspects of Venetian life. The government, which had to run the city and overcome private interests, found it expedient to stress the undifferentiated nature of communal life. Ideally, Venice was to be a place where all shared the burdens as well as enjoyed the benefits of municipal life. This was not, however, really the case. Legal status, occupation, wealth, honor, and prestige all served to differentiate Venetians from one another and to impose unevenly the burdens and benefits of civic life. Herein lay many challenges to the ideal of civic concord.

In retrospect the most striking feature of Renaissance Venetian society is the stratification of the populace into legally defined status groups. For this reason the date 1297 has long been recognized as critical in Venetian history. In that year a major change was made in the eligibility requirements governing membership in the Great Council, Venice's main deliberative body. Until then, membership in the Great Council was, theoretically at least, open to all male members of Venetian society. Men sat in the council by virtue of their past service to the government or because they were nominated to do so by a special nominating committee. In practice the core of the council was made up of men who belonged to distinguished families of ancient Venetian ancestry.

During the late thirteenth century pressure mounted for a change in eligibility requirements. One source of pressure was families that traditionally sat in the council. They feared that a rising tide of new men (many of whom grew wealthy in eastern trade) would swamp the council, depriving them of a place in it. The result was the law of 1297, which guaranteed a permanent seat in the council to all those who had served on it during the past four years; and, although it made special provisions for the acceptance of a few men not covered by the four-year rule, it excluded all others from the right to sit on the council. For this reason, the action taken in 1297 became known as the "closing," or Serrata, of the Great Council.

The closing of the Great Council did more than define eligibility for membership. It took on social significance as well. Membership in the council became synonymous with noble status; and since membership was restricted to those included in 1297, ascent to noble status was closed as well. The equation of council membership and noble status eventually found concrete expression in the *Libro d'Oro* (Golden Book)—the official register of noble births. As a consequence of the Serrata, Venice came to be ruled by a closed, hereditary aristocracy.[54]

The size of Venice's ruling class during this period is unknown. About 244 families enjoyed noble status during the period from 1293 to 1379, but that was not a constant figure. A number of families became extinct, and new families were inducted into the nobility. The largest induction took place in 1381 when, at the end of the War of Chioggia, thirty families were added. During the period 1297 to 1423 the population of the city varied a great deal. After reaching perhaps 120,000 persons before the Black Death in 1348, it ranged somewhere between 60,000 and 80,000 throughout the rest of the period. At its greatest, the nobility, including women and children, probably constituted about 5 percent of the total population. In 1311, 1,017 men sat in the Great Council. Hence only about one-twentieth of all Venetians enjoyed noble status, and only 1 percent of the population (the adult males) had the right to sit in the councils of government.[55]

The religious constituted another distinct group in Venetian society. Although they enjoyed fewer privileges and had less autonomy in Venice than in most cities, the clergy were nonetheless distinguished from all other Venetians. During the early Renaissance there were between 300 and 450 parochial clergymen in the city. To that number must be added the large number of monks and nuns who filled the city's monasteries. In the early fourteenth century Florence had a population of around 1,000 male and 500 female religious. Venice probably had an equal number.[56]

In addition to the nobility and clergy there was another legally defined status group in Venetian society—the class of cittadini (citizens). Like patricians they composed about 5 percent of the Venetian populace, and like patricians they enjoyed a number of privileges that set them apart from the rest of the populace. There were two categories of citizens. The first was *cittadini originarii*. These were men of ancient Venetian ancestry. Among the rights enjoyed by the cittadini originarii was the exclusive privilege of holding certain posts in the bureaucracy, most notably the post of grand chancellor. Since all government offices with the exception of the dogeship and the procuratorships of San Marco rotated on a frequent basis, the citizen-secretaries provided an important element of continuity in the government. Experts in writing and matters of protocol, cittadini originarii were especially valuable to the government as assistants on sensitive diplomatic missions. The other category included cittadini who enjoyed citizenship *de intus* or *de intus et extra*. These were grants of citizenship made to foreigners who had taken up residence in the city and paid taxes. Citizenship gave these men (most of whom were merchants) the protection and status of Venetians in their trading ventures. As a group then, the cittadini enjoyed a number of privileges denied to others in Venetian society.[57]

Below the cittadini came the mass of Venetian residents who enjoyed no special privileges or special legal status. What distinguished most popolani from one another was their occupation. Lacking any sort of census for the fourteenth and fifteenth centuries, it is impossible to calculate the occupational makeup of the Venetian populace. Nonetheless, a partial enumeration of the occupations in which they were engaged gives a sense of the variety within the Venetian laboring classes.[58]

Venice's involvement in the textile industries was not as great as that of Florence or the cities of Flanders; nonetheless, there were a significant number of people employed in the wool, cotton, and silk industries in the fourteenth century. Popolani found employment as weavers, shearers, dyers, combers, and carders and participated in the other processes involved in producing cloth. Women were especially active in certain aspects of cloth production, most notably spinning. The fur and tanning industries also employed significant numbers of Venetians. Venice was a major center in the international fur trade, and the city supported three distinct furriers' guilds.[59]

The city's marine economy provided employment for many other popolani. According to Doge Tommaso Mocenigo, in the 1420s the city employed 6,000 carpenters and caulkers. Carpenters, shipwrights, caulkers, oarmakers, sailmakers, ropemakers, and others were needed to build and equip not only the merchant cogs and galleys that sailed to distant ports but also to construct the gondolas and other small vessels that transported men and goods to other parts of the lagoon and to the terraferma.[60]

The city's rapid and continued growth throughout the late Middle Ages and early Renaissance provided opportunities for work in the building trades. A major construction project, such as the expansion of the Ducal Palace or the construction of a patrician palace, required many skilled workmen. Sixty-four artisans, including seven masons, forty stonecutters, ten carpenters, two painters, two blacksmiths, one windowmaker and two floorers or pavers, worked at one time or another building one of Venice's finest Gothic palaces, the Ca' d'Oro. Even a modest house required the service of carpenters and masons.[61]

Skilled workmen in the luxury trades gained for Venice an international reputation. Most famous were the glassmakers of Murano, whose furnaces turned out goblets, serving bowls, mirrors, window panes, and eyeglasses. Soapmakers produced a fine white soap, and druggists made an opium-laced product that was widely sought for its medicinal purposes. Goldsmiths and rock crystal carvers produced reliquaries and other objects for local consumption and for export.

The city also had a contingent of men who worked more with their minds than with their hands. Both the government and private individuals required the services of notaries to record their meetings and draft their personal documents. Most notaries were either priests or cittadini. Tutors and school teachers found work teaching the rudiments of reading and writing (in Venetian, if not in Latin) and the use of the abacus to the sons of nobles and artisans alike.[62] The city employed a number of physicians and surgeons, many of whom it lured to the city with promises of citizen status.[63]

The city also employed a large number of people in service industries. Bakers, butchers, food sellers of various sorts, cobblers, tailors, used-clothing dealers, barbers, and fuel and straw sellers all made a living meeting the daily needs of the populace. Tavern keepers, hostelers, and the like served both the native population and the merchants and pilgrims who visited the city.

In addition to these skilled workers, there were multitudes of unskilled or semiskilled workers in the city. They found work supplying muscle power. They worked as porters, stevedores, and balers, hauling cargos onto ships and moving goods from warehouses to workshops. Others transported people about the city; there was a large contingent of boatmen and ferry (*traghetto*) operators who kept traffic moving between the two halves of the city, between the islands of the lagoon, and between the city and the terraferma. People living on the periphery of the city and surrounding islands eked out a living from the lagoon. Some worked as gardeners and vineyard keepers, tending the gardens and orchards that supplied the city with fresh produce. Others harvested fish and fowl from the lagoon.

Women and the young found work as domestic servants. The prosperous household, whether patrician or popolano, had a large staff of servants, wet nurses, cooks, and stewards. Many of these posts were filled by slaves. The slave trade flourished in early Renaissance Venice; and with slaves costing as little as 25 or 30 ducats, it was possible for many Venetians to purchase them and use them in their households. Slaves constituted a legally defined group in Venetian society (slavery was hereditary), but the services they performed often made them indistinguishable from their free brethren who performed similar tasks.[64]

There also existed an underworld in Venetian society—a world of shysters, vagabonds, beggars, and thieves. They frequented Rialto, playing games of chance and waiting to relieve unsuspecting visitors of their money. Prostitutes had their headquarters in the parish of San Cassian. There they had easy access to the taverns and hostels of Rialto where they found customers for their services.[65]

The residents of early Renaissance Venice were thus divided into five different categories: nobles, clergy, cittadini, popolani, and slaves. Four of these, not counting the popolani, constituted legally defined status groups. This division gives Venetian society the appearance of rigidity and castelike stratification. Yet it also masks significant differences within these status groups.

The nobility, for instance, was a heterogeneous group in terms of ancestry and family size. Some members of the patriciate belonged to families of ancient origin, families that had served the city for generations. Members of the Tiepolo, Morosini, and Gradenigo families could trace their ancestry to the early days of the city, if not to Trojan families from which Venetian nobles sometimes claimed descent. Others came from upstart families whose ancestors had entered the Great Council as new men in the years immediately preceding the Serrata. The size of patrician families varied a great deal as well. Some, like the Morosini and Contarini, had many branches; others were represented by a single nuclear family. In 1379 at least fifty-nine members of the Morosini family owned property in the city and were assessed for government loans, and the prestigious Loredan family had sixteen members with enough wealth to be assessed; by contrast, Nicoletto Babilonio was the sole member of his family included in the assessment.[66]

The clergy and cittadini also exhibited a wide diversity. The clergy included men and women from patrician houses who won positions of power as abbots, abbesses, priors, and bishops. Yet a number of men from artisan backgrounds held clerical posts in the city's parish churches.[67] The cittadino class included men such as Raffaino de' Caresini, grand chancellor and friend of Doge Andrea Dandolo, and Pignol Zucchello, a merchant from Pisa who received a grant of citizenship and settled in the city.[68] Even the class of slaves included educated men who served as stewards of patrician households and newly arrived captives who were not baptized in the Christian faith and who did not speak a word of Venetian.[69]

Wealth was another factor distinguishing Venetians from one another. The absence of a source comparable to the Florentine *catasto* makes it difficult to calculate with much accuracy the distribution of wealth in Venetian society. Nevertheless two sources exist that give some clues to the matter.

The best source is the *estimo* or tax assessment of 1379. In order to assess loans for the War of Chioggia, the government ordered a census of immovable wealth in the city. All those having more than 300 *lire a grossi* worth of immovable wealth were to be assessed loans. Out of a population somewhere between 60,000 and 100,000 persons, 2,128 persons and 38 religious institutions qualified. Of the 2,128 persons (including widows) who were assessed, 1,211 were nobles, and 917 were commoners. The largest assessment went to nobleman Federico Corner of San Luca, who had property valued at 60,000 lire a grossi. Scores of other persons, including Corner's fellow parishioners nobleman Marino Dandolo and popolani Andrea Lavezer and Zanin Cataben, barely qualified with estimates of 300 lire. The wealthiest popolano was cittadino Bandino Garzoni, a merchant from Lucca who had an assessment of 50,000 lire. Garzoni received noble status in 1381, as a reward for his contribution to the war effort.[70]

Table 2.1 gives the breakdown of nobles and commoners assessed in different categories, as calculated by Gino Luzzatto. Several points are worthy of comment. First, the figures reveal a dramatic disparity in wealth within the noble class. Ninety-one nobles had fortunes worth over 10,000 lire, yet 817 (more than two-thirds) had fortunes below 3,000 lire. Fully a third ranked in the lowest category. Some nobles were too poor to be included at all—hence the difference becomes even more dramatic. But as Stanley Chojnacki has shown, a note of caution is warranted. Sometimes the disparity of wealth in the estimo reflects stages in the family cycle. Chojnacki notes, for instance, that future doge Michele Morosini had an assessment of 38,000 lire, yet his only son (and future heir) Giovanni had only 1,500 lire worth of immovable property.[71] For members of the larger families especially, the estimo may very imperfectly reflect both their own and others' perceptions of their actual wealth. Nevertheless, gradations in wealth within the patriciate could be very great indeed.

The second point to note is that a number of non-nobles were very wealthy men. Twenty-six popolani had assessments over 10,000 lire, placing them among the very wealthiest men in the city. Most of these men made their fortunes in trade. Pietro Regla of the parish of San Giacomo dall'Orio, who had an assessment of 14,000 lire, traded in grain; Nicolò Sturion of Santa Maria Nova (assessment 16,000 lire) was described in the estimo as a *spicier* (druggist). Very likely Sturion was a spice or drug trader rather than a mere apothecary. Many popolani with lower assessments also engaged in trade; Lunardo dall'Agnella, who had an assessment of 2,000 lire, was a *mercante de biave* (grain merchant).[72] Despite the great wealth of a few popolani, most had modest fortunes; the majority included in the estimo (541 of 917) had assessments in the lowest category.

Most of the popolani included in the estimo are identified by name alone, not by profession. Yet those who are identified by trade represent virtually all the skilled occupations in the city. The list includes butchers, cheese sellers, fruit sellers, soapmakers, cobblers, coopers, blacksmiths, goldsmiths, masons, carpenters, tailors, barbers, dyers,

TABLE 2.1 Breakdown of Wealth in the *Estimo* of 1379

Assessment (lire a grossi)	Nobles	Popolani
50,000 and more	1	—
50,000–35,000	4	1
35,000–20,000	20	5
20,000–10,000	66	20
10,000–5,000	158	48
5,000–3,000	145	88
3,000–1,000	386	214
1,000–300	431	541
Total	1,211	917

SOURCE: Luzzatto, *Storia economica*, 130.

hempmakers, tavern keepers, tanners, and others. This suggests two things: first, that there was not a strict hierarchy among the tradesmen of Venice. Although it is true that druggists and furriers were among the best represented (with 15 and 13 respectively), all trades shared in the wealth of the city.[73] Second, the information on professions indicates that a few members from nearly every occupational group were also members of the city's economic elite. Taken as a whole, the estimo of 1379 illustrates that the patriciate was not a monolithic class sharing common interests and also that a small but significant portion of the city's non-noble residents, drawn from many occupational groups, had a serious economic stake in the city.[74]

A second source that gives some sense of the distribution of wealth in the city is dowries. The dowry represented a woman's share of her father's patrimony and as such provides a useful, albeit rough, indication of her father's total wealth. A group of 681 dowries drawn up by non-noble families between 1309 and 1419 shows that for this period, the average dowry was 74 ducats; the mean was 50 ducats. The largest dowry was 80 lire di grossi or 800 ducats, which Margarita, daughter of Corado de Alemania, brought to her husband Angelino Longonasso in 1414. The smallest dowries were 10 ducats; there were two of these.[75]

Table 2.2 illustrates the distribution of dowry wealth among the non-nobles according to the dowry receipts. As the table shows, the total value of the 681 dowries is 50,674 ducats. Yet the top 20 percent of the non-nobles controlled almost one-half (47.59 percent) of the total dowry wealth. The 136 non-nobles who received the largest

TABLE 2.2 Distribution of Dowry Wealth, 1309–1419

Decile of Sample (by dowry size)	Dowry Value (ducats)	Percentage of Total
1	16,246	32.06
2	7,872	15.53
3	6,163	12.16
4	4,881	9.63
5	3,993	7.88
6	3,342	6.59
7	2,777	5.48
8	2,242	4.44
9	1,908.5	3.77
10	1,249.5	2.46
Total	50,674.0	100.0

SOURCE: ASV, Cancelleria Inferiore, Notai.

dowries received dowries totaling 24,118 ducats. By contrast, the 136 poorest popolani received dowries equalling only 3,158 ducats, or 6.23 percent of the total. When one considers that the very poorest Venetians (those with tiny dowries or those who had no dowries at all) were the least likely to go to a notary, then it becomes clear that the diversity in wealth among Venetian commoners was very great indeed.[76]

The data from dowries also warrant some comparisons with the data from the estimo. First, it is not surprising to find that some of the wealthiest men in the dowry group were included in the estimo. Bartolomeo de Ugolin, a furrier from San Pantalon, received a dowry of 350 ducats from his wife Agnes. Bartolomeo was one of thirteen furriers included in the estimo, in which his immovable wealth was assessed at 1,000 lire. Francesco Bereta of San Simeon Grande, who got a dowry of 250 ducats from his wife, had an assessment of 500 lire in the estimo.[77] Second, the dowry data strengthen a conclusion drawn from the estimo, namely that wealth among the popolo was not tied to particular occupations. For although it is true that goldsmiths received an average dowry of 106.1 ducats (based on nine dowries) and cobblers received dowries averaging only 51.7 ducats (based on nineteen dowries), there was also tremendous disparity within particular trades. Dowries for goldsmiths ranged from 35 to 200 ducats and for cobblers from 13 to 130 ducats. Even boatmen (*barcaruoli*) showed quite a disparity. The dowries they received ranged from 20 to 120 ducats. Again it appears that the practice of a particular trade did not, by definition, exclude one from membership in the city's economic elite.

Given the sources available, it is impossible to reach any definitive conclusions about the distribution of wealth in Venetian society. Yet the presence of 917 non-nobles in the estimo shows that wealth was not confined to the patrician class. And an average dowry figure of 74 ducats suggests that many popolani, including artisans and laborers, made an adequate living. Perhaps as a trade center Venice enjoyed a greater influx of capital than its industrial and banking neighbors. Although the Venetian economy was susceptible to economic down turns, Venice was able to recover from them more quickly than most cities. The fact that Venice recovered more rapidly and completely from the Black Death than did Florence, Siena, or the other Tuscan towns supports this conclusion. Prosperity may in turn have been shared with a slightly larger percentage of the populace than in other Italian cities.[78]

The evidence presented shows that there was no absolute correlation between wealth and membership in a particular status or occupational group. Furthermore, it suggests a different division of Venetian society than that defined by legal status. The significant division was not among nobles, cittadini, and popolani, but rather among nobles, well-to-do commoners (the *popolo grande*), and workers (the *popolo minuto*). Since this is the division that will be used throughout this study, it seems worthwhile to explain briefly the characteristics of each group.[79]

The characteristics of the nobility, of course, are largely self-evident. Nobles were those who had the right to sit in the Great Council. Although there were great differences within the nobility in terms of wealth, family size, and antiquity, noble status conferred so many privileges that even the poorest patricians stood apart from the rest of society. Certain forms of charity were reserved for impoverished patricians, and patricians alone had the right to hold political office.

The second group, well-to-do commoners or the *popolo grande*, is a diverse group with imprecise boundaries. This group included some cittadini, such as Grand Chancellors Raffaino de' Caresini and Benintendi de' Ravagnani and merchants Bandino Garzoni and Pignol Zucchello, but did not include the lowliest notaries of cittadino status, who had salaries of only 30 ducats per year. Moreover, men who did not enjoy cittadino status but who owned workshops, possessed property, employed several workers, or in some other way dis-

URBAN FORM AND SOCIAL STRATIFICATION 37

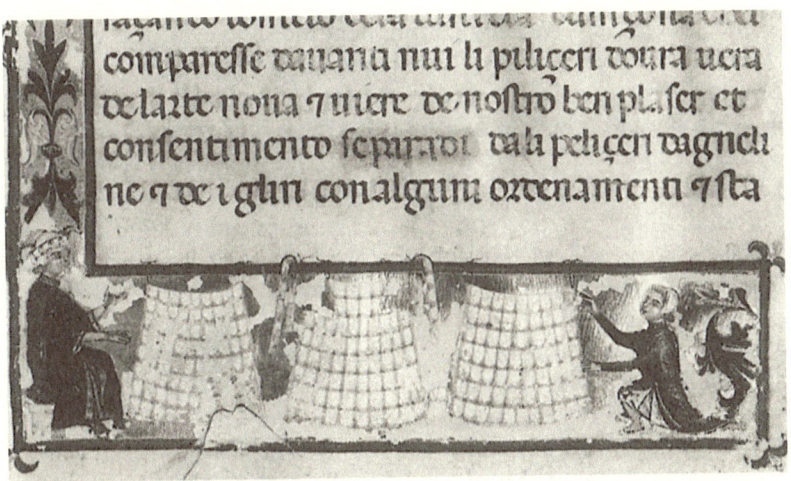

PLATE 2 A master furrier and a worker. Detail from the Capitulary of the Vair Furriers' Guild. Photo: Museo Civico Correr.

tinguished themselves from the great mass of Venetians were popolani grandi. What we can say with certitude is that in 1379, the 917 non-nobles included in the estimo represented the solid core of the popolano grande group.

The third group, the *popolo minuto*, included everyone else. The city's workers, whether skilled or unskilled, were members of this group. They were artisans, including master craftsmen who worked for others, and day laborers who found work as they could. Servants, slaves, and the poor who received charity completed this group. (Plate 2).

This tripartite division of Venetian lay society into nobles, popolani grandi, and popolani minuti allows us to take into account not only the one truly significant status difference in Venetian society (nobility), but also differences in the distribution of wealth. What is more, it seems to accord with contemporary Venetian usage. During much of the fourteenth century Venetians were less concerned with legally defined status differences than is often supposed. In private documents, for instance, nobles almost always referred to themselves as such, using the title *nobilis vir dominus;* yet cittadini rarely used their honorific title *circumspectus et providus vir*.[80] Indeed, it is their failure to identify themselves as such that makes it so difficult to determine the contours of the cittadino class in the early Renaissance and that calls into question their status-consciousness.

Both nobles and wealthy commoners did, however, use the term *dominus* to describe themselves. It was most frequently the appellation applied to patricians, yet it was sometimes used by non-nobles as well. Bernardo Bedoloto, a wealthy merchant from the parish of San Giacomo dall'Orio, was described as dominus, as was his father Giacomo; and Natalia Zana referred to her father who was a doctor (*physicus*) both as *discretus vir dominus* (possibly signifying cittadino status) and as *dominus magister* (calling attention to his learning).[81] Nobles and well-to-do commoners constituted the *domini* of Venetian society. In his will, dated 1349, Marco Arian from a prominent cittadino family left a bequest of 300 ducats for the construction of wells in the parish of San Raffaele. He stated that the wells were to serve the needs of "the poor and the good men of the parish" (al povolo e a boni homeni de la contrada). In Arian's mind there were two categories of people in the parish—the poor and men of standing—and these categories had little to do with legal status.[82]

Public documents indicate that the patrician government generally divided the city into two groups: *nobiles et populares*.[83] Yet there are indications that the government also recognized distinctions between *populares*. In 1394, for instance, the Great Council voted to make physical improvements to the market at Rialto comparable to those recently made at piazza San Marco. The council justified this beautification plan by noting that it was at Rialto that "nobles, our merchants, and generally all foreigners" gather (nobiles et mercatores nostri ac generaliter omnes forenses).[84] Nobles and merchants were not synonymous, yet both, along with foreign visitors, counted for a great deal in the government's estimation. And in a law concerning the festival of the *Marie*, the officials in charge of the festival decided that if a parish did not have sufficient nobles to fund the event, then "popolani owning property" (populares habentes possessiones) were to do it.[85]

The indifference of cittadini to honorific titles, the flexible use of the term *dominus*, and the government's own tripartite division of the populace show that during much of the early Renaissance legal status counted for less than has often been assumed. The Serrata did mark (more or less) the political closure of the Venetian government, but social closure, including the development of exclusive aristocratic and cittadino mentalities, took much more time to complete. The signs of this change came late, at the end of the fourteenth century. As we shall see, when these changes did occur, they signaled a major transformation in the social foundations of the Venetian Renaissance state.

THREE

Family Structure and Marriage Ties

On the twenty-second day of June, 1312, Nicoleto Rosso of the parish of San Simeon Grande went to the notary Domenico, priest of San Maurizio, and had an agreement with his wife, Biancafiore, drafted. Nicoleto agreed not to beat or verbally abuse Biancafiore under threat of a 50 *lire di piccoli* fine. In the past Nicoleto had abused Biancafiore "so inordinately and evilly" (inordinate et malo modo) that she had fled their home and returned to her father's house in Treviso. Wishing "for you peacefully to stay with me while you live," Nicoleto, with the consent of his relatives, now encouraged Biancafiore to return. He did, however, insist upon one stipulation. He stated, "If you do not obey my precepts and orders, then I want the right to correct and castigate you moderately and decently."[1]

Twenty-seven years later, on 18 October 1339, nobleman Leonardo Michiel went to the notary Felice de Merlis and had a surprisingly similar document drafted. According to the charter, Leonardo had "without cause" abused his wife Maddalena so harshly that she had fled their household and did not wish to return. Leonardo promised that if Maddalena returned, he would keep her in "legitimate matrimony," and that if he broke the agreement, he would pay a fine of 100 lire for each infraction. The money was to be paid to Maddalena outright to do with as she pleased.[2]

These two charters, one drafted by a popolano, the other by a patrician, provide insight into Venetian family life and attitudes toward marriage. Husbands sometimes beat their wives and cursed them so badly that the women took the only recourse open to them—flight. When this occurred, there was a crisis in family relations that kinsmen acted quickly to correct. Nicoleto's relatives (meis heredibus) took an active part in the agreement between Nicoleto and Biancafiore. Not only were they parties to the agreement between the spouses, they were also liable for the fines that would be incurred if the agreement were broken. Leonardo Michiel's relatives also intervened to negotiate the agreement. Both sets of relatives would have agreed with the sentiments of the Florentine poet Antonio Pucci, who wrote:

> La femmina fa l'uom viver contento:
> gli uomini sanza lor niente fanno.
> Trista la casa dove non se stanno,
> però che sanza lor vi si fa stento.[3]

Despite the obvious similarities between the two cases, there were marked differences as well. The expectations that popolano Nicoleto Rosso and nobleman Leonardo Michiel had for the future differed considerably. Nicoleto expected the relationship between himself and Biancafiore to be, if not cordial, then close, even paternal; he expected his wife to obey his orders, and if she did not do so, then he believed he had the right to correct her actions, and, further, to instruct and educate her. By contrast, the future relationship between Leonardo and Maddalena was to be purely formal. Leonardo was concerned only with maintaining a "legitimate matrimony" with a "legitimate wife." There was no expectation that the couple would be close, much less cordial. Indeed, Leonardo agreed that if he broke the agreement and failed to pay the fine, he could be put in jail. Furthermore, Maddalena and her relatives were careful to stake out an independent position for her. They carefully noted that any fines levied on Leonardo were to be hers alone, to do with as she pleased (de sua re libera et propria ad sue beneplacitum voluntatis). The purpose of this agreement was simply to restore the couple to a state of legitimate matrimony.

These two examples of families in crisis illustrate that patricians and popolani had differing expectations of marriage. For popolani, marriage was to be a close, working relationship between spouses; for patricians, marriage was more clearly an alliance between kinsmen in which the alliance—the *matrimonium* itself—was paramount.

This chapter explores the differences in family orientation among early Renaissance Venetians. The family stood at the center of Venetian life, with marriage serving as its constitutive act.[4] Family structure and kinship ties secured Venetians in their social world, influencing and shaping other social bonds they created. Hence any understanding of the associations of early Renaissance Venetians must begin with an examination of kinship networks.

The Patrician Family

Patricians are the only group in Venetian society whose family life has been studied in any detail. Studies of individual patricians and family institutions such as the *fraterna*, the joint holding of the patrimony by brothers, have illuminated ways in which patricians used kinship and marriage ties to promote their economic fortunes. Other family strategies, including restriction of marriages, allowed patricians to maintain family fortunes over long periods of time.[5]

The family figured prominently in the political machinations of patricians as well. Unable to dominate the councils of government by themselves, patrician families sought allies through marriage, with women serving as the connective tissue between families. Each lineage pursued a strategy designed to move it closer to the center of power within the patriciate. The cumulative effect of these overlapping and cross-cutting ties was to bind the patriciate together and promote intraclass harmony. In Robert Finlay's words, "assemblies of the Great Council amounted to the congregation of large, interlocking family complexes based on both lineage and affection, *parenti e consorti*.[6]

What all this meant to the individual patrician and how it affected his social contacts, especially with persons outside the patriciate, is somewhat harder to determine, given the lack of sources comparable to the Florentine family diaries. The sources that are available suggest that Venetian patricians did, like their Florentine counterparts, live in two familial worlds: one centered around the household, the other focused on the lineage.[7] The patrician's primary attachment was to his immediate family—those who made up his household—yet he also moved in a larger world of kinship—the patriline. The experience of patrician Marino Badoer nicely illustrates this dual orientation.

Marino Badoer, who lived in the first half of the fourteenth century, was a member of one of Venice's premier patrician families. As a *casa vecchia*, the Badoer family traced its ancestry to the early days of Venice. Marino came from a branch of the family that resided in the parish of San Giacomo dall'Orio. At the beginning of the fourteenth century, the Badoers already had a venerable past in the parish, having been the principal benefactors of the church in the thirteenth century.[8]

Marino was the son of Marco Badoer, nicknamed Belleto. Marco and his brother Ruggiero represented the San Giacomo branch of the family. Marco Badoer had four children who survived to adulthood: three sons, Marino, Nicolò, and Marco, and a daughter Zana. Marino married Sofia Ghisi, member of a large and powerful family that resided in the neighboring parish of San Simeon Grande. Together Marino and Sofia produced four children: three daughters, Sclava, Eufemia, and Zana, and a son Nicoleto. Marino also had an illegitimate son named Marco (Figure 3.1).[9]

Various acts recorded in notarial registers provide glimpses into the family life of Marino Badoer. Like other patricians, he used marriage as a means of allying himself and his kinsmen to other noble *case*. His own marriage to Sofia allowed him to cultivate the Ghisi.[10] He borrowed money from both Pietro Ghisi of San Simeon and from Sofia Ghisi, a nun; and in 1325 he entrusted full power of attorney over his affairs to Nicolò Ghisi.[11] Marino also maintained close ties with his sister Zana, who married nobleman Francesco Querini of Santa Giustina. In his will he left a bequest of 50 ducats to help dower Zana's daughter Agnesina and a small bequest to help support another niece—a nun at San Giovanni de Torcello.[12] Although Zana's marriage to Querini had immediate and short-term benefits for Marino, it should also be seen in the context of the lineage. The marriage cemented a bond between the two patrilines which had begun at least a generation earlier; Marino's and Zana's aunt Tommasina, wife of their uncle Ruggiero, was herself a Querini.[13]

Marino's three daughters provided him with further opportunities to ally himself with other families. In 1342 Marino made arrangements with Pietro Contarini for the marriage of his daughter Sclava to Pietro's son, though it is unclear whether the marriage ever took place.[14] In the meantime, however, Marino managed to marry another of his daughters, Eufemia, to nobleman Nicolò Contarini. Thus the Contarini connection remained secure.[15] Marino married his third daughter, Zana, to nobleman Nicoleto Soranzo.[16] In this way he reestablished a link to the Soranzo family that his father had begun a generation earlier by marrying Marino's own brother Marco to Beriola Soranzo.[17] The Contarini and Soranzo families, like the Badoer, were *case vecchie*. Marino was able to marry his daughters into venerable and powerful families.

Marino also maintained close ties to his brother Nicolò. One of the most distinctive features of patrician family life was the fraterna. According to law, brothers who lived together and engaged in business were treated as partners, unless they went through a formal act of separation. Maintenance of a joint residence often reinforced this legal bond; and in some instances, marriage was limited to the eldest brother in order to protect the patrimony from dispersal. The rela-

FIGURE 3.1 The Badoers

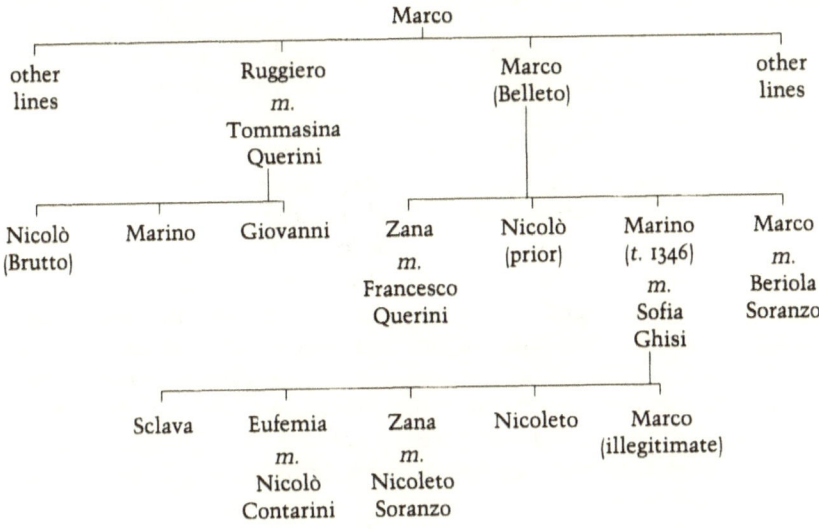

t. = testament
m. = married

tionship between Marino and Nicolò accorded with several of these practices. Nicolò did not marry; instead he became prior of the hospital of San Giovanni Evangelista, to which the Badoer family had long had close ties. The family was its principal benefactor and had the exclusive privilege of selecting the prior from among its members.[18] In this generation, the incumbent was Marino's brother Nicolò.

Two property divisions involving Marino and Nicolò illustrate how real estate interests linked not only brothers but also members of the casa as a whole. In March 1320 Marino and Nicolò made an agreement dividing twenty properties in San Giacomo. This property division, which may have been one step in the dissolution of the fraterna linking them, was done "for the sake of peace and in order to avoid trouble."[19] For his share, Marino got a large property (*proprietas magna*) and a row of buildings (a *ruga*) containing eight dwellings. Nicolò also got a large property, seven row buildings and three houses which "used to be of wood but now are of mortar." The brothers rented most of the dwellings to popolani. Marino's properties bordered those of his first cousins (the heirs of his uncle Ruggiero) and the property of his former sister-in-law, his brother Marco's widow.

She held the property as surety for her dowry. Property bound together brothers, cousins, and in-laws.

Sixteen years later, in 1336, there was another division. This time Marino and Nicolò acted together to divide properties between themselves and their cousins Nicolò (son of Ruggiero) of Santa Giustina and Enrico and Ziani (sons of Giovanni Badoer, count of Arbe), also of Santa Giustina. The properties were in the parish of San Stin (near San Giovanni Evangelista) and across the Grand Canal in Santa Giustina.[20] The three parties subdivided a large property in San Stin into three units. Provisions were made for the building of walls to delineate boundaries and for the continued communal use of certain entrances. Marino and Nicolò got as their joint share one part of the large property in San Stin and part of a ruga in San Stin. Enrico and Ziani held another share. In return, Marino and Nicolò relinquished their share of the property in Santa Giustina, which until then they had held jointly (habebamus pro indiviso) with their cousins. By this action, the brothers consolidated their holdings on the Rialto side of the Grand Canal.

Unlike the first property division, this was a joint division rather than an individual one. The Badoers of San Giacomo divided property with their cousins, the Badoers of Santa Giustina. This was done even though Marino and Nicolò were not living together. Nicolò stated that he was from San Giacomo, but that he lived at the hospital of San Giovanni Evangelista, "since I am prior of the place." Despite his position, Nicolò continued to identify with the San Giacomo branch of the family.

Marino Badoer's will provides further illustration of the complex familial world in which a Venetian patrician lived. On 8 November 1346 Marino had presbyter Felice de Merlis record his testament.[21] Marino named as his executors his wife Sofia, his daughters Eufemia Contarini and Zana Soranzo, his cousin Marino Badoer, his niece Agnesina da Canal, and his son Nicoleto. His brother Nicolò was already deceased. Marino's main concern was to provide for his children, both legitimate and illegitimate. He left a yearly allowance to his bastard son Marco and the *residuum* (balance) of his estate to his legitimate son Nicoleto. But Marino also took an interest in the welfare of more distant members of ca' Badoer. Fifty ducats from his estate were to be used to help support one of his cousin's sons. Furthermore, Marino noted that a dispute had developed between the Badoers and the bishop of Castello over the priorate of the hospital of San Giovanni Evangelista. If the case were settled in favor of ca' Badoer, then Marino wanted 40 of the 60 lire owed him by the hospital to be remitted to San Giovanni Evangelista, "for the soul of Nicolò, my dead brother and prior of the said place, and for my soul." If the Badoers lost, he wanted his executors to remit only 20 lire to the hospital.

In his will Marino also made provisions for the disposition of his properties. He left them to his legitimate son Nicoleto, as part of the residuum of his estate. However, in the event that Nicoleto should die without male heirs, Marino wanted the properties to pass not to his daughters or his bastard son, but to the heirs of his cousins Enrico, Zanino, and Ziani Badoer. And he stated that the properties were never to be sold. Instead they were to go "always to the male heirs of this house of ca' Badoer."[22] Marino wanted to keep the properties within the patriline.

Marino was not alone in his concern for other members of the lineage. In 1370 Maffeo Badoer of Santa Giustina made elaborate provisions for his properties. He left them to his sons; in case of their deaths, to his daughters; and in case of their deaths, to his nephew Giacomino. But if Giacomino were to die without male issue, Maffeo wanted his properties to pass to Nicoleto, son of Marino Badoer of San Giacomo dall'Orio.[23]

The experience of Marino Badoer shows that members of great patrician houses, like their counterparts in Florence, were entwined in complex family webs. The first concern of these men was the welfare of their immediate family—the kinsmen with whom they shared a roof and strong ties of affection. Beyond the household lay the larger kin group—the lineage. Meetings of the Great Council, ancestral palaces, and patronage of particular churches and hospitals reinforced the bonds uniting members. The solidarity that bound one member of the Badoer family to all other members found concrete expression in a commemorative plaque that they erected at San Giovanni Evangelista in 1349. The Badoers placed the plaque there in thanksgiving for the end of the plague and "for the good of the scuola and the aid of our brothers." The signatories were from many branches of the family. They included Giacomo Badoer from Peraga, the new prior; Marco Badoer of San Stin; Giovanni Badoer, also of Peraga; Maffeo Badoer of San Stin; Filippo and Alberto Badoer; and Marino Badoer of San Giacomo dall'Orio.[24]

The lineage-consciousness of patricians was most evident in the concern they expressed for keeping property in the family. Nobleman Angelo da Pesaro bequeathed his magnificent palace—the present-day Fondaco dei Turchi—to his son with the proviso that the palace never be alienated from the family. Marco Loredan made provision for his estate to pass to the "propinquos magnos" of "domo Lauredano." And Marco Barbaro left his "chasa granda" to his grandsons.[25]

The significance of this attachment to lineage becomes clear when we turn from the experience of a large family like the Badoers to that of a small family like the Dalle Boccole of Santa Trinità. Unlike the Badoer family, which enjoyed great antiquity, the Dalle Boccole family was one of the "new" families among the patriciate. There is no record of family members having held important government posts before the Serrata; indeed, it is likely that the family's prominence derived from their inclusion in the Serrata.[26]

One of the earliest references to the family is found in the will of Nauticherio Christiano, dated July 1312. Christiano, a wealthy resident of Santa Trinità, named Giovanni Dalle Boccole, whom he described as his *nepos* (nephew or grandson), as his executor. The two were business associates and held properties jointly in Venice and elsewhere. Christiano left a bequest of 2,000 lire to a certain Nicolò Dalle Boccole, whom he also described as a *nepos*. Only Giovanni has survived in the record (Figure 3.2). In his will, Christiano also made provisions for the construction and endowment of a hospital in Santa Trinità that was to house twenty poor and infirm persons. The hospital was known as the "hospital of miser Natichlier de cha Christian."[27]

The Giovanni Dalle Boccole named in Christiano's will was a wealthy man. In his own will, dated 1321, he mentioned properties that he held in Venice and in the countryside around Treviso and Ferrara, and he bequeathed 3,000 lire for the enlargement of San Zanipolo.[28] Giovanni asked to be buried at San Zanipolo in the chapel of Saint Nicholas. According to his will, Giovanni had at least six children: two sons, Marino and Pietro, and four daughters, Francesca, Caterina, Beatrice, and Beriola. He married his daughters well. Francesca married nobleman Ermolao Balbi, Beriola married Filippo da Molin, and Beatrice married into the huge Morosini family.[29] Caterina's fate is unknown. The sons, Marino and Pietro, maintained close contact throughout their lives, although they did not live under one roof. Marino lived in Santa Trinità, whereas Pietro lived for a time in Sant'Aponal and for a time in San Moisè.[30] The brothers entrusted power of attorney to one another; stood pledge for one another, and engaged in a variety of joint commercial ventures. And they looked to their relatives, especially their sisters, for business capital. The relationship between the brothers and their widowed sister Francesca Balbi was especially close. Pietro borrowed a great

FAMILY STRUCTURE AND MARRIAGE TIES 47

FIGURE 3.2 The Dalle Boccole

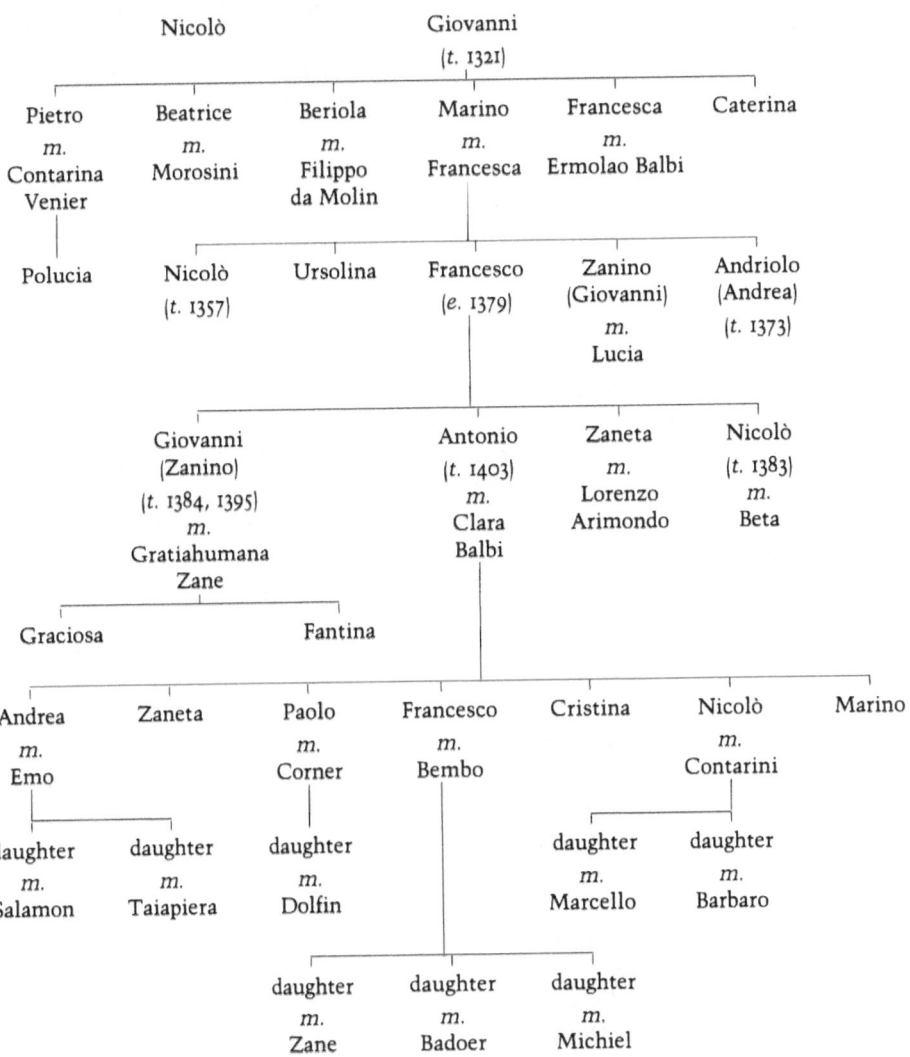

t. = testament
m. = married
e. = estimo

deal of money from Francesca, and in 1340 he granted her power of attorney. When Francesca was widowed, Marino and Pietro tried to protect the interests of her son, their nephew, Franceschino.[31]

Judging from the activity of the two brothers, the fortunes of the Dalle Boccole prospered in the second quarter of the fourteenth century. In 1348, responsibility for putting on the festival of the *Marie* passed to the parish of Santa Trinità. The Council of Forty awarded the privilege (or burden) of staging the festivities to three families in the parish: the Celsi, the Sagredo, and the Dalle Boccole.[32] The Celsi and Sagredo were two of the oldest and most distinguished families in the parish. Both contributed to the construction of the church in the eleventh century.[33] The inclusion of the Dalle Boccole with these families reflected their growing power and prestige in the parish (and their ability to pay for the festival).

Only Marino had sons and so the bulk of the family fortune passed to his children. He had four legitimate sons: Francesco, Andriolo, Zanino (Giovanni), and Nicolò. According to their wills, both Nicolò and Andriolo died without male heirs; and the bulk of the estate passed to their brother Francesco.[34] Francesco was the only member of the Dalle Boccole family included in the estimo of 1379. His assessment of 10,000 lire a grossi made him the second wealthiest man in the parish. Only popolano grande Nicolò Strevian, whose assessment was 12,000 lire, surpassed him.[35]

Unlike their father's generation, which seems to have worked uncommonly hard, this third generation (of the fourteenth century) showed a proclivity for crime. In 1351 Nicolò and Zanino ran afoul of the law when they helped their bastard brother resist the guards of the signori di notte.[36] And in 1357 Francesco was tried and severely punished for raping a little girl with the assistance of her mother.[37] Nobles frequently attacked patrolmen and committed rape. Commission of these crimes suggests an arrogance on the part of the Dalle Boccole brothers that may indicate that the brothers felt more secure about their place within the city's elite than had their father or grandfather.[38] Marino Dalle Boccole may have sensed this change in attitude among his sons. In his will, he stated that Zanino could use his father's goods in commerce, "if he conducts himself like an honest man" (se regat bonum hominem).[39]

The fourth generation consists of the children of Francesco, namely, his sons Giovanni, Nicolò, and Antonio, and a daughter Zaneta. Antonio married Clara Balbi, thereby recreating the link to the Balbi family that had existed in his grandfather's generation. Giovanni married Gratiahumana Zane. The wills of the brothers are extant and allow us to assess the position of the family at the end of the fourteenth century. Nicolò drew up a will in 1383 and died shortly thereafter without heirs.[40] Giovanni drew up two wills: one in 1384, another in 1395.[41] In both instances, he named his wife and brother Antonio to be among his executors. In the will dated 1384, he stated that he wished for any daughters he might have to be endowed with dowries of 1,400 ducats; sons were to get the residuum of his estate. If he failed to have sons, the residuum was to pass to his brother Antonio and his heirs. In the will dated 1395, he simply stated that his house in Santa Trinità was to be divided among his children. Antonio, who was *podestà* of Torcello, drafted his will in 1403.[42] He left the balance of his estate to his children equally. Then he noted that if his children died, he wanted his estate to be divided into four parts. Two-fourths were to go to his nephews Nicoleto and Lorenzo Arimondo, sons of his sister Zaneta; one-fourth was to be distributed for his soul; and one-fourth was to be given to his niece Fantina, daughter of his deceased brother Giovanni. Antonio asked to be buried in the family tomb in the chapel of Saint Nicholas at San Zanipolo. This was the same place where his grandfather Marino and his great-grandfather Giovanni had asked to be buried.

In their family life, the Dalle Boccole pursued many of the same practices of the larger and older Badoer family. They tried to extend their contacts through marriage, and brothers maintained close relations. But what distinguished the Dalle Boccole from the Badoers was the small size of the family—the absence of a large kin group. When he drafted his will in 1403, Antonio Dalle Boccole knew that if his sons died without male heirs, the patriline would become extinct. In that event, he had little choice but to leave the bulk of his estate to another patriline—the Arimondo family. Marino Badoer, by contrast, was confident that if his own sons died without male heirs, the family would continue through a collateral line. In the end, Antonio Dalle Boccole had four sons who married, but not one of them produced a male heir. On the death of Antonio's son Francesco in 1483, the Dalle Boccole family became extinct.[43]

The size of patrician families had a profound impact on the way they perceived themselves and others. As Stanley Chojnacki has shown, a disproportionate share of offices and total patrician wealth went to the larger families. The greater the size of the family, the greater its prestige and status within the patriciate.[44] Members of great houses like the Badoer lived in a family world that transcended space (they were widely dispersed throughout the city) and time (the family extended through generations). They viewed the family as a "continuum of outstanding men."[45] Size provided a kind of insurance against demographic catastrophe and allowed certain families to rule the city with confidence. Small families did not share this confidence. With family extinction an ever-present possibility, their position was precarious. They were forced into the role of clients to the larger families. Membership in a family affirmed a patrician's place in society, but the size of the family often determined his standing within the patriciate itself.

The *Popolano Grande* Family

Popolano grande families shared a number of characteristics with patrician families. Like patricians, the popolo grande placed great emphasis on the fraternal bond; they used marriage as a way of furthering their economic fortunes; and they saw palaces as symbols of the kin group. Yet in one respect the orientation of popolano grande families differed markedly from that of patricians. Unlike patricians, for whom family was an affirmation of place within society, the popolo grande viewed the family and in particular marriage as a vehicle of upward social mobility.

The history of the Disenove family illustrates this pattern of upward social mobility. Cittadino Marco Disenove was a wealthy man actively engaged in overseas trade. At the time of his death in 1354, he left four children: an elder son Francesco, a daughter Cristina, a younger son Pietro, and an infant or unborn daughter Chiara. In his will, he requested that his house in San Giacomo dall'Orio remain in the family.[46] In the same year, the elder daughter Cristina married nobleman Marco Soranzo.[47] At about the same time, Francesco got into trouble over some financial irregularities and went into exile. He apparently died shortly thereafter.[48] In 1358, at age nineteen, Pietro married noblewoman Orsa Trevisan, who brought with her a dowry of 1,000 lire a grossi.[49] In 1361 Chiara, who was still a minor, died, and her share of the estate passed to Pietro.[50] With Pietro's death, before 1376, the Disenove family, like the Dalle Boccole, became extinct.[51]

What is most striking in this unusually complete picture of a fourteenth-century cittadino family are the marriages between Marco Disenove's children and patricians. His daughter Cristina married into the Soranzo family and his son Pietro married into the Trevisan family. Prominent patrician families accepted the offspring of a respectable cittadino family as suitable spouses for their own children. Why was this the case? The marriage between Marco Disenove's daughter Cristina and Marino Soranzo is fairly easily explained. Cristina brought with her a dowry of at least 800 ducats, which in the year 1354 was competitive with, indeed higher than, most noble dowries.[52] The Soranzos stood to gain considerable economic advantage from the marriage since legally a woman's dowry was at the disposal of her husband. The marriage between Marco's son Pietro and Orsa Trevisan is more of a surprise since offspring of the union would not be patricians (noble status was based on the patriline) and since in this instance it was incumbent on the patrician family to supply the dowry. The explanation may lie in the size of Orsa's dowry—1,000 lire a grossi or about 400 ducats. While a respectable sum, it was not competitive even with the dowry of a wealthy cittadina like Cristina Disenove. Marriage into a respectable popolano grande family may have been the best the Trevisans could afford for their daughter Orsa.

There is no source that allows us to determine the incidence of intermarriage between patricians and popolani in the early Renaissance, but the examples that appear in various records suggest that it was not uncommon. To cite a few: the Lucchese silk merchant Tommaso Nardi, who received a grant of *cittadinanza* in 1365, married his daughter Loica to nobleman Domenico Gossoni. A certain Pietro, a fruit seller (*frutarolus*), married his daughter Agnolla to nobleman Giovanni Guorro. Grand Chancellor Benintendi de' Ravagnani married two daughters to patricians. Nobleman Nicoleto Soranzo married his daughter Cecilia to non-noble Pietro Berardino. Popolano Marco a Cagnolis married Catarucia, daughter of nobleman Raffaele Civran; and cittadino Alvise de Garzoni married the daughter of nobleman Giovanni Dalle Boccole.[53] According to Marco Barbaro's compilation of noble marriages, in the fifteenth century, 5.6 percent of noble marriages were with popolani.[54]

The marriages contracted by the wealthy non-noble Bedoloto and Regla families provide further evidence of intermarriage between patricians and popolani and allow us to chart the fortunes of the families over several generations (Figures 3.3 and 3.4). The Bedoloto family derived from stock that at the turn of the century included a man who served as procurator or treasurer of the parish and as a guard for the signori di notte.[55] Through heavy involvement in trade the fortunes of the family rose considerably, and by the third quarter of the fourteenth century the two brothers who represented the family contracted good marriages. Ludovico (Alvise) Bedoloto married noblewoman Chiara Michiel, and his brother Bernardo married noblewoman Fiordelise da Riva.[56] Bernardo Bedoloto was then visited

FIGURE 3.3 The Bedolotos

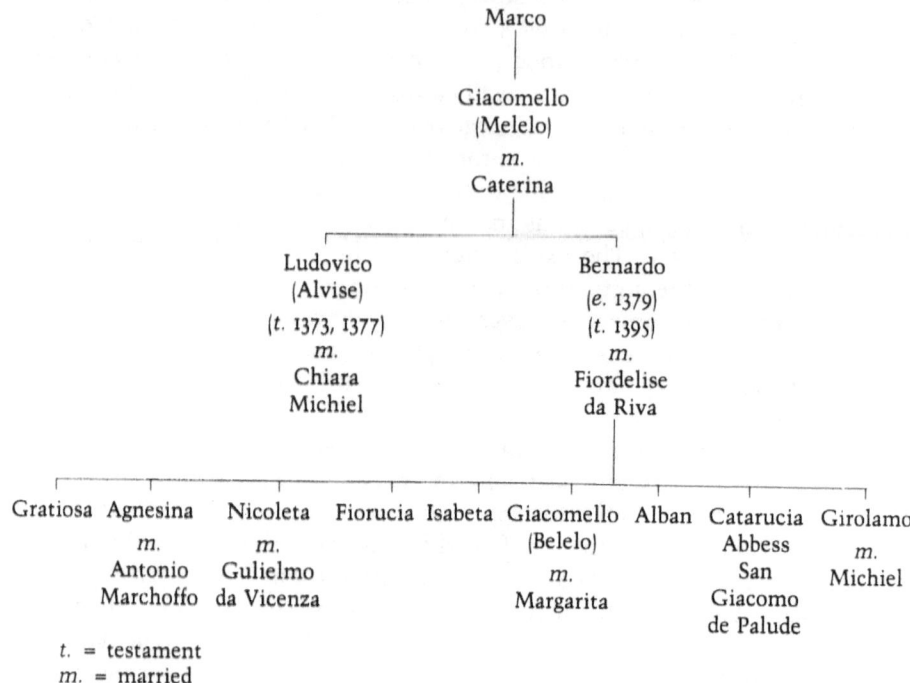

t. = testament
m. = married
e. = estimo

by one of the misfortunes feared by fathers in Renaissance Italy—the birth of many daughters. Probably for this reason he was unable to contract marriages to patricians for his daughters (at least for those whose marriages we can reconstruct). He settled at least one in a convent, and he gave to another (Agnesina) a dowry of only 250 ducats—a very small sum.[57] But he did manage to marry his son Girolamo into the prominent Michiel family.[58]

The Regla family marriages were more spectacular. Giovanni Regla had three children. We know how he married two of them. His daughter Maddalena married non-noble Marino de Raynaldo from a trading family of Triestine origin. His son Francesco married into the noble Marango family, a small family that became extinct before the end of the fourteenth century.[59] Nevertheless, it was a marriage into the nobility and perhaps added some prestige to the Regla family. In turn Francesco Regla had eight children; one of his daughters, Leonarda, married nobleman Marco de Mezzo; nothing can be said for

FAMILY STRUCTURE AND MARRIAGE TIES   53

FIGURE 3.4 The Reglas

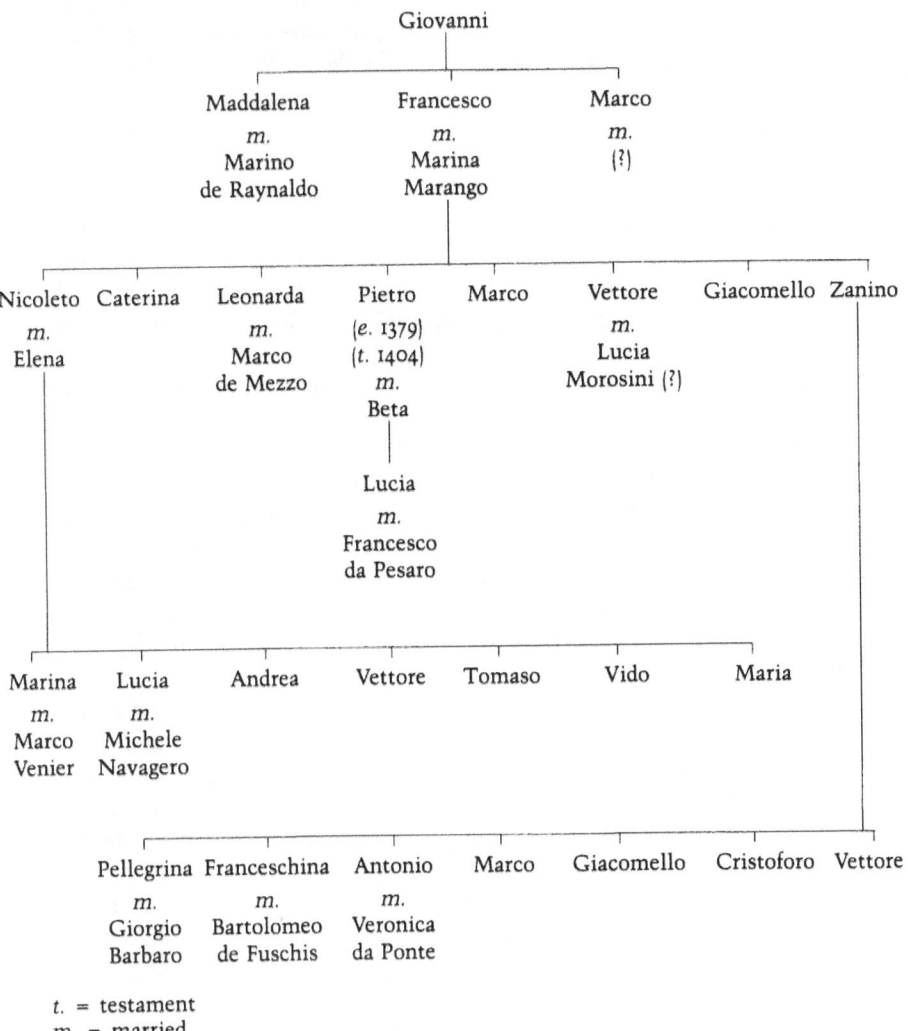

t. = testament
m. = married
e. = estimo

certain about the other marriages, although it appears that his sons Zanino and Pietro married into noble families.⁶⁰

In the next generation, the Regla family made a series of outstanding marriages. Nicoleto and Elena Regla had six children: three sons and three daughters. They married their daughters Marina and Lucia into the noble Venier and Navagero families respectively. The youngest daughter Maria, who was unmarried at the time her mother made her will in 1421, was to be provided with a dowry of 900 ducats—a fairly competitive sum.[61] Nicoleto's brother Pietro, the second wealthiest man in the parish of San Giacomo dall'Orio in 1379, had only one daughter, Lucia, who married nobleman Francesco da Pesaro.[62] A third brother, Zanino, had seven children. Using their share of a 10,000 ducat legacy left them by their wealthy uncle Pietro, the girls found husbands. Franceschina made what was perhaps an undistinguished marriage to Bartolomeo de Fuschis, but her sister Pelegrina married nobleman Giorgio Barbaro of Santa Fosca.[63] And in 1417 their brother Antonio married noblewoman Veronica da Ponte, who had a dowry of 800 ducats.[64]

The marriages of the Regla family illustrate an interesting evolution. In the second generation, the non-noble Reglas married into a lesser noble family, the Marangos. In the third and fourth generations, they married into some of Venice's premier families: the Veniers, de Mezzos, Navageros, Pesaros, and Barbaros. In the second generation, Francesco married above his station, whereas the noble Marangos married below theirs. In the third and fourth generations, the Regla women, well-dowered daughters of a non-noble family, married into the nobility. The history of the family in the trecento can be viewed as a steady rise in prestige.

The marriage arrangements made by the Bedolotos and Reglas for their daughters reveal a familiar pattern of social mobility found in European societies, namely that wealthy daughters of men without status marry the sons of men with status.[65] Marriage to the well-dowered daughters of non-nobles provided a means by which patrician families could replenish the family fortune. Yet the Bedoloto and Regla sons also married nobles; this less familiar pattern of intermarriage requires further comment.

Patrician fathers had three options to choose from when deciding the future of their daughters: they could arrange marriages for them, they could place them in convents, or they could allow them to remain spinsters. The last option seems to have been fairly uncommon in the early Renaissance. Notions of family honor required that daughters be suitably placed, and the high mortality rate associated with the plague made spinsterhood risky.[66] In addition, spinsters living with their brothers represented a continuous drain on the resources of the patriline. Many fathers therefore chose the second option, placing one or more daughters in convents. The entry fees required by convents were considerably lower than dowries, so fathers could settle their daughters in convents without depleting the estate.⁶⁷ Marriage was the third alternative, and as we have seen, some noble fathers chose to marry their daughters below their station rather than place them in convents. One reason is the cost of marrying a daughter to a popolano may not have been much greater than the cost of placing the girl in a convent. The dowry that Orsa Trevisan brought to Pietro Disenove was only half what Pietro's sister took with her. In addition, noble fathers stood to gain economic advantage from these unions. Both the Bedolotos and Reglas were active in overseas trade; both at least for a time had substantial amounts of capital.⁶⁸ The promise of business contacts and potential partners coupled with the desire to protect the family honor may have been the inducements patricians needed to marry their daughters to popolani.

In addition, although it is true that noble families did not gain much prestige from such marriages, they also did not lose much. The decision by patricians to marry their children outside the nobility is further evidence that Venetians of the trecento were less status-conscious than is generally thought. The fear of losing prestige by marrying non-nobles was not great. In addition, many of the social customs of patricians and popolani grandi were similar. When the sons and daughters of patricians married into popolano grande families, they did not move into a different social milieu. Patricians and popolani grandi often moved in the same social circles. For instance, both Ludovico and Bernardo Bedoloto had friends among the patriciate.⁶⁹ And patrician and popolano grande women shared a life focused on the household and children. Patricians had something to gain and little to lose from such unions.

If the reasons patricians contracted marriages to popolani are complex, the reasons the popolani grandi married patricians are more simple. The non-noble who was fortunate enough to marry his daughter to a patrician would have nobles for grandchildren. And marriage of a son to a patrician opened the door to political favors, especially grazie, from the wife's kinsmen.⁷⁰ Marriage into the nobility opened both direct and indirect avenues to the centers of power in Venetian society, and access to power is clearly what wealthy commoners wanted. Both Pietro Regla and Girolamo Bedoloto tried unsuccessfully to enter the ranks of the nobility.⁷¹

The family life of the popolo grande reveals much about Venetian society during the early Renaissance. Popolano grande families mimicked as much as possible their noble counterparts. Indeed, one of the writers who gave expression to the patrician family ideal was cittadino Giovanni Caldiera.[72] Marriage between nobles and popolani indicates that there was fluidity in social ties. Marriage served not only to bind the patriciate together but also to ally patricians with those immediately below them. Finally, the experience of the popolo grande reveals a striving for status among non-nobles. When the notary who was recording his will asked goldsmith Francesco Bedoloto what he wanted to happen if his wife gave birth to a daughter, Bedoloto responded that he wanted the girl to be given 1,000 ducats for a dowry, "in a style of noblewomen" (more nobili domine).[73] Nothing better illustrates the aspirations of this intermediate group in Venetian society.

The *Popolano Minuto* Family

It is only when we move from a consideration of the elite of Venetian society to a consideration of the popolo minuto, the vast majority of Venetians, that we encounter a marked and significant change in family structure and ideals. The familial experience of artisans and the poor of Venice contrasted strikingly with that of patricians and the popolo grande. For the popolo minuto the nuclear family, in particular the conjugal bond, was the focus of family life. The working-class family goal was a close working relationship between husband and wife.

There are no census data that allow calculations of life expectancies and family size in Venice in this period; yet if demographic patterns were similar to those of other Italian cities, the households of the popolo minuto were small and often truncated. According to the catasto of 1427, the average Florentine household numbered 3.8 persons and the average Pisan household 4.2 persons. In 1395 the Bolognese household had an average of 3.5 members, while in the Veneto, Veronese households averaged 3.68 persons in 1409.[74] In Venice the pattern was almost certainly the same. Evidence from artisan wills suggests that on the average artisan couples produced fewer than two children.[75] And guilds recognized that members might not have any kinsmen. The capitulary of the used-clothing dealers stated that members were to escort the relatives of deceased members to the funeral, "if the deceased has any relatives" (s' el ne averà).[76]

Not only were artisan households small, but artisans themselves were isolated from a larger kinship network. Generally, they were not enmeshed in complex family webs, like the patricians (and to a lesser extent the popolo grande). This can be illustrated in artisans' selection of executors for their estates. Table 3.1 summarizes the selection of fiduciaries in 120 wills drawn up between 1297 and 1423 by artisans and their wives and widows. The table shows that in a group of 50 married artisan males, 40, or 80 percent, named their wives as sole or joint executor of their estates. Among relatives, artisans looked most frequently to their sons, brothers, and brothers-in-law. None selected their fathers and only one his mother. Only one artisan named his uncle as an executor and two named their cousins. Women relatives were named infrequently.

These data call for several comments. First, the absence of fathers as fiduciaries suggests that most artisans' fathers were dead by the time their sons drafted their wills. In Florence and Genoa artisans married relatively late, and their fathers often were deceased by the time their sons reached testamentary age. Second, the figures show that men relied little on distant relatives as fiduciaries. Either artisans did not have distant relatives or they did not feel close enough to them to name them as executors. The first possibility is more likely given demographic patterns and the large number of coparents (the godparents to one's children) and nonrelatives named as fiduciaries. We would expect artisans to look first to kinsmen and only afterward to non-kin to protect their patrimony. Lacking kinsmen, artisans looked for support to those linked to them through fictive kin ties or friendship.[77]

The pattern among artisan wives differed somewhat from that of men. After husbands, mothers and sisters were the most frequently named executors of married women (named by six and five women). Fathers and brothers were next, named by three women each. Children and in-laws were named infrequently, whereas two women chose their uncles as executors. None named their aunts. Nonrelatives were almost as popular with married women as with men, but coparents were not. A significant number of wives (five) chose clerics to be executors. Only one man chose a clergyman.

These figures too call for comment. First, women testators probably were on average younger than male testators since many drew up their wills during pregnancy. This may explain their greater reliance on parents and siblings, and the relative absence of children as executors. Second, like their husbands, artisan women seldom found executors among more distant kin. Again this suggests the minor role that distant kin played in the family life of working-class Venetians. Third, women too looked to friends and neighbors for support.

Artisan widows' wills are informative, for they show where women turned when the conjugal bond was broken. For widows, the most common choice for an executor was not in fact a relative.

TABLE 3.1 Selection of Fiduciaries among Artisans

	Married Artisan Men (total 50 testators)		Married Artisan Women (total 50 testators)		Widowed Artisan Women (total 20 testators)	
Spouse	40[a]	40	38	38	0	0
Mother	1	1	6	6	3	3
Father	0	0	3	3	1	1
Brother	8	7	3	3	0	0
Sister	1	1	5	5	4	4
Son	10	5	1	1	1	1
Daughter	3	2	2	2	1	1
Mother-in-law	0	0	0	0	1	1
Father-in-law	3	3	1	1	0	0
Son-in-law	0	0	0	0	1	1
Daughter-in-law	0	0	0	0	0	0
Aunt	0	0	0	0	1	1
Uncle	1	1	2	2	0	0
Brother-in-law	4	4	2	2	1	1
Sister-in-law	0	0	0	0	1	1
Cousin	2	2	1	1	0	0
Cleric	1	1	6	5	2	2
Coparent	11	6	2	2	2	2
Procurators of San Marco	0	0	1	1	0	0
Unspecified nonrelative	26	14	16	13	18	11
Unspecified relative, either nephew or grandson	3	3	3	3	1	1

[a]The first set of figures represents the total number of fiduciaries named in each category. The second set of figures represents the total number of testators who named fiduciaries in that category. For example, among artisan men, five named sons as fiduciaries, but together they named a total of ten sons.

SOURCE: ASV, Cancelleria Inferiore, Notai; ASV, Archivio Notarile, Testamenti.

Eleven of the 20 widows chose one or more persons unrelated to them as fiduciaries. Among kin, sisters were the most common choice, followed by mothers. Coparents and clerics were relatively more popular with widows than they were with wives. When marriage ended, women turned to nonrelatives, coparents, and clerics, but among relatives they favored the immediate family.

The evidence presented in Table 3.1 suggests that the Venetian artisan family did not have much contact with a wide kinship group.

This contrasts with the experience of great patrician families who maintained contact with and relied on distant kin. A group of 26 testaments from the Ghisi family (13 men's wills and 13 women's wills) shows that 4 chose cousins to be executors, 2 chose aunts, and 1 a maternal uncle.[78] Together 120 artisans, artisans' wives and widows, chose only 3 cousins, 2 uncles, and 1 aunt. To compensate for their isolation from kinsmen, artisans looked to friends, clergy, and coparents. But first they turned inward. As the overwhelming selection of spouses indicates, artisans relied heavily on the marriage bond.[79]

More than any other event, marriage marked an artisan's entry into adulthood. Twelve was the legal age of majority in Venice, yet a variety of sources show that the working classes did not generally consider their children to come of age until later. Testators often decreed in their wills the age at which their children would receive their legacies. This could range up to twenty-five years of age. The capitulary of the coopers' guild stated that sons could not take over their deceased fathers' workshops until age seventeen.[80]

Regardless of legal and customary notions of adulthood, artisan men reached de facto adulthood when they married, for it was often at that time that fathers released their sons from their legal tutelage. Marriage and filial emancipation sometimes occurred simultaneously. On 4 June 1315, for example, Lamfranco of the parish of San Samuele emancipated his sons Servodeo, Amatore, and Marco. On the same day Marco and Servodeo drew up charters accepting dowries from their wives.[81] When Zanino, an immigrant from Mantua, remarried and accepted his wife's dowry of 100 lire, he emancipated his sons Azolino and Marco.[82] Fathers and sons did not want to be liable for each other's debts and deeds.[83] The same was true for daughters. Once daughters received their dowries (which constituted their share of the patrimony), their fathers' legal obligation to them ended.[84]

Some sons, however, remained under their father's tutelage after marriage. A young man sometimes accepted his wife's dowry in his father's presence and with his father's blessing. Bartolomeo de Boateriis even received power of attorney from his father to have a dowry receipt drawn up for his wife Margarita.[85]

Other times, a mother or brother would stand with the groom when accepting a dowry.[86] In these instances, the groom probably did not have the wherewithal to establish a separate household; and the bride's parents may have wanted the entire family to take responsibility for receiving the dowry.

For still others, the issue was moot. Dowry receipts show that many young men and women married after the death of their fathers. Death, rather than legal separation, cut them off from their kin. For immigrants, distance created practical, if not legal, separation from parents. Immigrants who came to Venice to find work often married, remained, and lost contact with their kin, whether they were legally emancipated from them or not.[87]

After marriage, popolano minuto couples adopted a wide variety of living arrangements. Giovanni Ruzerii and his wife Giovannina lived with her father and brother. A cobbler named Lorenzo and his wife Anna lived with Anna's mother until fear of creditors drove them away. Zanino de Ragono and his wife Caterina maintained in their house Caterina's niece and her husband Marco Donato. The household also included Zanino's three-year-old adopted daughter and his slave Anna.[88] Other couples lived by themselves, finding their own accommodations. Many popolano minuto families, like the Baxerio family, were dispersed throughout the city. Michele Baxerio and his sons Giovanni and Pelegrino were all masons. Yet the three lived in different parishes: Michele in San Trovaso, Pelegrino in Sant'Angelo, and Giovanni in San Giacomo dall'Orio. The brothers Zulian and Giovanni Moro were rock crystal carvers; one lived in San Zulian, the other in San Salvador.[89] Since most popolano minuto families did not own property, there was no traditional hearth that could serve as the psychological and social focus of family life. This contrasted with the experience of many patrician families who, even though dispersed throughout the city, felt attachment to a particular palace.

Among the laboring classes, marriage could serve to link nuclear families—that is, the bride's immediate family and the groom's immediate family. Sometimes there was a practical motive for creating such ties. When marriages were contracted between families engaged in the same trade (and this happened quite infrequently), the families may have wanted to pool their resources.[90] An artisan with no male offspring might contract a marriage for his daughter so that his patrimony could be put to good use. A more important consideration, however, was the desire to create ties of dependency to another kin group; ties that could be used in times of trouble.[91] Marriage provided a way for isolated nuclear families to create a support system.

The primary goal of marriage, however, was the creation of a new nuclear family centered on the conjugal bond. The conjugal unit became the economic and emotional mainstay of working-class life. Common goals and interests, in particular children and the patrimony, led the husband and wife to rely on each other.

Economic necessity contributed much to the development of close ties between spouses. In order for the working-class family to meet its subsistence needs, both the husband and wife had to work. Dissolution of a marriage could mean financial disaster for the poor, especially widows.[92] Marriage, more specifically the income of two working partners, was the popolo minuto's best insurance against economic hardships.

Women contributed to the family income in a variety of ways. They participated in most trades in trecento Venice, performing the less skilled tasks. They were excluded in most cases from controlling workshops (except as caretakers for their sons).[93] Women also found employment in areas of the economy largely reserved for them. The textile industry employed many women who performed various tasks needed to turn raw wool, silk, and cotton into finished cloth.[94] Other women worked in food retailing or as seamstresses and tailors; and the poorest women found work as servants and wet nurses.[95]

Through their dowries and employment then, working-class wives contributed to the income of their families. The income supplied by women helped keep the family above the level of subsistence. In turn, the earning power women enjoyed strengthened their hand in the marriage. Because wives contributed to the family income, husbands could not easily discount their opinions. In 1321, for instance, Giacomina, wife of Gelfo da Reggio, forced her husband to sign over to her some property near Ferrara. Gelfo originally had purchased the property in her name (perhaps as surety for her dowry) but had not ceded it to her. Giacomina pressured Gelfo into making the cession, fearing that she would not be able "to do with it [the property] as she pleased."[96]

Nowhere is the working-class wife's importance more evident than in power of attorney contracts. When a Venetian artisan went about the task of selecting someone to act as proctor for his affairs, he had to select someone who would have his best interests at heart. He wanted to be sure that his patrimony would be protected, especially if he had children. Notarial records show that time and time again, working-class men selected their wives. In 1322, for instance, a shearer named Marco gave his wife Filippa special power of attorney to handle money owed him for his service on a ship of the noble Capello family.[97] Other men gave their wives plenary power of attorney. In 1312 a goldbeater named Biagio gave his wife full power of attorney; similar grants were made by many other artisans.[98] In some instances grants to wives may indicate that artisans had no reliable male kin or friends to whom they could entrust their affairs, but more likely husbands believed that their wives had the acumen and experience needed to handle their affairs. After all, they had contributed to the growth of the patrimony. Economic necessity coupled with the dissolution of kin ties served to make marriage the material focus of working-class family life.

Attitudes toward widowhood provide further insight into working-class views of marriage. Popolano minuto husbands, like their patrician counterparts, frequently included incentives in their wills (in the form of larger legacies) for their wives not to remarry. Some feared that if their wives remarried, their children would be neglected or deprived of their legacies by stepfathers. But honor and reputation were also concerns, for even childless men tried to entice their wives to remain widows. When the bale binder Matteo drafted his will in 1379, he left the usufruct of four pieces of land in the area around Treviso to his wife Caterina. Upon her death, the land was to be ceded to the scuola grande of San Giovanni Evangelista. However, if Caterina remarried, the land was to go immediately to the scuola.[99] Franceschino de Croce, a sailor, made similar provisions. He named his wife Marina as his sole executor and left her his entire estate. But he warned that if she remarried, she would receive only her dowry and his estate would be handled by Giovanni dal Suto, a boatman.[100] Neither man mentioned children in his will. Both hoped that their wives would remain widows, probably as a sign of respect for their deceased husbands' souls.[101]

Despite encouragement to remain widows, many popolano minuto women remarried. The reason was quite simple; unlike patrician women, who could use their dowries to live quite comfortably, popolano minuto women could not afford to remain widows.[102] In fact, widows made ideal wives. Not only did they have their dowries, which by law had to be returned to them, but often they had some additional inheritance from their husbands. Stepchildren as well often had inheritances that could be placed at their stepfather's disposal. When Michele Corezario married Caterina, widow of Bartolomeo de Floravante, he got use of his stepson's inheritance of 20 ducats.[103] Popolano men as a group found widows perfectly acceptable as wives. Economic realities overcame cultural attitudes toward widowhood, for it was in marriage that the artisan or laborer was more secure from the vagaries of life.[104]

A final example that illustrates the significance of marriage to working-class Venetians is the case of the artisan wife Margarita. In

1397 Margarita, wife of Cristoforo Quattropani, a boatman, drew up her will. She named her husband Cristoforo and another boatman named Bartolomeo as her executors; and she left the residuum of her estate to Cristoforo. But he died first and by 1399 Margarita had remarried, taking as her new husband Giovanni de Plan, a goldsmith. In September of that year Margarita revised her will, not by drawing up a new one but simply by crossing out Cristoforo's name and substituting Giovanni's. For Margarita marriage was her station in life; the husbands were interchangeable.[105]

Margarita's apparent facility in changing husbands does not in any way diminish our evaluation that working-class marriages were characterized by mutual dependence and support. Rather it illustrates how crucial the marriage bond was to the popolo minuto. It was in marriage, regardless of the partner, that the isolated artisan found a measure of security.

Kinship and marriage ties had broad significance to Venetians in the early Renaissance. The nature of familial experiences did much to determine the psychology and outlook of both patricians and popolani and, as we shall see, influenced in turn their other social contacts. Social interaction in early Renaissance Venice can only be understood in the context of familial and kinship experience.

For patricians the family was an affirmation of their place in society. All actions undertaken by the kin group, including marriage alliances, patronage of religious sites, construction of palaces, and cultivation of clients, were seen within a familial context and were designed to enhance the prestige and honor of the house. In a society where esteem and honor were paramount, patrician families were one in their desire to appear the most esteemed and honorable. Only large families, however, enjoyed the demographic security that allowed them to pursue their familial strategy with confidence and aplomb.

For the popolo grande, the kin group was the vehicle for social mobility. Unable as individuals to enter the ranks of the nobility, wealthy commoners sought to ally themselves by marriage to patricians. Business contacts, friendship circles, and offices in various institutions provided contacts that could lead to marriages with patricians. The family became the focus of the popolo grande's social aspirations.

For the laboring classes the family and in particular the marriage bond provided a measure of security. Isolated from fellow kinsmen and susceptible to the vagaries of life, the popolo minuto sought in marriage a working partnership between spouses that would allow them to meet the challenges of life. In contrast to some patricians, for whom the family was a source of confidence, the family situation of the popolo minuto points to their essential insecurity, which may in turn have contributed to their political and social impotence.

In light of these findings the actions of popolano Nicoleto Rosso and patrician Leonardo Michiel come more sharply into focus. Both men risked their honor in order to get their abused wives to return to them. Michiel (and his kinsmen) wanted his wife to return because her flight threatened not only to disrupt contact between the two lineages, but also because it threatened the prestige and honor of the families. Michiel's only concern was to restore his wife to a state of legitimate matrimony. The future relationship between the spouses was unimportant, only the fact of the relationship mattered. For Rosso, by contrast, the relationship was paramount. Rosso depended on his wife to be a partner with him. For this reason he continued to insist on his right to instruct and correct her. Rosso's future security depended on a working and workable relationship with Biancafiore. These two instances of Venetian families in crisis point to the centrality of the family in Venetian life. Yet they also illustrate that the very concept of the family differed dramatically among the patricians, the popolo grande, and the popolo minuto.

FOUR

The World of Work: Guild Structure and Artisan Networks

In his chronicle *Les Estoires de Venise* Martino da Canal described in detail the reception that the artisan guilds gave the newly elected Doge Lorenzo Tiepolo and his wife the dogaressa in 1268. Each guild marched to the ducal palace, where the guildsmen saluted the doge and wished him victory and long life. They then proceeded to the Tiepolo palace at Sant'Agostin, where they repeated their salutations to his wife. For this occasion the guildsmen wore their finest robes and dressed their apprentices and workers richly as well. Some of the guilds chose to put on elaborate spectacles. The barbers dressed two of their members as knights errant who had rescued damsels in distress; the combmakers presented the doge with a lantern that when opened released a flock of birds. Other guilds used the occasion to display the products of their craft. At the head of each procession came the gonfalon or banner of the guild. The gonfalon, which was used on other ritual occasions as well, symbolized the spirit of fraternity that guildsmen wished to emphasize on this occasion.[1]

Processions were only one of many means by which guilds promoted solidarity. In their statutes, guilds tried to prevent rivalry among members by limiting competition. They regulated the number of workers a master could employ, limited the days and hours members could work, and promoted equitable distribution of raw materials. The religious activities undertaken by the religious arms of the guilds, the scuole, also cultivated a sense of community. Guildsmen helped dower the daughters of deceased or poverty-stricken members, recited prayers for the souls of their deceased brothers, and attended their brethrens' funerals. These were activities traditionally associated with kin. Yet as we have seen, many artisans did not have a secure family life. By adopting these activities as their own, guilds gave their members a sense of belonging. Nowhere in Venetian society was the emphasis on community and solidarity more pronounced than in the guilds (Plate 2).[2]

This chapter explores the associations and networks forged in the world of work—in the marketplaces and workshops of the city. The analysis is divided in two parts. The first section examines the industrial organization of the city and the internal organization of the guilds. It shows that, contrary to widely held opinion, Venetian guilds were not communities of equals. Instead they were hierarchic, and in some instances oligarchic, institutions over which certain great guildsmen maintained control. Furthermore, it shows that the patrician regime fostered these tendencies and protected leading guildsmen. The second section analyzes the social world of Venetian artisans. Here it is demonstrated that shared work experiences and acts of charity did not forge guildsmen into tight-knit communities. Instead, artisans tended to divide along lines of wealth. Wealthy artisans (the popolo grande) associated with one another and with patricians, whereas the workers (the popolo minuto) forged their own informal ties with one another. Despite their claims to the contrary, Venetian guilds were not highly integrated close-knit communities of interest. Rather, in the world of work, Venetian society was sharply divided between the popolo grande and the popolo minuto; and the tension generated between masters and workers had important consequences for the patrician regime.

Production Techniques and Guild Structure

Giovanni Monticolo, the leading authority on Venetian guilds, once wrote,

> Venetian artisan guilds lacked a real contrast between the masters and workers in the sense in which the interests of the one were opposed to those of the other; the economic interests of masters and workers did not interfere with the normal state of affairs which was concord between members—concord which was reinforced by social benefits, by devotional practices and by the action of the State.[3]

Monticolo's formulation of Venetian guild history has had a profound influence on the writing of Venetian history for the later Middle Ages and Renaissance. His belief that the guilds lacked striking contrasts between masters and workers and that guilds were subordinate to the state through the authority of the giustizieri vecchi has been accepted by the leading authorities on Venetian history and has contributed to the view of the Venetian popolo as essentially undifferentiated and passive masses.[4]

The idea that there was not a sharp contrast between the interests of masters and workers was perhaps correct for some Venetian guilds. Certain guilds, especially those involved in food selling, tailoring, and construction, may indeed have approached the guild ideal of a fraternity of equal members. This was due to the kind of work they performed, consumer expectations, and levels of technological development. Tailors, for instance, worked for individual consumers who wanted to purchase custom-made goods. Although a master tailor might employ one or two workers who could be kept busy cutting cloth and doing stitching, it was difficult for him to anticipate demand and move into large-scale production. Furthermore, once workers gained a certain level of technical proficiency, they could set themselves up in business with a minimal amount of capital and take commissions of their own. Food retailers, such as cheese sellers, butchers, and bakers, found themselves in a similar position. Their trade depended on a steady stream of customers who came regularly (often daily) for the purchase of a few items. In these trades differentiation of tasks and stratification of workers was impractical.[5]

In the construction industry, production techniques inhibited specialization and stratification. As Richard Goldthwaite has noted, the structure of the building trades remained largely unchanged until the nineteenth century. They were stubbornly resistant to new forms of industrial organization. In the Middle Ages and Renaissance most construction projects required the services of a few master craftsmen specially trained in each aspect of building. Given the level of technology, there was no way to quicken production by dividing workers into a class of accomplished masters and unskilled laborers. A similar situation prevailed in the shipbuilding industries. Most caulkers and ship carpenters held the rank of master.[6]

The situation in other sectors of the Venetian economy, such as glassmaking and the fur and wool industries, was quite different. These industries required large amounts of capital for the acquisition of raw materials and the purchase of equipment. Often the same raw material had to be worked by a variety of craftsmen specially trained in different tasks. The exigencies of these industries facilitated the division of members into a class of great masters who controlled the production processes and large numbers of workers (many of whom were masters themselves) who worked for wages. Furthermore, each of these industries required close cooperation between master craftsmen and noble merchants.

Glassmaking was Venice's most renowned industry. It required a high degree of technical competence and large capital expenditures.

The success of Venice's glass industry depended on the technical expertise of master glassmakers who knew what proportions of certain materials were needed to produce fine glass products. Much of the other work, including tasks such as stoking fires and hauling wood, could be performed by semiskilled or even unskilled laborers. Glassmaking also required a large capital outlay for equipment and supplies. Venetian glass manufacturers worked with many different kinds of furnaces and imported raw materials. To secure these materials, glassmakers had to rely on merchants, many of whom were members of the patriciate. A number of noblemen owned furnaces and rented them to glassmakers. Venice's reputation as a glass center thus depended on the successful cooperation of nobles and master craftsmen for the importation of raw materials, the production of objects, and the exportation of finished glassware.[7]

The fur industry also required extensive cooperation. Furs were a staple of the wardrobe. Government officials and the wealthy dressed in ermine, marten, and lynx, whereas the less wealthy kept warm in garments made of squirrel and lamb. Fur garments were expensive but practical and were among the items frequently bequeathed in wills. The demand for large quantities of pelts fostered an international trade in furs. Pelts from the Baltic and Russia were shipped to Europe and the Near East, while other kinds of furs (especially sheepskins) from southern Europe made their way to ports in the north. As was often the case, the Venetians found themselves in an unusually propitious position at the intersection of the fur trade routes. The fur trade became a major sector of the Venetian economy. During the third decade of the fifteenth century hundreds of thousands of pelts valued at tens of thousands of ducats were passing through Venice annually.[8]

Many of the furs entering Venice did not remain in the city but were exported, after working, for sale elsewhere. This offered many opportunities for employment; and Venice became a major center of the fur industry, with three different guilds (based on the kind of pelts used) devoted to that trade.[9] Production was so efficient that it was even profitable for Venetian merchants to ship raw furs from Crete to Venice and then ship them back to the eastern Mediterranean.[10]

When merchants imported furs to Venice, they made arrangements with the city's furriers to have the pelts processed. In some instances, merchants simply sold raw pelts to furriers and that was the end of their involvement. The furriers then finished the skins and sold them on the retail market. Often merchants retained ownership of the pelts, entrusting them to master furriers who acted as their agents (known as *compari*). The compari farmed the furs out to workers for finishing and then handled their reexport. According to Robert Delort, the *compare* was nothing more than a "frontman" for the merchant. Yet the arrangement was mutually beneficial. The merchant got his product finished while avoiding legal entanglements with the guild (only guild members could sell at retail), and the master furrier got a steady supply of pelts to work. Although some furriers themselves engaged in overseas trade, many depended on noble merchants.[11]

The textile industries, especially the wool industry, showed the greatest specialization and differentiation of all. The wool industry was controlled by drapers whom Frederic Lane has likened to "merchant-employers." The drapers bought the wool and put it out under the domestic system of production for carding, spinning, weaving, and washing. Throughout the process the drapers retained ownership of the wool, paying workers (some of whom were highly skilled craftsmen) according to piece rates. The cotton industry was organized in much the same way: certain merchant-employers (the *fustagnarii*) retaining ownership of the cotton while it was worked by others.[12]

The glass, fur, and textile industries varied considerably in their production techniques. What is noteworthy about them, especially when compared with some of the more traditional industries, is the wide variation in the level of skills and economic involvement of persons participating in these trades. The wool industry, in particular, included a few master-employers and large numbers of subordinate salaried workers. Unlike the victualling and construction industries, there was a wide variation in the status of members. In addition, these industries were heavily dependent on capital supplied by merchants, many of whom were nobles. The patrician merchant Andrea Barbarigo, for example, worked closely with several drapers, including Lorenzo da Vigna and Alvise de Stropi, who retailed cloth for him.[13] In each of these industries and in others such as goldsmithing, craftsmen depended on merchant investors to supply them with raw materials and capital and with means by which to export and market their wares.[14]

There were certain organizational characteristics that all Venetian guilds shared. At the head of each guild was a group of officials known as *sovrastanti*, *giudici*, or *degani*. Some guilds, such as the guild of the vair furriers (*varotarii*), had one supreme officer, the *gastaldus*, who was assisted by five subordinate officers known as *giudici* (judges). In other guilds, the officers may have ruled as an undifferentiated board.[15]

Guild officers held office for one year and had a number of responsibilities. Their primary duty was overseeing the guild. The gastaldus and his assistants were supposed to regulate membership in the guild. They had to see that members swore to uphold the rules of the guild and that apprentices and workers were registered with the giustizieri vecchi.[16] Guild officials were supposed to ensure that members knew and followed the rules of the corporation. To do this they convoked members twice a year to hear the capitulary read and discuss guild business. These meetings were usually held in a church, although in later centuries they were held in guild halls.[17]

Guild officers also had judicial responsibilities. They were available once a week to settle minor disputes between guildsmen, provided the disputes involved small sums of money. The judges of the vair furriers' guild could only handle cases involving less than 5 lire worth of goods; the procurators of the drapers' guild had jurisdiction in cases involving 100 soldi di piccoli or less.[18] Cases involving greater sums had to be taken to the giustizieri vecchi or the *consoli dei mercanti* (consuls of the merchants) for adjudication. The government limited the penal powers of guild officers. The judges of the vair furriers were only permitted to levy fines up to 40 soldi.[19]

Guild officers were responsible for supervising the business practices of guildsmen. Many guild capitularies included detailed regulations about the kinds of products produced and the production methods employed.[20] Guild officers were to ensure the observation of these rules. They conducted weekly or monthly inspections of members' workshops, and members had to report promptly cases of fraud, theft, or illegal dealings. In addition to controlling production, the officers oversaw retailing. They had to inspect market stalls at San Marco and Rialto; and in some guilds such as that of the vair furriers, they were responsible for assigning stalls to members.[21] Some guilds assigned specific duties to specific officials. For instance, the drapers' guild was presided over by three procurators who heard disputes between members, three inquisitors who inspected workshops and markets, a scribe who recorded all guild acts, and a *bolladore* who marked all products with the seal of the guild.[22]

In theory then each guild functioned as a *communitas*.[23] United by professional and fraternal bonds, members were expected to work together to ensure the reputation of their craft and a fair share of business for each member. In practice, guilds were unable to live up to this ideal, for guildsmen used a variety of tactics to gain unfair advantage over their fellow members. They formed cartels fixing prices, worked during forbidden hours and feast days, avoided paying customs duties, and concealed shoddy or defective goods.[24] In addition, guilds encroached on each others' territory. During the fourteenth and early fifteenth centuries, disputes developed between the rock crystal carvers and glassmakers and between the caulkers and carpenters over who had a monopoly on the production of certain products and tasks.[25] In 1385, the tailors and jacketmakers actually came to blows. In order to help maintain peace, the government ordered the jacketmakers to hold their procession on the eve of Saint Mark's feast and the tailors on the feast day itself.[26] Conflicts of this sort created tension between guilds and within the Venetian artisan community itself.

A greater threat to harmony, however, was the division that developed within guilds between masters who enjoyed full guild privileges and workers who had little or no say in guild affairs. This was especially the case in the more profitable sectors of the economy. Certain masters, with the tacit approval of the giustizieri vecchi, turned what were supposed to be egalitarian institutions into hierarchic, even oligarchic, ones.

In more traditional trades differences between masters and workers were not very pronounced. All were inscribed in the guild. And although workers enjoyed fewer privileges than masters, they also bore fewer burdens. In particular they made smaller contributions for such things as the *luminaria*—the tax designated to support illumination of the scuola's shrine.[27] It is unclear whether or not workers had a voice in guild affairs, although that seems unlikely. In most guilds, however, workers were clearly subordinate to masters. They were denied a voice in guild matters, for they were prohibited from voting in guild meetings. The smiths' and cobblers' guilds, for instance, granted the right to vote only to heads of workshops (capud cuiuslibet stacionibus). The fustian guild did the same. The bellfounders' guild only allowed "masters and heads of workshops" (maistri e chavi de botega) to attend elections.[28] Although workers enjoyed the social benefits of scuola membership, they were denied a voice in the actual governance of the guild.

The most striking example of domination by masters was in the woolen cloth industry. In this particular industry the government authorized the formation of only one guild—that of the drapers—the merchant-employers who owned the wool and put it out for processing. Teasers, fullers, spinners, and others involved in producing woolen cloth were not allowed to form guilds and were only tangentially tied to the drapers' guild. The wool guild was unabashedly a union of employers. Any draper who for a time worked for others was himself disqualified from guild membership. In order to be readmitted to the guild, he had to testify that he no longer did piece work for others.[29] In an industry that employed hundreds and perhaps thousands of workers, only the small circle of drapers had guild representation. When the guild held its meeting in 1391, forty men were in attendance.[30]

Not surprisingly, masters used their control to protect their interests against those of workers. Many guilds restricted the freedom of workers to move from one master to another. They were not allowed to do so until they had fulfilled all obligations to the master who first employed them.[31] This allowed employers to control the flow of labor and kept masters from luring away each others' employees. Several guilds, including the carpenters and caulkers, stipulated that if a worker failed to agree on a wage before beginning a job, he had to be content with whatever wage the employer decided to pay.[32] In the fustian guild, workers were encouraged to denounce other workers who tried to defraud their masters.[33] And a rule written into several guild statutes had a chilling effect on worker protests. It stated that if a worker brought a suit against his master before the giustizieri vecchi and lost, then the worker had to pay the officer any damages he incurred.[34]

The drapers' guild maintained the tightest control over its workers. In 1377 the *provveditori di comun* (superintendents of commerce and certain crafts) approved several new rules. One made it illegal for a worker living with a master to buy wine for any worker or master not living in the master's house. More importantly, the provveditori approved a measure that made it illegal for workers (or masters) to gather outside of their homes in groups of eight or more. The law promised a reward to informers who reported these meetings and amnesty to participants who revealed them. The prologue stated that these measures were being issued, "to avoid the many questions, quarrels, and disputes that occur daily."[35]

These ordinances are especially noteworthy when viewed in light of similar measures taken in Florence. In 1446 Cosimo de' Medici spearheaded legislation that led to a reorganization of the *gabella del vino* (wine sales tax). Among the reforms was a law prohibiting workers in the wool and silk industries from taking more than one fiasco of wine to work.[36] Apparently the authorities feared that drink would incite the workers. The Venetian prohibition on workers congregating needs no explanation. The government clearly feared that workers would gather together and perhaps riot. What is significant is the date of the Venetian law—1377—just one year before the explosion of the Florentine Ciompi. Large numbers of immigrants, especially from Tuscany, had come to Venice to work in the textile industries. Apparently they brought with them their desire to be organized as a guild and to have some say in political affairs. Clearly, the Venetian drapers believed that the immigrants would find a sympathetic ear among their own salaried workers.[37]

When regulating the guilds, the giustizieri vecchi, the consoli dei mercanti, and the provveditori di comun found themselves in the difficult position of having to balance the interests of the government with those of masters and workers. On one hand, as the representatives of the ruling merchant class who had close financial ties to certain industries, they naturally tended to favor the rights of masters over workers. On the other hand, the patricians had to be careful lest masters become so powerful that they would demand a share of political power, as happened in other cities.[38] At the center of this dilemma were guild election procedures and eligibility requirements for office-holding, for through control of electoral procedures, certain masters might gain unchallenged control over the guilds and use them as a base on which to build political power.

As originally established, most Venetian guilds had election procedures that did just that. The retiring officers either selected the new officers themselves or selected the men who would be the electors. This system facilitated the creation of an inner circle of great masters who controlled the guilds.[39] In some guilds, certain families may have dominated the elections, creating dynasties of guild officials. The patrician government soon recognized the danger of this system and took steps to stop it. In 1265 during the height of popolano unrest in the city, the Great Council passed a law limiting the term of office for gastaldi to one year.[40] This law was designed to prevent the formation of an on-going class of leaders within the guilds. Even with this reform, electoral procedures still facilitated the creation of an oligarchy within the guilds. As a consequence, during the later years of the thirteenth century most guilds either voluntarily changed or were forced by the justices to alter their electoral procedures. They substituted for the old system a more equitable method of choosing electors by lot.

The barbers' guild is fairly typical. According to the capitulary of 1270, the retiring gastaldus selected five men who together with the gastaldus selected the new officials. In 1300 the giustizieri vecchi ordered this system changed. The new law required the retiring guild officials to call to election all masters over twenty years of age. The officers were to put ballot balls equal to the number of men in attendance into a hat. Nine of these balls were gold, and the masters who drew the gold balls were the electors. The law enjoined them to select "the best and most able" men to be the new officers. In order to be elected, a candidate had to gain the approval of six of the nine electors. To protect against family collusion, the law stipulated that none of the electors could be related to one another. Fathers, sons, brothers, in-laws, and cousins were prohibited from sitting on the same electoral board. The election procedure of 1300 was modified slightly in 1315 when the number of electors was raised from nine to twelve; and a candidate had to get nine votes in order to be elected.[41]

Although the barbers' guild was fairly typical, in some guilds the modification of electoral procedures was not so dramatic. The glassmakers, for example, modified their system to the extent that the retiring officials were to choose twenty men who were reduced by lot to five electors. The retiring officials still enjoyed a large amount of control, for they selected the pool of potential electors.[42] A similar system was established in the stonecutters' guild in 1363. Arguing that men were attending the election who "do not know the owners [of stoneyards] nor the masters of this trade," the giustizieri vecchi approved an election procedure in which the old officers selected forty electors who were to choose the new officials. This was done so that "the mystery not fall into ruin to the detriment and injury of all."[43] And in some guilds the masters were able to prevent any interference with election procedures. In the drapers' guild no modification was made to an electoral procedure that allowed the three retiring procurators along with three "other good men" to select the new officials. Only the consoli dei mercanti, to whom the drapers reported, had a veto.[44]

The electoral procedures utilized by Venetian guilds exhibited great variety. The procedures were changed and adjusted (with the consent of the giustizieri vecchi) to meet the changing demands and pressures of the guilds and the patrician government. Yet despite the variety, a pattern is apparent. During the late thirteenth century, when the threat of popular unrest was greatest, the giustizieri vecchi intervened in electoral procedures in order to make them more egalitarian. This may have been done in response to pressure from members who were not getting their fair share of offices, but more likely the real motive behind this period of reform was the desire on the part of patricians to prevent the domination of the guilds by a small clique of masters who might then demand a voice in government. During the fourteenth century, when the guilds were quiet, the government allowed modification of the electoral procedures in some guilds so that certain masters again enjoyed a disproportionate say in guild affairs. And in the drapers' guild the patricians were content to let the small number of masters who constituted the guild run their own affairs.

In addition to electoral procedures, there were other methods certain masters used to maintain control of crafts. Many guilds denied full participation in guild government to newly inscribed masters. The cobblers' guild required that a master be a resident of Venice for four years before participating in elections. The caulkers' guild prohibited foreigners with less than eight years' residence from voting or holding office. The smiths had severe eligibility requirements for becoming gastaldus; one had to be either a native-born Venetian or a foreigner with twenty-five years' residence in the city to qualify.[45] Admission standards were another weapon in the masters' arsenal. They could deny entry into the trade to anyone who they felt was not "sufficiently learned in the trade."[46] And by controlling the distribution of shops and market stalls, guild officers had indirect control over retail trade and could use their discretionary power to reward friends and hurt enemies.[47]

Much of the time the giustizieri vecchi allowed certain masters to run the guilds with little actual interference. They only intervened when those who suffered from these policies were able to mount sufficient pressure for intervention or when violations were too flagrant to be ignored. In 1305, for instance, the giustizieri vecchi had to intervene in the cobblers' guild and lay down rules about the timing and location of the guild's annual meal. Apparently guild officers were using the meal as an opportunity to buy the votes of poorer members.[48] The fifteenth-century capitulary of the bell-founders included a provision prohibiting apprentices and workers from attending elections. It appears that masters were packing the election hall with unqualified voters.[49] And the giustizieri vecchi had to add a measure to the caulkers' statutes prohibiting any man from holding the office of gastaldus more than once every five years, "when it was brought to the attention of the giustizieri vecchi that the office of gastaldus of the caulkers was going to a few men year after year." The giustizieri vecchi intervened in order to ensure "quiet and peace among the men of the guild."[50] Under normal circumstances, they would have let the guildsmen handle their own affairs.

This brief examination of industrial organization and guild structure reveals several things. First, it shows that in many industries there was a marked difference in the status and economic interests of masters and workers (including masters who worked for wages). The owner of a glass furnace, the draper with wool to be processed, and the furrier with a contract to fill had very different interests from the workers whom they hired to stoke fires, spin thread, and finish hides. The interests of the employers were often more closely tied to those of merchants than they were to their employees who worked for wages and piece rates. Despite Monticolo's claim to the contrary, there were significant differences in the interests of employers and workers. Second, guilds did not represent equally the interests of masters and workers. Workers had little more than a nominal voice in most guilds, and in some they had no voice at all. Even among masters, there were differences. Many guilds were controlled at least informally by a small circle of masters who manipulated elections, restricted entry, and controlled retailing. Many guilds were hierarchic, even oligarchic, institutions.

And for the most part the city's patricians, through their officials the giustizieri vecchi, maintained the status quo. Except in cases of serious abuse they allowed employers to pass measures favorable to themselves, and they accepted electoral procedures that were open to manipulation. They did this because in many industries there was a community of interest between merchants who imported raw materials and craftsmen who had it worked. The fur industry with its merchant importers and compari is a good example. In return for their service to merchants, these craftsmen got a relatively free hand in running their trades. As long as the guilds did not become the focus of political discontent, the patricians were content to allow great master craftsmen to run them any way they pleased.

None of this would appear surprising to students of guilds in other European cities, yet for Venice a tradition has developed that guilds were essentially harmonious social service organizations and that the government maintained a discrete balance between the interests of masters and workers. In fact there was tension between masters and workers, as the attempts by the woolworkers to congregate in the 1370s shows. Most of the time the patricians sided with the masters. The workplace was filled with tension — tension that extended to the social world of Venetian artisans.

The Social World of Venetian Artisans

The problems involved in trying to reconstruct the social contacts of any group in Venetian society, especially any group below the nobility, are legion. To the problems of unsystematic and spotty sources, which are applicable to all groups, we must add difficulties unique to the laboring classes. These include unsystematic use of surnames, variant spellings of surnames, lack of identification by trade, and failure to note status within a trade. When examining the laboring classes, there is seldom enough information about particular individuals to reconstruct their lives. Less satisfying collective biographies must be substituted instead. And one must often rely on qualitative examples where quantitative data would be preferable. Despite these limitations, it is possible to draw a picture of the social world of Venetian artisans using a variety of sources such as notarial records, court cases, guild capitularies, and government legislation. The picture may not be finely etched, but the general outlines are clear.

Just how much did Venetian artisans associate with one another? Did a shared profession forge guildsmen into tight-knit communities? We can begin to answer these questions by examining several factors — professional endogamy, residence patterns, and charitable activities — that shed light on artisan behavior.

The group of 681 dowry receipts drawn up by popolani between 1309 and 1419 allows us to measure the incidence of professional endogamy. Given the primacy of marriage to working-class life, levels of professional endogamy and exogamy provide a useful clue to the solidarity of guildsmen.[51]

Of the 681 dowry receipts examined, 73 list the profession of both the groom and his father-in-law and therefore allow for comparison. Of these 73 marriages, only 4 (a mere 5.5 percent) are professionally endogamous. Yet even that figure may be too high, for one of these marriages may not have been, strictly speaking, endogamous. In the group, a glassmaker from Murano married a glassmaker's daughter, a cutler married a cutler's daughter, a baker married a baker's daughter; and there is the case of Dorico, described as an *unctor pellium*, who married Orsa, daughter of a furrier. In all likelihood, Dorico was actually a tanner.[52] The rest of the cases (69, or 94.5 percent) are professionally exogamous. Although there are instances of marriages between persons in allied trades (wool shearers marrying the daughters of dyers, painters marrying the daughters of stonecutters, and linen-workers marrying into weavers' families),[53] there are also instances of marriages in which there is no connection between the husband's profession and that of his father-in-law. Stonecutters married into silk-working families; boatmen married the daughters of cutlers, and potters married the daughters of sailors.[54] The evidence shows that in the aggregate, profession was not a crucial consideration when artisans went about the task of selecting spouses.

The reasons for this low incidence of professional endogamy are not entirely clear. There would seem to have been a number of advantages to endogamous marriages, especially from the point of view of the groom. If he married the daughter of a man in the same profession, he could, in all likelihood, expect his wife to have acquired at least some rudimentary skills in the trade. Furthermore, a marital tie to another member of the trade might provide useful opportunities to pool resources and contacts. Father- and son-in-law could purchase raw materials in larger quantities and divide them among themselves. There might also be advantages within the guild itself. Although relatives were prohibited from sitting together on electoral boards, there was nothing to prevent relatives from lobbying other guildsmen on their kinsmen's behalf. And a husband stood to reap fairly substantial rewards if his father-in-law died without male heirs. He was likely to inherit his father-in-law's tools, raw materials, perhaps even his clients.[55] The advantages to be gained from exogamous marriages are harder to see. The clearest advantage was that an artisan could extend his contacts beyond his particular profession, but how important this was to artisans, most of whom could not take advantage of Venice's economic opportunities, is uncertain. All that can be said with certitude is that the incidence of professional endogamy among Venetian artisans was surprisingly low. This suggests that there was not a high degree of solidarity among members of the same profession, for when they went about the all-important task of choosing spouses, profession did not loom very large in their considerations.

Residential patterns provide a second criterion for judging solidarity among Venetian artisans. According to some analysts, what distinguished the preindustrial city from its industrial counterpart was the identity in the preindustrial city of workplace and residence. According to this view, the preindustrial city was composed of a series of unique, occupationally distinct neighborhoods. Artisans who lived and worked together developed a strong sense of solidarity.[56]

In Venice each guild or craft had a *ruga* (street of market stalls and workshops) at Rialto where guildsmen could congregate, exchange wares, and keep an eye on competitors. But the residential patterns of artisans were more complex. In some trades, artisans did live and work in the same place; in others they did not.

The glassmakers of Murano provide a good example of Venetian artisans for whom residence and workplace were identical. This is understandable since glassmaking was prohibited elsewhere in the city and since the distance between Murano and Venice made a daily commute between the two islands impractical, especially in winter. Residence seems to have played a role in creating a sense of group identity among glassmakers. According to the statutes of the glassmaking guild, glassworkers were not permitted to work on the feast of San Donato—patron of Murano. The glassmakers' guild was the only guild to include his feast day as one of its holidays.[57] This indicates that in the guildsmen's eyes their place of work and place of residence were inseparably linked. The two factors may have served to create a sense of community among guildsmen.

A similar situation existed among another group of artisans, the tanners of the Giudecca, who also for reasons of public safety found their occupation confined to a specific part of the lagoon. According to the statutes of their guild, the tanners were not allowed to work on the feast of Sant'Eufemia—patron of a major church on the Giudecca.[58]

In some trades members were widely dispersed. A list of bakers from the year 1402 shows there were bakers living in virtually every part of the city.[59] Demands of the trade probably account for this dispersal. Bread was a product that had to be procured daily—hence every neighborhood had need of a baker.

In most trades residential patterns were more complex. In many guilds there was a tendency for guildsmen to favor certain parishes as their residences, yet in no case did all members of a trade live in those parishes. Nor were any parishes exclusively inhabited by one occupational group. The coopers provide a good example. Several coopers lived in the parish of San Cassian, near Rialto, site of the coopers' ruga. At least five coopers had property in the parish in 1379, the year of the estimo. Yet coopers lived in other parts of the city as well.[60] The ropemakers were also dispersed throughout the city. When officials drew up the rules for the annual reading of the guild's statutes, they decided that the readings were to alternate between Santa Croce and San Martino—parishes located at opposite ends of the city.[61]

One hundred ten wills drawn up by furriers and their wives and widows for the period 1311 to 1418 provide clues to their residential patterns. Twenty-nine different parishes are listed as places of residence by the testators. Table 4.1 gives the breakdown by parish.

The table shows that furriers were distributed throughout at least twenty-nine of the city's seventy parishes. Yet there were heavy concentrations in two parishes—San Giacomo dall'Orio and San Pantalon. Furthermore, with the exception of Sant'Angelo, all of the parishes containing three or more furriers were in the same general vicinity—on the Rialto side of the Grand Canal. Despite this concentration, furriers could be found living on the opposite side of the city from the majority of their fellows. Three lived near the Arsenal: two in the parish of Santa Trinità, one in Sant'Antonin.

The reasons for this concentration of furriers on the Rialto side of the city are unclear. It is not too distant from the Giudecca, where their industrial allies the tanners lived. That part of the city was also more sparsely settled than the central zone from Rialto to San Zaccaria. This may have offered the furriers the room they needed to perform their tasks. Tradition may also have played a role; from an early date furriers seem to have preferred the Rialto side of the canal.[62]

Some Venetian artisans lived in one part of the city and worked in another. Nicolò Tedesco lived at the eastern end of the city in the parish of San Pietro di Castello but worked near Rialto in the parish of San Lio.[63] Workers at the Arsenal came from throughout the city. Giovanni Rosso, a caulker at the Arsenal, lived in the sestiere of Cannaregio in the parish of Santa Fosca. Another caulker at the Arsenal named Raffaleto lived across the Grand Canal in the parish of San Barnaba.[64]

Workplace and residence were only two of many focal points in the working lives of Venetian artisans. The rhythms of work and guild activities took them frequently to other parts of the city as well. Again the furriers provide a good example. The varotarii had their ruga in the parish of San Giovanni de Rialto; the *peliparii* (furriers of domesticated animal skins) had theirs across the bridge in the parish of San Bartolomeo.[65] But both groups of furriers also maintained stalls in the market at the piazza San Marco. Guild regulations stipulated that the varotarii set up their stalls at the end of the piazza near San Marco; the peliparii at the opposite end, near San Gimignano.[66] In addition, guild activities took furriers to other locations in the city. The varotarii held their biannual meetings at the church of San Giovanni de Rialto, but their scuola met at the church of Santa Maria dei Crociferi—one of the farthest spots in the city from the residential concentration of furriers (Map 2).[67] The caulkers were in a similar situation. Large numbers of caulkers worked at the Arsenal,

TABLE 4.1 Residential Patterns of Furriers

San Giacomo dall'Orio	26
San Pantalon	24
Santa Croce	10
San Simeon Grande	7
Sant'Angelo	6
Santa Margarita	5
San Polo	3
San Trovaso	3
21 other parishes	26
Total	110

SOURCE: ASV, Cancelleria Inferiore, Notai; ASV, Archivio Notarile, Testamenti.

but their scuola was located across the Grand Canal at Santa Maria della Carità (the present day Accademia).[68]

It is difficult to assess the impact the geographic arrangement of residences, workplaces, and guild sites had on Venetian artisans. On one hand, residential clusters and a common street at Rialto may have promoted a sense of community among craftsmen. They saw each other in their home parishes and at work. On the other hand, trips to Rialto, San Marco, and the scuole tended to pull Venetian artisans beyond professional and parochial spheres and into a larger orbit. Economic specialization and functional diversification did not transform the city of Venice into a series of closed, occupationally defined neighborhoods; it probably did not, except in a few instances, reinforce guild solidarity.[69]

Charitable contributions to fellow guildsmen provide a third index of guild solidarity. Most guilds required their members to make yearly contributions to the scuola attached to the trade. The money was used for illumination of the scuola's altar, care of sick fellows, and burial of poor brethren. Of course artisans also had the option of making bequests to their guild scuole in their wills. These legacies would benefit not only members of the confraternity, but also the testators' own souls.

An examination of the 120 artisan wills examined in chapter 3 shows that of the 120 testators, only 2 (a mere 1.6 percent) left a charitable bequest to their guild scuola. Both bequests were made by men; none of the wives or widows did so.[70] The 110 wills of furriers and their wives and widows yield similar results. Of the 110 testators examined, 20 (18.2 percent) left a bequest to at least one confraternity, but of these only 5 (4.2 percent) included the scuole of the furrier guilds. Again, only men did so. Matteo Polo and Franceschino Ven-

MAP 2 Site of Vair Furrier Associations

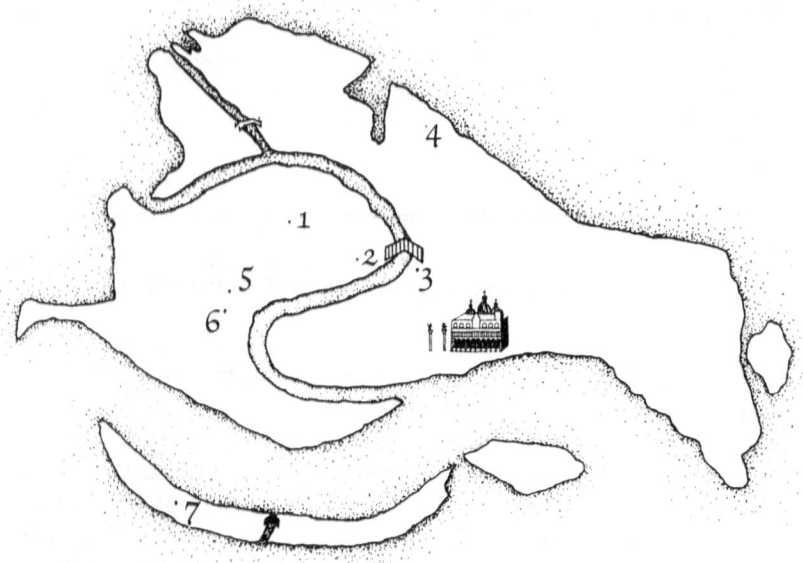

1. San Giacomo dall'Orio
2. San Giovanni de Rialto
3. San Bartolomeo
4. Santa Maria dei Crociferi
5. San Pantalon
6. Santa Margarita
7. Giudecca

delino left bequests to the scuola of the varotarii; Pietro de Bonaventura, Biagio Rizzo, and Giacomo de Cristoforo remembered the scuola of the peliparii.[71] Looking at men only, 5 of 39 testators (12.8 percent) remembered their fellow furriers with charitable bequests.

These three indices—professional endogamy, residential patterns, and charitable contributions—present mixed results; yet on balance they indicate that the level of solidarity within guilds was low. The reasons for this low level of group solidarity, however, are still unclear. Was it due to a general feeling of apathy among Venetian artisans (a result of their exclusion from politics) or was it related in some way to the hierarchic and oligarchic structure of the guilds themselves? And can a low level of solidarity among guildsmen be equated with actual antipathy between them? In order to answer these questions, it is necessary to make a detailed analysis of the social contacts of one professional group—the furriers of early Renaissance Venice.

There is no way to know how many furriers there were in early Renaissance Venice, but their numbers must have been fairly great. According to several rubrics of the capitulary of the *varotarii*, the number of masters who voted when the chapter met varied from 30 to 34. At the same time, the guildsmen complained that their numbers were declining. If we estimate that each master employed two workers, then we may assume that around 100 persons were employed in the wild fur (*vair*) industry. The number of persons working in the domesticated fur industry was probably as great, while there were fewer *glirarii* (furriers of dormouse skins). It seems reasonable to assume that around 250 persons worked in the fur industry in this period.[72]

At the top of the profession stood a few great master furriers. One such man was Bartolomeo Brocha, who lived in the parish of San Giacomo dall'Orio. Brocha was a wealthy man; he was one of 13 furriers included in the estimo of 1379 (assessed at 1,000 lire) and one of the 16 richest men in his parish.[73] Brocha was actively involved in the fur industry. He maintained a workshop on the street of the furriers at Rialto, and in 1364, he rented warehouse space (a *volta*) in the vicinity.[74] The rhythms of his life, traveling from San Giacomo to Rialto, brought Brocha into daily contact with this fellow master furriers and with patrician merchants who traded in pelts.

Brocha's family life was closely intertwined with the trade. Indeed, he seems in some ways to have tried to secure his bond to the guild through his family. Brocha had his son Bernardo follow him in the trade. Hereditary succession (sons following in their fathers' footsteps) was not automatic among Venetian artisans; it occurred in only 52 percent of observable cases among furriers.[75] Although a slight majority of fathers had their sons take up the same profession, many chose not to. Lorenzo, son of furrier Benedetto, became a mason; and Giacomo, son of another furrier, worked in the wool industry. The furrier Abeardo had two sons; one became a furrier, the other a cobbler.[76] Bartolomeo Brocha had a choice in his son's future occupation; he chose his own.

When it came time for his daughter to marry, Brocha selected as his son-in-law a furrier named Nicoleto who lived across the Grand Canal in the parish of Sant'Angelo.[77] We have already noted the low incidence of professional endogamy among Venetian artisans, so Brocha's decision again probably reflects his desire to tie his family's fortunes to those of the guild. We do not know the profession of Brocha's own father-in-law, but two furriers served as witnesses to the will of Brocha's wife Fantina.[78] In all likelihood these were friends of the family who came when called or were employees who were close at hand when Fantina decided to dictate her will. In his familial and daily life at least, Bartolomeo Brocha associated freely with fellow guildsmen and found security for his children in the guild.

But an examination of other contacts shows that Brocha's connections were not only circumscribed by profession—parish residence and membership in a confraternity put him in touch with other social worlds as well. Brocha's position as one of the wealthy inhabitants of his parish gave him standing in the parochial community; as a property owner he had the right to sit with noble and other non-noble property owners in parish business meetings. Perhaps because of his position in the community, fellow parishioners and those in surrounding parishes turned to Brocha for assistance. For instance, one neighbor, a paver (terazarius) by the name of Marco, entrusted his personal affairs to Brocha when, in 1371, he granted him general power of attorney. And another neighbor, a caulker named Antonio Rosso, had Brocha and two priests from San Giacomo witness his wife's dowry receipt.[79] Brocha, in turn, looked to those more powerful than himself for favors. Three times he was able, through the assistance of unnamed noble patrons, to secure grazie or pardons for crimes that he and his son Bernardo committed.[80]

Brocha may have met these noble patrons in the scuola grande of San Giovanni Evangelista, of which he was a member. He shared membership in the confraternity with noble and non-noble men from throughout the city, including his fellow parishioners the Badoers. Brocha could claim many of the leading citizens of his parish and the city as his ritual brothers.[81]

Thus the social world of the furrier Bartolomeo Brocha had a number of axes around which it rotated. In his familial and daily life, Brocha moved in a world of fellow furriers, but he was in no sense restricted to that world. His standing in his home parish and his membership in one of the city's scuole grandi put him in contact with men from various social classes and occupations throughout the city.

Two other prominent furriers, Bartolomeo Trevisan and Tiziano, shared many of the same characteristics. Both men were comparatively well off and were established members of the community. They were popolani grandi. Tiziano held property in his home parish. In his will, he noted that he had acquired some of the property from his relatives (ex parentella); the rest he had bought for the sum of 500 lire di piccoli, which he paid out of his own pocket (de meis propriis denariis). Trevisan, a slave owner, had business dealings with butchers who supplied him with skins. In 1384 the Senate voted to give Trevisan, an immigrant from Treviso, the privilege of cittadinanza.[82]

Like Bartolomeo Brocha, Trevisan and Tiziano had significant kinship ties to other furriers. Tiziano followed his father Marco in the profession and himself married the daughter of a furrier.[83] Trevisan and Tiziano also had furrier cofathers, to whom they looked for help with their affairs. Tiziano selected his cofather, Moreto de Donato, a fellow furrier from San Giacomo, as one of the executors of his estate, and Trevisan chose to grant power of attorney over his affairs to his cofather, the furrier Natale.[84] This spiritual kinship tie provided a way for furriers to secure themselves to others in the trade.

Both Trevisan and Tiziano moved in friendship circles with furriers as well. Tiziano named another furrier, Pietro de Bonaventura of Santa Croce, as executor of his estate and had still another, Luciano Datale, witness the document. And Trevisan was selected by Caterucia, wife of furrier Gulielmo de Pavia, as an executor.[85]

Yet like Bartolomeo Brocha, these two well-to-do furriers also had ties to institutions that pulled them beyond the orbit of the guild. Tiziano had significant ties in the parish community; he named his parish priest Paolo Re as one of his executors and had a wealthy fellow parishioner, goldsmith Giovanni a Via Nova (assessed in the estimo at 3,000 lire), witness the will. Tiziano left several bequests to the parochial clergy and also made provisions for a *caritade* (love feast) to be given to the poor of his parish. Tiziano had close attachments to the parish church; he specifically noted that he wished to be buried in the family tomb, which was located under the portico of the church. If the priests refused him burial there, then he wished to be buried at the scuola grande of Santa Maria della Carità of which he was a member.[86] Trevisan also had significant attachments to his parish. He held the post of gastaldus or prior of the local confraternity in San Giacomo. His election to that post reflected his prestige and authority within the parish.[87]

These men were not the only furriers to hold positions of importance in various institutions. Furrier Bertuccio Merlo, whose brother was parish priest of San Simeon Piccolo, twice held the post of guardian of the scuola grande of San Giovanni Evangelista. Giovanni Bono, a furrier from San Giacomo, was gastaldus of the scuola of Santa

Caterina at San Stae; furrier Nicoleto held the same post for the scuola of Sant'Angelo. Giovanni Saimben, one of the furriers included in the estimo, held the important post of procurator for his home parish; and Luciano Datale (mentioned earlier as a witness to Tiziano's will) served as prior of the hospital of San Giovanni de Murano.[88]

The furriers Bartolomeo Brocha, Bartolomeo Trevisan, and Tiziano are representative of a small group of wealthy master furriers who stood at the top of the profession in early Renaissance Venice. These men were tied by bonds of marriage, coparentage, and friendship to others in the Venetian furrier community. But just as importantly, they had significant attachments outside the trade. Parishes and confraternities provided other spheres of activity and other contacts for them. Many held positions of authority in the significant social institutions of Renaissance Venice.

For the mass of furriers who manned the Venetian fur industry— the popolo minuto of the trade—the situation was very different. The circumstances of their lives were much less secure. These were poor men and women who often lived near the edge of subsistence; the gap separating them from master furriers was often dramatic. In contrast, for instance, to Tiziano, who bequeathed 300 ducats for each of his daughters to marry, and to Marco Rosso from Santa Croce, who left 50 ducats in goods and money as a dowry for his slave, furriers such as Canciano, an immigrant from Udine, and Giacomo, an immigrant from Bologna, received dowries from their wives valued at 13½ and 20 ducats respectively.[89]

Most of the popolo minuto were too poor to buy property which, as we have seen, conferred a degree of social standing and a sense of place on its owners. Instead, they were itinerants in the city, moving from parish to parish seeking lower rents and trying to avoid creditors. For many the sense of alienation was heightened by the fact that they were immigrants who had come to Venice seeking work. Although the flow of immigrants increased after visitations of the plague, there was a constant need for new workers in the city because furriers, like other Venetian artisan groups, were unable to reproduce themselves. The furrier couple produced on average less than two children.[90] For rich and poor furriers alike, families were small; there were few ties to more distant relatives, such as cousins and uncles. These people faced insecure lives. They lacked an economic stake in the community, permanent homes, and the security that ties to an extended kinship network could provide.

These characteristics affected the social lives of the popolo minuto of the fur industry. Because of their poverty and their itinerant existence, they did not develop the same attachments to parishes and scuole that more established furriers had. Instead, they developed friendship and kinship ties to those in similar circumstances. Sometimes the bond uniting workers was professional—they found friends and associates in workshops and marketplaces. For instance, two varotarii, Sander from San Pantalon and Giovanni Spagnolo from San Stae, were friends.[91] For others, the shared experience of immigration may have been the bond uniting them. Francesco of Modena and Giovanni of Udine became friends.[92] But associations of workers were not determined by professional ties alone; they formed friendships and married into the families of workers in other trades as well. The furrier Melio married his daughter Agnes to Miorino, a silkworker; and Giacomo de Stephano, a poor furrier from San Giacomo, named his friend Antonio, a soapmaker from the neighboring parish of San Simeon Grande, to serve as his executor.[93] Often friendship circles encompassed men from various trades. In 1417 a group of men, including three varotarii, a cheese seller, and a barber, went to the parish of San Barnaba for the purpose of disrupting the wedding feast of a goldsmith.[94]

While shared profession, common status, or common background might bring workers together, one institution, the tavern, helped seal the bonds between them. Artisans met in the taverns clustered around San Marco and Rialto to drink, gamble, and relax. It is not difficult to imagine that these men sought in the conviviality of the crowd, in the wine and cards, the sense of community that was conspicuously lacking in their lives. For its part the government feared the violence and possibly even the conspiracies that workers (homines Venecie vilis conditionis) might foment in taverns and, as a consequence, kept then under tight control. The number of taverns was regulated by law, and a variety of government officials had them under supervision.[95]

Compared to that of their more prosperous fellow tradesmen, the social world of workers in the Venetian fur industry was more isolated from the mainstream institutions of Venetian society and more class-bound. Unlike master furriers who claimed noble merchants as business associates and rubbed shoulders with patricians in parish meetings and confraternities, workers in the fur industry moved more exclusively with workers from their own trade and from other trades. Even the places of meeting were different. While nobles and well-to-do popolani dined and drank in the houses of friends, workers congregated in taverns. The associative characteristics of Venetian furriers therefore mirrored the two-tiered organization of the Venetian furrier guilds. Outside the workshop, the social world of prominent master furriers and the workers in their employ had little intersection.

The same was true in other professions. In each trade there were a few men who enjoyed a degree of wealth and social standing that set them apart from their fellow tradesmen. The ranks of the goldsmiths included well-connected men like Zanino, who married the illegitimate daughter of nobleman Paolo Morosini, and Matteo Simiteculo, who came under the special protection of the noble Zancani family. Yet the profession also included men like Andrea from the parish of Santa Maria Mater Domini who got a dowry from his wife valued at only 35 ducats.[96] The wool industry was controlled by drapers like Francesco Rabia, who in 1382 was elected gastaldus of the guild. He married his daughters to members of the patrician Belegno and Soranzo families, and his son Paolo became a guardian of the scuola grande of San Giovanni Evangelista.[97] In 1419 Rabia received a grazia from the Senate when it was discovered that he had not paid customs duties on some cloth.[98] Yet the textile industry over which men like Rabia presided was manned by poor men and women like Balsarino of Milan, described as a "vagabundus laborator fustanitorum," who shared a room with two German fustian workers.[99]

The Venetian artisan community consisted of men with vastly different experiences, expectations, and interests. The masters, with their ties to noble merchants and positions of authority in guilds, parishes, and scuole, had an interest in the status quo and were ready and able to work through personal channels, especially the grazie procedure, to secure their ends. Life was very different for the workers. For them, the masters who controlled piece rates and workshops often appeared a more immediate threat to their well-being than did the patricians.

Usually the tension between masters and workers simmered below the surface and was mediated by paternalistic ties and by guild-sponsored charitable activities; and sometimes relations between masters and workers were good. For instance, Nicolò, a painter, named his former *discipulus* Pasqualino as one of his executors and bequeathed him five ducats.[100] At other times tension boiled over into acts of violence, as criminal cases in the records of the signori di notte and *avogadori di comun* (the Venetian state attorneys) illustrate. One case involved Benevenuto de Venzono, a cobbler from Santa Maria Nova, and his worker (*laborator*) Nicolò de Udine. One day Benevenuto and Nicolò began arguing over wages. According to Nicolò, Benevenuto owed him 50 soldi, yet had only paid him 30.

Nicolò drew a knife on his master and killed him. Witnesses included two of Benevenuto's other workers, Pietro de Cremona and Zoanuto de Cremona, and the workman of another cobbler, Domenico de Cremona.[101] A second case involved master tailor Michele di Andrea of the parish of Santa Maria Formosa and his worker (*lavorente*) Giacomo Tempesco. Michele was in his workshop at San Zanipolo when Giacomo arrived and began arguing with him. Giacomo had seen his master speaking with Zanino Contarini and, according to Michele's testimony, must have jumped to the conclusion that the conversation concerned a piece of property Giacomo wanted to rent from Contarini. The murder occurred when the workshop was full; the witnesses included two other workers, one of whom was an immigrant from Belluno, and two apprentices, both about age thirteen.[102] A dispute over wages and fear of losing a property were the precipitating events that led to the crimes. Yet it seems that an attitude of suspicion and fear between masters and workers contributed to the crimes as well.

A third incident involved the draper Francesco Rabia discussed above. On 5 December 1417, while he was paying his "laboratoribus et aliis manualibus," Giovanni the German, a wool teaser, approached Francesco and demanded his pay. Francesco responded that he would pay Giovanni when his turn came. The two started to scuffle; and when Francesco's son Paolo came to help his father, Giovanni stabbed him. Paolo survived the wound, and Giovanni managed to escape. The avogadori di comun voted to prosecute Giovanni if he could be found. In this case a dispute over wages pitted an immigrant worker against a well-established member of Venetian society.[103]

Another incident occurred on 10 September 1373 and involved master furrier Nicoleto Bianco and his employee Francesco of Modena. On that day Nicoleto got into a fight with Francesco in which he accused Francesco (described as a *laborator*) of not working. Francesco vowed revenge on his master swearing, "by God, I'll get you for this." Later that evening, while Nicoleto was at home drinking with his friend Alvise de Rastello (a government functionary) and another friend, Francesco appeared (along with his companion, the furrier Giovanni of Udine). The quarrel resumed, and Francesco mortally wounded his master. The immediate cause of the crime was hot tempers aggravated by drink, yet it is likely that a worker's pent-up frustrations also contributed. This murder may well reflect the resentment that immigrant workers such as Francesco and Giovanni felt toward men such as Nicoleto (a master furrier) and Alvise (a government official)—men they perceived to be on the inside of Venetian society.[104] As these examples illustrate, the artisan workshop was rife with tension.

Given all this, the political impotence of the guilds in early Renaissance Venetian society is easier to understand. Venetian guilds operated under a double liability: they were not only legally excluded from participating in politics, but also hampered in their ability to apply unified political pressure by conflicts between and within guilds.

The social characteristics of the Venetian artisan community compounded these problems. Artisans exhibited a low degree of professional endogamy and a moderate degree of hereditary succession. The same families did not intermarry generation after generation, and sons did not automatically follow in their fathers' footsteps. Hence it was difficult for a sense of common identity and interests to develop over time. Demography worked against artisans as well. Unable to reproduce themselves, they had to rely on immigrants to replenish the trade. The open nature of the professions placed artisans at a clear disadvantage when dealing with patricians. Each new generation of guildsmen naturally had to produce its own leaders, yet they lacked the consciousness of themselves as an elite (which arose from family and community traditions) and thus the self-confidence with which to challenge successfully the patricians.[105] Their situation contrasted with that of patricians who were a closed "caste"—or at least were becoming one. Through generations of mutual association and intermarriage patricians were developing a sense of class identity and interests. The institutional nature of the guilds, the exigencies of trade and commerce, and the associative and demographic characteristics of Venetian artisans interacted to ensure the impotence of guilds in Venetian society.

In this regard the contrast with Florence is instructive. Florentine guilds also had diverse memberships with differing interests and orientations. Yet in Florence the corporate view of politics provided an ideology around which all artisans, even the *sottoposti* of the wool industry, could rally.[106] In Venice, guildsmen lacked a political tradition that would allow them to overcome their internal differences and mount a viable alternative to patrician rule. On important ritual occasions like the one described by Martino da Canal, Venetian guildsmen did march as corporate bodies, bearing the banners of their guilds and professing unity. Yet the ideal of community that those occasions expressed was a chimera. In the world of work, conflict as often as not triumphed over community; and this helped ensure the stability of the patrician regime.

FIVE

The Parochial Clergy and Communities of the Sacred

Thus far we have examined familial and artisanal associations in early Renaissance Venice and have seen that family structures and workshop relations tended to separate Venetians from one another as often as they drew them together. We now turn our attention to the religious life of early Renaissance Venetians and ask, did religion—in the sense of both spiritual sentiments and religious institutions—provide a sense of solidarity that could allow Venetians to overcome these divisions? In order to answer this question, we shall examine the place of the parish clergy in Venetian society and the relationship between society and the sacred.

The Parish Clergy as Social Intermediaries

The clergy constituted in some ways the most distinctive social group in Venetian society. Clergymen were set apart from the rest of society by their physical appearance (the tonsure and clerical garb), by their immunities from civil law, and by the identity they enjoyed as members of various religious entities, including mendicant orders, parish chapters, and the nine congregations of secular clergy.[1] In an ideal sense the clergy were to be servants to but not members of the society that they served; they were to tend their flock but not become involved in the problems that beset it. Yet Venice was heir to a tradition of Byzantine caesaro-papism in which church and state were closely intertwined; and the clergy, the parochial clergy in particular, became in some ways the most "connected" members of society.[2] They were involved in virtually all aspects of their parishioners' lives.

The parish clergy were drawn from a variety of social backgrounds. It is possible, using the list of parish priests (*plebani*) compiled by Flaminio Cornaro in his *Ecclesiae venetae antiquis monumentis*, to gain a general sense of the social composition of the clergy. An examination of Cornaro's list for the period 1297 to 1423 yields the names of 488 parish priests. Of these 488 individuals, 111 (22.7 percent) have noble surnames, possibly indicating noble status; 358 (73.4 percent) have either no surname or non-noble surnames. The names of 19 individuals (3.9 percent), including names such as Nicolaus Iustus and Guido de Bernardo, are ambiguous and do not fit clearly into either category.[3]

Cornaro's list poses two major problems that make anything more than tentative conclusions hazardous. First, popolani often had the same surnames as patricians; names such as Bon and Trevisan were common in Venice. Someone having a noble surname may not in fact have been a patrician. Second, the list contains the names of plebani—of men who reach the top post in the parishes. Nobles may have reached that position in greater proportion than popolani. Hence the list of plebani may not faithfully reflect the social composition of the parish clergy as a whole. Nonetheless, the list does provide a rough indication of the clergy's social origins and shows that the parochial clergy did not come from only one social group. Perhaps as many as one-fourth of the parish clergy were patricians.

An examination of individual parish clergymen bears this out. Some came from distinguished noble families. Two members of the Querini clan, one of the case vecchie, served as plebani or parish priests for the ancient and wealthy parish of Santa Maria Formosa. Bartolomeo Querini held that post in the 1270s before becoming bishop of Castello; many years later in the 1340s Francesco Querini held the same post before himself becoming patriarch of Grado.[4] Other case vecchie families also contributed members to the parochial clergy. Cardinale Morosini served in the 1310s as plebanus of the large and wealthy parish of Sant'Angelo; Tommaso Tiepolo was the plebanus of San Martino; and Giovanni Zane served as plebanus of the parish of San Luca in the 1350s.[5]

Less venerable patrician families also had sons who served in the ranks of the parish clergy. Giacomo Diedho was plebanus in the parish of Santa Lucia in the 1340s; Leonardo Vendelino was a priest in the parish of Sant'Agostin in the 1320s; Marino Civran was plebanus of Santa Margarita; and Nicolò Staniario held the same position in the parish of San Fantin.[6] Barnaba dalla Fontana served as parish priest for the parish of San Basilio in the 1340s; he was also a canon of San Marco.[7] Careers in the clergy remained an outlet for sons of the patriciate throughout the life of the republic.[8]

Many popolano families also found careers for their sons in the church. Some came from the sizeable and relatively well-off non-noble families that constituted the popolo grande. In 1386, Pietro Spirito, a member of the cittadino Spirito family, was elected parish priest of San Marcuola.[9] Other popolano families such as the Cavazza, the Graciano, and the Barbafella contributed members to the parish clergy during the early Renaissance.[10] Many of these families enjoyed cittadino status and made their livelihoods in the world of trade.

Other parish clergy came from the ranks of the artisans—albeit from the ranks of prosperous artisan families. Presbyter Felice de Merlis, who in 1333 became plebanus of San Simeon Piccolo, came from an artisanal background. His brother Bertuccio was a furrier, yet a distinguished one.[11] As we have seen in chapter 4, Bertuccio twice was elected guardian of the scuola grande of San Giovanni Evangelista. Presbyter Pietro Rosso of San Cassian was the son of another furrier (a glirarius) residing in the same parish; and Paolo Bedoloto, a furrier (and unrelated apparently to the Bedolotos of San Giacomo dall'Orio), had a son Giacomo who became a priest. Giacomo's uncle (Paolo's brother) was a goldsmith.[12] Basilio, subdeacon and later deacon in the church of San Giacomo dall'Orio, was the son of Cristoforo de Artusio, a cheese seller (chaxarolus). Cristoforo was, however, a respected member of the parish community—he was elected to the post of *procurator* (overseer) of the church's property.[13]

Other members of the clergy came from the ranks of the popolo minuto. Antonio, a cleric (clericus) in the parish of San Giacomo dall'Orio, was the son of a barber; and Lorenzo, a priest in the parish of San Severo, had a sailor (marinarius) for a brother-in-law.[14] It was not uncommon for wealthy Venetians, especially women, to leave bequests in their wills for the outfitting of young clerics with the materials necessary to be priests (robes, chalices, books, etc.). For example, Polluzia, wife of Olivero Darpo, made provisions for the endowment of Nicoleto, son of silkworker (samitarius) Luciano, and Nicolota Venier left 30 soldi for the outfitting of a priest.[15] Hence it was possible for particularly devout or precocious popolano minuto boys to find a patron who would finance their career in the church.

Clergymen of noble origin served not only in the wealthier parishes of the city but also in poorer ones. Wealthy parishes were not the exclusive domain of patricians. Francesco Querini was preceded in the post of plebanus of Santa Maria Formosa by popolano Giovanni Parmacini and succeeded by popolano Nicolò Greco.[16] Nobleman Giovanni Foscarini served during the 1370s in the poor parish of San Leonardo as plebanus.[17]

Many clergymen were recruited from families residing in the parish in which they served or from adjoining parishes. The brother of Donato, plebanus of San Barnaba, lived in San Barnaba; the mother of Zaneto, a priest in San Giovanni Novo, was a resident of the parish; and both the mother and sister of Gregorio Bruno, priest in Santa Trinità, lived in the parish.[18] Stefano Pianigo, plebanus of San Stin, was the son of *ser* Giacomo Pianigo, a glassmaker who resided in the contiguous parish of Sant'Agostin. Stefano's brothers lived in Sant'Agostin—one of them, Marco, was included in the estimo with an assessment of 300 lire.[19] The parents of nobleman Nicolò Staniario, priest in Santa Trinità, lived in the neighboring parish of Santa Giustina, and Gasparino Favaccio, plebanus of Sant'Agostin, had two brothers in the neighboring parish of San Giacomo dall'Orio.[20]

The transfer of clergy from one parish to another also reflected some tendency toward localism. Clergy, especially in the lower ranks of cleric, subdeacon, and deacon, seldom went far when accepting new posts or promotions. Many clergymen remained in one church for years, slowly moving up the ecclesiastical ladder. For instance, in the parish of Santa Trinità, a certain Zaccaria, who in 1339 held the post of cleric, had by 1346 advanced to the position of deacon.[21] Francesco Rizzo was a cleric in 1346 but by 1347 was serving as subdeacon for the church.[22] The chapter of San Stae selected a certain Zanino as subdeacon when his predecessor, Bartolomeo Sconer, advanced to a new position.[23] Graciano Gracian, who in 1340 was a cleric in San Canciano, had by 1372 become the plebanus.[24] Mobility between parishes seems to have increased for those reaching the ranks of presbyter and plebanus, yet even here there was some tendency toward localism. Plebanus Stefano Pianigo came to the parish of San Polo from the nearby parish of San Stin.[25] Presbyters Felice de Merlis and Marco Dartico both moved from San Giacomo dall'Orio to the contiguous parish of San Simeon Piccolo.[26] Plebanus Pietro Bacchari of San Pietro di Castello served first as presbyter of San Martino where, according to his will, his grandfather, father, and other relatives were buried.[27] Even when clergy moved a great distance, they often had some connection to the place where they were called. Before becoming plebanus of San Stin, Pietro Zane was a presbyter at Santa Maria de Murano. In 1406 he became plebanus of Sant'Agostin, and in 1428 was recalled to Santa Maria de Murano as plebanus.[28]

The availability of posts in the church was especially important to one group in Venetian society—the popolo grande. Sacerdotal positions represented an outlet for the ambitions of popolano grande families and individuals. Through ecclesiastical posts, families gained social and in some instances political prestige. For instance, the nephew of Bartolomeo Recovrati, plebanus of San Giacomo dall'Orio, became a canon of San Marco in the first half of the fourteenth century. This represented a great honor for the Recovrati family as reflected in the fact that Bartolomeo asked in his will that his name be inscribed in the registers of the canons and his soul remembered in their prayers.[29] The education that other priests acquired gained them access to the highest circles of society — circles that might otherwise have been closed to them. Hence Gasparino Favaccio, priest of Sant'Agostin, moved in Petrarch's Trevisan and Venetian circle of friends, a circle that included Doge Andrea Dandolo.[30]

Popolano grande families gained a number of advantages from having a family member hold ecclesiastical office. The entry of sons into the clergy meant the patrimony was more secure from subdivision. Clerics could expect a much smaller share of the family's wealth. Also important were the economic opportunities offered by ecclesiastical positions. The business activities of the clergy will be considered more fully below. At this point let it suffice to say that clerics had commercial opportunities unavailable to most popolani. Clerics were often asked to accompany government officials overseas either in their capacity as notaries or as chaplains. This meant they had direct access to the world of international trade. Stationed at strategic stops along Venetian trade routes, priests were in a position to gather vital information and to ship merchandise to friends and associates in Venice. At home many priests found posts in the bureaucracy as notaries. These offices carried salaries and placed priests near the centers of power. In a world in which information was passed by word of mouth, being at the center of news was critical.

Sacerdotal posts were not the only positions of authority and prestige in the parish, however. Each parish had a procurator who was responsible for overseeing the church's property and wealth. The procurator was selected by the parish chapter.[31] Sometimes the chapter entrusted the parish's financial resources to one of its own members. In 1359 the chapter of San Giacomo dall'Orio gave responsibility for the church's property to presbyter Pietro Paolo Dente.[32] At other times, priests gave the job to a layman. Nobles served as procurators. Both Giovanni and Pietro Orio, members of one of the leading families in the parish of Santa Trinità, held the post of procurator for the parish.[33] Other noble procurators included Giovanni Bondemiro in

San Tomà, Martino and Marco Capello in Santa Maria Mater Domini, Bartolomeo da Molin in San Marcuola, Marco Moro in Sant'Agostin, and Minello Condolmer in Santa Lucia.[34] Yet priests also conferred the post on prominent popolano parishioners. We have already noted in chapter 4 that Giovanni Saimben, a wealthy furrier, held the post in San Simeon Grande; and in chapter 3 that the first member of the Bedoloto family about whom we know anything—a certain Marco—served as procurator of San Giacomo dall'Orio during the 1290s.[35] The list is easily expanded. Marco Tranquillo, a wealthy popolano from Santa Croce (included in the estimo at 2,500 lire), served as procurator for his home parish; ser Giovanni Graciano served in Santa Trinità; ser Nicolò de Zane, a potter, was procurator for San Moisè, and ser Benedetto, a tailor, was procurator for San Silvestro.[36]

The selection by parochial chapters of popolani grandi as procurators reveals two things. First, along with the evidence of intermarriage, it suggests that the distinction separating patricians and the popolo grande was not as great in the early Renaissance as it would later become. It was in the interest of the clergy to select competent, respected, and diligent men as procurators—men who could be trusted to administer the resources of the church carefully and, if necessary, to defend those interests in court.[37] The clergy believed that popolani were as capable of the task as nobles. In addition, the choice shows once again that the parish in its various manifestations provided an outlet for the ambitions and energies of the popolo grande. As we shall see in the next chapter, noble males showed surprisingly little interest in neighborhood affairs. However, for the popolo grande, who were excluded from most forms of political power, the parish was one of the few arenas where they could actively exercise authority.

A parishioner's first official contact with the clergy came on the day of his baptism. Little is known about baptismal rites in medieval and early Renaissance Venice. In the notarial records of Felice de Merlis, there is, however, rare notice of a baptism performed in the church of Sant'Agnese by the parish clergy. In 1319 presbyter Marco Sclapado of the church baptized Simone, son of Tixe de Buzzacarini, an immigrant from Padua.[38] The act shows that baptisms were performed in parish churches (a point disputed by some historians[39]) and broadens our knowledge of the ceremony. Two men, Marco Ruzzini and Marco da Riva, presented the child at the baptismal font; two others, Marco Baseggio and Pietro Tolomano, received him from the font. The child's uncle, a monk at the nearby monastery of San

Gregorio, placed a "good candle of wax" on the altar in thanksgiving. The notary was careful to record that the ceremony was performed "according to the rite and form of the Roman church."[40] Baptism marked the formal entry of a newborn child into the Christian community. The child was presented to the church by godparents and received from the church by godparents as well. The child's parents and relatives were present in this ceremony of admission, which was presided over by one of the parish priests.[41]

The paucity of sources prevents us from following closely the progress of Venetians' lives in the church. There are few extant records such as parish registers (which become common in the sixteenth century), which record parishioners' spiritual transit through life. Nonetheless, the records are not entirely mute. They show that Venetians especially looked to the parish clergy for absolution of their sins and for intercession on behalf of their souls after death.

Most Venetians had a special relationship with one member of the parish chapter, known as the *patrinus* or *parin*, who served as their confessor or spiritual father. Franceschina, wife of Iacobello de Tomaxin, made this aspect of the relationship clear when in her will she bequeathed 2 ducats to "mio parin de penetentia," the presbyter Pasquale.[42] The patrinus's duty was to counsel his flock, to hear their confessions, and generally to help guide them through their life in the church.

In the majority of cases, a person's patrinus was a member of the local parish chapter. In a few instances, however, he came from another parish or from one of the city's monasteries. Lucia, widow of Ermolao Venier of Santa Trinità, looked to presbyter Leonardo of San Giovanni Degolà for spiritual guidance; and Tiziano, a friar at San Zanipolo, was "patrinus meus penitentie" to Bonafemina Alectis of San Gimignano.[43]

The testaments of fourteenth-century Venetians contain numerous bequests to patrini, usually given in return for the recitation of masses after death. An examination of 333 wills made by parishioners from San Giacomo dall'Orio shows that slightly more than 17 percent of all testators remembered their patrini with bequests.[44] The prominent place assigned to confessors in wills indicates that patrini held an important place in Venetians' religious lives. It also suggests that confession was the preeminent sacrament for laymen—a view held by the church throughout the Middle Ages. Venetians went to the great monastic churches such as the Frari and San Zanipolo to hear preachers, and to scuole to participate in religious exercises and pageants, but they generally went home, to their parishes, to take the sacraments. The parish clergy performed the routine yet vital cure of souls.

Although the relationship between an individual and his or her patrinus was primarily a religious one, in some instances, depending on the temperament of the individuals involved, it became much more than that. Like their lay counterparts, godparents and coparents, patrini formed part of an extended family or fictive kin group that individuals could call on in times of need. For instance, the plebanus of San Giacomo dall'Orio, Paolo Re, was not only confessor to Tiziano, a furrier examined earlier, but also an executor of his estate. Tiziano's other executors were his wife, his cofather (compater) Moreto de Donato (a fellow furrier from San Giacomo), and another furrier, Pietro de Bonaventura from Santa Croce.[45] Tiziano included his patrinus in a group closely tied to him by marital, professional, and neighborhood bonds. As we have also seen, clerics and coparents were popular choices as fiduciaries for widows. With the death of their husbands, they often looked to these individuals to provide not only spiritual comfort but also practical assistance.

Other members of the clergy, in addition to the patrini, played a role in the lives of their parishioners. The parochial chapter was a group to which Venetians could turn for various kinds of assistance. Since one member of the parochial chapter usually served as a notary, parishioners made a series of visits throughout their lives to the clergy for legal purposes. Just as they went to see the priest for baptisms, confessions, and funerals, so they also went to see the priest *cum* notary when they wanted to draft marriage contracts, charters of filial emancipation, testaments, and other kinds of documents that charted their legal transit through life. If the individual failed to bring the necessary witnesses, the notary would gather his fellow clergy to witness the acts he had drafted. Consequently, clergy were present at many of the major events in their parishioners' lives, either in their sacred role as priests or in their legal role as notaries and witnesses.

Perhaps because of this association of the clergy with the law, many Venetians, especially popolani, entrusted legal authority to clergymen. In addition to naming clergy as executors of their estates, they gave power of attorney over their affairs to clergy during their lifetime, through grants of proctorship. In April 1316, a resident of San Giacomo dall'Orio by the name of Andrea de Corado gave power of attorney to his wife Giacomina and to presbyter Pietro of San Giacomo. In August of the same year, Andrea drew up a new charter; this time, however, he entrusted responsibility solely to Pietro.[46]

Benevenuto, a ragpicker from San Polo, gave power of attorney to Damiano Balbi, plebanus of Sant'Agostin, and Francesco, a cobbler from San Giovanni Novo, named Giovanni Forte, a priest in Sant'Angelo, as his proctor.[47] Some Venetians gave power of attorney to relatives who were members of the clergy. Marco de Marchese granted a proctorship to his brother, presbyter Pietro; and presbyter Nicolò Bon, a priest from San Giacomo, received power of attorney from his brother, sister, and brother-in-law.[48]

The choice of a clergyman as the recipient of power of attorney was a wise one for popolani, especially the popolo minuto, for several reasons. First, clergymen were familiar with legal procedures. If problems arose, if decisions had to be made, they were in a position to make them both quickly and wisely. Second, the clergy enjoyed a degree of power and prestige in society unknown to most popolani. If disputes arose, they had a better chance of protecting their clients' interests than did laymen. In the example cited above, Nicolò Bon received power of attorney from his relatives, who recently had emigrated from Venice to the terraferma. They must have believed that Nicolò, not only as their brother but also as a clergyman, could best protect their interests in Venice. Of the grants made to clergy, few were made to clergy below the rank of presbyter.[49] This strengthens the contention that the motive in granting power of attorney to clergymen was the hope that they would use their position to protect their clients' interests. It made little sense to grant such power to mere deacons and subdeacons. Nobles sometimes granted power of attorney to clergy. For instance, nobleman Francesco Morosini gave power of attorney to plebanus Marco Dartico of San Simeon Piccolo and to a fellow nobleman from Santa Fosca; and noblewoman Lucia Zeno named Bartolomeo, plebanus of Santa Trinità, as her proctor.[50] Yet nobles usually granted power of attorney to fellow nobles. That was wise, since in general nobles had more influence than did clergy.

Venetians also turned to the clergy as a source of loans and investment money. One problem for Venetians, especially the poor, was to find sources of small low-interest loans. Venice did not have a *Monte di Pietà* like other Italian cities; and Jews, a common source of such loans, were banned from the city during much of the fourteenth century. The alternative for those in need of money was to find private lenders. One source was the parochial clergy who made loans known as free loans—so called since they were made "causa amoris et dillectionis." In spite of their name, the loans actually concealed an interest payment.[51]

In a charter dated 22 July 1315, the plebanus of San Giacomo dall'Orio,

Bartolomeo Recovrati, loaned "causa amoris et dillectionis" 20 soldi di grossi to Bartolomeo Tataro, a glassworker from Murano. Tataro had use of the money until the following Easter.[52] Presbyter Nicolò Bon of San Giacomo loaned 10 soldi di grossi to Menica, a servant from the contiguous parish of San Giovanni Degolà; and presbyter Giacomo Padanno loaned 8 soldi di grossi to a shearer (cimator) Rigeto and his wife Marchesina.[53] The brothers Francesco, a cutler, and Giacomo, a jacketmaker, borrowed 50 soldi di grossi from Nicolò Beccario, priest of San Cassian; Francesco Bonin of Santa Maria Nova got a loan of 40 soldi di grossi from the priest Zanoto; and Giovanni, a fruit seller (frutarolus) in Sant'Agostin borrowed 5 ducats from the parish priest Damiano.[54] In his will dated 1410, Marino, a priest in San Giacomo, notified his executors that several parishioners, including Alessio de Durazza and Zafredo, to whom he had loaned 8 and 6 ducats respectively, owed him money.[55] These were small loans, made to humble people to help tide them over bad times.

Another kind of loan was the local *colleganza*. Unlike the free loan, which on rare occasions may not have earned interest, the local colleganza was clearly a profit-making business loan in which the lender expected a secure return on his or her investment. Because of their safety (they could be used only in Venice, unlike regular colleganze which entailed high risk international trade), local colleganze were especially popular with widows who used them to increase their often small fixed incomes.[56] Widows were not the only source of these loans, however. Nuns, nobles, and parish clergy provided a steady source of such loans for a wide variety of people. Unlike the recipients of free loans, the recipients of local colleganze tended to come from the more prosperous ranks of Venetian society. Both nobles and commoners saw local colleganze as a means of raising capital to be used in a variety of commercial ventures. Plebanus Bartolomeo Recovrati of San Giacomo made local colleganza loans to a variety of people, including the furrier Scalco and his son Martino.[57] Andrea Çoto received 100 lire in local colleganza from presbyter Nicolò of Sant'Agostin, and presbyter Lorenzo della Turre loaned 10 lire di grossi (100 ducats) to a resident of Santa Maria Formosa.[58] Omenbono, plebanus of San Giacomo in 1348, loaned 500 ducats to Marco Disenove, the well-to-do cittadino.[59] And Andrea Briça, priest of San Stae, gave money in regular colleganza to noble parishioners Marco da Molin and Donato Grioni.[60] In the lending of regular and local colleganze, clergymen had contact with a different range of people than those to whom they made free loans. Colleganze were made to popolani and nobles who had the resources and connections needed to turn that capital to a profit. Free loans, on the other hand, were frequently made to help the destitute.

Clergy were active not only as lenders of money but also as borrowers: since they were fully involved in the commercial life of Venice, they had occasion to go to others, either fellow clergy or laymen, for capital. In 1337, for instance, Andrea, priest of Santa Trinità, borrowed 3½ lire di grossi from Belladonna, a resident of San Lorenzo. In this particular instance, Andrea borrowed the money on behalf of his sister-in-law.[61] Leonardo Verde, priest of Santa Trinità, received a loan from his parishioner Benedetta, widow of Giovanni Caldera. Leonardo offered his missal as collateral for the loan.[62]

The clergy like others borrowed money in order to invest it in commercial ventures. A letter written to the priest Felice de Merlis while he was serving in the entourage of the Venetian *bailo* (governor) to Ayas by his friend and fellow priest Nicolò Bon contains evidence of the clergy's commercial activity. The two used the opportunity presented by Felice's tour of duty overseas to engage in several trade ventures. They invested in various commodities including pistachio nuts and cotton. Nicolò tried to summarize how he had managed Felice's money. He wrote,

> I gave your aunt 4½ soldi di grossi and 3 soldi di grossi to Bogatino [a presbyter at San Giacomo]. Of the other 3 soldi, I gave 2 to Tasso the furrier, 12 grossi I put toward the debt of 32 grossi which you owe me ... our plebanus got his cope yesterday and gave me 2 soldi di grossi. I still have 4 grossi which I will give to the plebanus or your aunt. ... Let us move to other things. I gave your aunt 3 soldi di grossi. Item 12 grossi. My intention with the next voyage is to satisfy Marco Trevisan for the 15 grossi which he seeks, he says that he gave them to you on my account.[63]

Overseas tours provided opportunities not only for the priests themselves, but also for friends and associates. In 1378 nobleman Giacomo Venier of Santa Trinità gave power of attorney to presbyter Giovanni Gazo, chaplain of the Venetian governor of Coron and Modon, to collect money that Enrico Barbarigo owed him.[64]

In Venice proper clergymen invested in property and served as landlords. Over the years parish churches accumulated properties through pious bequests, which they then rented. In the estimo of 1379, "le case del piovan de S. Lio" were assessed at 1,500 lire, those of San Zulian at 6,000, and those of Santa Maria Zobenigo at 300. For the tenants of these houses, the parish clergy were their landlords. Yet some clergy owned properties privately. In his will, the plebanus of San Giacomo dall'Orio, Bartolomeo Recovrati, was very concerned that this distinction be understood; he stated that he had bought and maintained certain properties "with my own money, at my own cost and expense."[65]

Recovrati's will shows that he was attentive to the condition and disposition of these properties. He left them under the jurisdiction of his executors, going so far as to inform them that rents were due twice a year—on the feast of Saint Peter in June and on the feast of the Circumcision. Furthermore, he enjoined his executors to maintain his properties in good condition ("in suo bono statu"). He was a strict landlord. In the 1320s he took a case before the *giudici di petizion*, one of the city's civil courts, and tried to extract 3½ soldi di grossi in back rent from the executors of a certain Pietro Bono of San Salvador. Before his death, Bono had rented a property in San Giacomo from Recovrati.[66]

In their various guises the parish clergy constituted part of what Paolo Prodi has called the "largely undifferentiated socio-ecclesiastical structure of medieval Venice."[67] Drawn from a wide variety of social backgrounds and participating fully in the life of the city as landlords, creditors, litigants, friends, and opponents, the clergy were part and parcel of the communities they served.

Nevertheless, their status as ecclesiastics did distinguish the clergy from their flock. Their special relationship to the holy as dispensers of the sacraments and intercessors through prayers made their status in some sense "neutral" and so allowed all Venetians, regardless of their own status, to approach them. Patricians, popolani grandi, and popolani minuti alike looked to the clergy to meet a variety of personal needs. The presence of these intercessors and intermediaries at nearly seventy sites throughout the city may have helped lessen the social tensions present in the parish communities.

Communities of the Sacred

The chief characteristic and in some sense the great strength of the parochial clergy was their familiarity. Actively involved in the life of their parishes, the clergy were able to serve as social intermediaries, ministering to the needs of their flock, rich and poor, noble and commoner alike. Yet the quotidian quality that was so essential to the parish clergy was in some ways antithetical to the sacred. For the sacred to make its impact fully felt, it had to be set apart from the everyday, removed from the structures and rhythms of daily life. It had to reside beyond or above the parish.[68] This section explores the location and the role of the sacred in Venetian society. It also delineates the composition of the groups that congregated both physically and spiritually around holy places to form what might be termed "communities of the sacred."

If the holy did not reside, or at least was not seen to exercise its full *potentia* in the parish, then where did it reside? Where was the sacred located?[69] The answer is in monasteries and scuole. Monasteries were places where the *opus dei*—the work of God—was carried out. Monks and nuns dedicated their lives to a regimen of prayer, work, and meditation. Monasteries therefore represented a place set apart—a locale where the sacred could be experienced more fully. Religious confraternities, which from the thirteenth century on became an important aspect of the Italian religious experience, were another locus of the holy. Yet the holiness of the scuole derived not so much from the places themselves as from the spirit of religious fraternity created among laymen. The exercises the brethren performed were designed as a way for members to earn salvation not only for themselves but also for their deceased fellows. Thus it was either through the efforts of the regular clergy or through the activities of the confraternities that Venetians felt the impact of the holy. Venetians approached the holy not as individuals acting alone but as members of a community.

It may seem strange to assert that Venetian monasteries and convents with their reputation for corruption and moral laxity were places where the holy was perceived to be more fully present.[70] Yet the high incidence of sexual criminality associated with those places is itself testimony to their power. The taboos associated with the violation of convents were very great, yet the frequent violation of those taboos indicates that the convents had an attractive power that in many instances Venetian males found irresistible. The proximity of the sacred and the sexual (with the two inseparably linked) served to heighten rather than diminish the distinctiveness of these locales.[71]

It was on women, rather than men, especially patrician and popolano grande women, that convents exerted their strongest influence. Many patrician women had friends and relatives who were members of religious orders. To cite just two examples: Ysabeta da Mosto (née Falier) had a sister who was a nun at the convent of Santa Maria della Celestia and a niece who was a nun at San Giovanni Evangelista de Torcello; and Zana Contarini had a sister and an in-law who were nuns at the Celestia and a daughter who was a nun at San Giovanni Evangelista de Torcello.[72] In general only the daughters of nobles and wealthy commoners could enter convents; entry fees were too high for most artisans, and the demands of the family economy dictated marriage for most working-class girls.⁷³ Thus convents were institutions with a decidedly elite female focus. In convents Venetian patrician women could and did hold positions of power and authority. In the early years of the fifteenth century the abbess of the Celestia was noblewoman Agnesina da Molin, the prioress Marchesina Geno, and the sacristan Lenucia Pisani. Among the nuns were representatives of the da Canal, Boldu, Morosini, and Bragadin families.⁷⁴

Convents also exercised a strong influence on women because they offered a refuge from the structures and restrictions of male-dominated society. In the convents women were able to create their own culture. For laywomen convents represented one of the few socially acceptable places beyond the family palace where they could venture without risk to their reputation. Convents represented a refuge from the world.⁷⁵

Some women either entered tertiary orders in widowhood or asked to join religious orders at the time of death. When she drafted her will, Beta, wife of Pietro Regla, asked to be accepted into the order of and buried at Santi Biagio e Cataldo, where her sisters Franceschina and Franca were nuns. When she drew up a new will in 1427, she still wished to be buried in the habit of nuns, but this time in the Augustinian order of the convent of Sant'Andrea de Zirada.⁷⁶ Pace, widow of nobleman Andrea Navagero, asked to be buried in the habit of the nuns at the convent of the Vergini. Her mother was buried at the same spot.⁷⁷ Maria Malipiero of Santa Trinità sought burial in "lo habito dele done" of the convent of the Celestia.⁷⁸

Venetians of all social ranks enlisted the support of the regular clergy as intercessors for their souls, though the practice was especially common among the elites. Noblemen Giovanni Dalle Boccole and Tommaso Sanuto of Santa Trinità left bequests to the Franciscans, Dominicans, Servites, Carmelites, and Augustinians, as did noblemen Nicoleto Moro and Marino Badoer of San Giacomo dall'Orio.⁷⁹ Noblewomen often remembered all of these orders as well. Popolani grandi such as Cristina, wife of Nicoleto Barbafella, and the furrier Tiziano also included all these orders in their wills.⁸⁰ Artisans and the poor usually did not have the resources to endow masses at all these establishments, so if they chose to endow masses, they usually selected one or two sites. Caterina, wife of the furrier Stefano of San Giacomo, endowed masses at the Frari; and Caterina, a servant from Santa Trinità, left money both for construction and for masses at San Zanipolo.⁸¹

Venetians tended to favor with endowments those orders that were located close to them. For instance, in a group of 333 parishioners of San Giacomo dall'Orio who drafted wills between 1297 and 1423, 38 (11.4 percent) left money to the Franciscans, followed by the Dominicans with 18 endowments (5.4 percent), the Carmelites with 16 (4.8 percent), the Augustinians with 15 (4.5 percent) and the Servites with 13 (3.9 percent). The church of the Frari located near San Giacomo captured the loyalty of the residents. Across the Grand Canal in the parish of Santa Trinità, similar patterns are visible. The evidence from 90 wills shows that the Dominicans received the largest number of endowments (10, or 11.1 percent), followed by the Franciscans with 7 endowments (7.8 percent), the Servites with 6 (6.7 percent), and the Carmelites and Augustinians with 5 endowments (5.6 percent) each.[82] Santa Trinità was near the Dominican house of San Zanipolo.

Yet the great monastic houses were not the only places receiving support. Venetians tended to look with special regard on smaller monastic and pious establishments near their homes. For the residents of San Giacomo such a place was San Giovanni Evangelista, location of one of the city's scuole grandi and site of a hospital. As we have seen, the noble Badoer family had special patronage rights over the site—the right to select the prior of the hospital from among its members. Many residents of the parish were members of the scuola and left bequests to it or the hospital. Zana, wife of Marco Zane, left money so that shirts could be purchased for the poor of the hospital. Daniele, a potter, asked to be buried at San Giovanni Evangelista.[83] And Beata, widow of a furrier, left the residuum of her estate to the "loco Sancti Iohanis Evangeliste" in memory of her soul, that of her husband, and those of her other deceased relatives.[84]

The convent of Santa Maria della Celestia adjacent to the parish of Santa Trinità had a special attraction for residents of that parish. Several noblewomen remembered the convent with bequests. Ysabeta, widow of Andrea da Mosto, left 2 grossi to each nun at the Celestia (she also left a ten-pound candle each to the churches of the Frari, San Zanipolo, Santo Stefano, and Santa Maria dei Servi); Nicolota, widow of Giacomo Venier, named the abbess of the Celestia as one of her executors and endowed the convent with several bequests.[85] Popolano Nicolò Furlan left a bequest of 100 lire di piccoli to the Celestia, and popolano minuto Paolo Duracino, who left his shoes to his brothers, left a bequest to the Celestia to pay for his funeral.[86] The nearby Franciscan monastery, San Francesco della Vigna, occasionally garnered bequests from residents of Santa Trinità. Gerita, wife of Giovanni Çio, left 1 ducat to be distributed between

San Francesco, Corpus Christi, and Sant'Andrea de Zirada.[87] Beria, wife of Masini Areçiis, wanted a three-pound candle to be used at San Francesco for the elevation of the Eucharist.[88]

In spite of this tendency to look with special regard on monasteries and convents located near their homes, Venetians did endow monastic houses farther from home. A number of residents of Santa Trinità left bequests to the Augustinian monastery located on Murano; and Daniele, the potter from San Giacomo dall'Orio, who left bequests to San Giovanni Evangelista, also endowed the monasteries of San Giacomo de Galicia and Santa Maria dei Angeli—both located on Murano.[89] Giovanni Dalle Boccole of Santa Trinità, who left 3,000 lire for the "amplificatione" of San Zanipolo, bequeathed certain properties in the area around Treviso to the convent of Sant'Eufemia on the island of Mazzorbo. In addition, he left 10 lire to every monastery and hospital "from Grado to Cavarzere."[90]

Scattered throughout the city and the islands of the lagoon, monasteries and convents represented to Venetians of the early Renaissance sacred locales where the holy was perceived to be more fully present than in their own parishes. At these spots, communities of men and women performed the opus dei. For those on the outside, the religious performed the crucial task of praying for the souls of the deceased. Although the special province of nobles and the popolo grande, the monasteries even appealed to the popolo minuto as *luoghi sacri* interwoven throughout the fabric of the city.

Unlike the monasteries, which were sacred places with communities of religious attached to them, the scuole were communities of spiritually oriented laymen and laywomen who through spiritual exercises hoped to approach the holy. During the fourteenth century the scuole remained true to the ideals upon which the first penitential confraternities, the *scuole dei battuti*, were founded. According to Brian Pullan, these ideals reflected the "deeply pessimistic atmosphere" of the latter half of the thirteenth and early fourteenth centuries. The primary task of the scuole was "to prepare for death and to maintain a bond with the dead: to commemorate them and, through the celebration of Mass for the souls of the living and of the dead, to speed their passage through Purgatory."[91]

The scuole also promoted a sense of community among the living. The capitulary of the scuola piccola of the Virgin and Twelve Apostles, dated 1288, enjoined members to "live honestly in peace and love, without deceit, pride or commotion, keeping always in mind the example of the holy Apostles whom Christ commanded to love peace and charity and to love your neighbors as yourselves."[92] Initiation ceremonies reinforced the sense of brotherhood. The candidate for admission knelt before the scuola's altar and upon rising received a kiss from the scuola's guardian. In some confraternities a brother who wished to relinquish membership was treated as if he had died. He was placed on a catafalque and carried around the church. Such ceremonies emphasized the special relationship that bound members of the confraternity as ritual brothers.[93] The ever-vigilant government recognized the strength of the confraternal bond and in 1360 placed the scuole under the jurisdiction of the Council of Ten.[94]

To what extent did the scuole of Venice represent true communities—places where Venetians of all social ranks could come together in a spirit of fraternity and where social tensions could be defused? It is difficult to provide a precise answer to that question, yet even a cursory examination indicates that the scuole drew their members from a variety of professions and social groups, even including the popolo minuto.[95] Indeed, the earliest list for the scuola of Santa Maria della Carità (dated 1260) lists members not alphabetically by first name (the usual procedure with such lists) but by occupational categories. One such category included furriers, cobblers, jacket-makers, and tailors, and another was made up of traghetto operators, laborers, and porters. The classification of members by profession suggests once again the strength of the guild movement in Venice during the 1260s. A new membership list begun in 1353 deemphasized occupation by assigning each occupational category an insignia (a cross, a hammer, etc.).[96]

Table 5.1 lists by occupational category the professions of a sample of members drawn from the capitulary, or *mariegola*, of the scuola grande of Santa Maria della Valverde (also known as the Misericordia) compiled in the fourteenth century (as well as of the members of the scuole piccole, discussed below).[97] The sample contains the names of 178 members, of whom 90 (50.6 percent) list their occupations. To facilitate comparison Table 5.1 adopts the same occupational categories used by Pullan in his analysis of sixteenth-century lists. The most notable aspect of the fourteenth-century list is the fairly even distribution of members across a variety of professions. This contrasts with the sixteenth century, when 25 percent of the members of San Rocco and 12.6 percent of the members of San Marco were Arsenal workers, seamen, or boatmen. Only 2.8 percent of the Valverde's members belonged to that category. The inclusion of only one porter in the Valverde sample suggests that in the fourteenth century, like the sixteenth, the scuole grandi accepted few members from the ranks of the popolo minuto.[98]

TABLE 5.1 Occupational Composition of *Scuole*

	Valverde		Celestia		Sant'Anna		Santi Apostoli	
Professions and higher civil servants	0	0.0%	1	0.7%	0	0.0%	1	0.6%
Luxury trades, books, jewelry, art and music	10	5.6	7	4.6	3	1.8	3	1.9
Groceries and drugs	1	0.6	1	0.7	2	1.2	4	2.6
Traders, brokers, unspecified merchants	6	3.4	1	0.7	0	0.0	1	0.6
Arsenal workers, seamen and boatmen	5	2.8	7	4.6	10	6.1	8	5.2
Textiles and clothing	12	6.7	7	4.6	11	6.7	17	11.0
Footwear and leather	10	5.6	6	3.9	5	3.1	5	3.2
Victuals and wine	9	5.1	5	3.3	4	2.5	7	4.5
Building, construction and furnishing	16	9.0	4	2.6	5	3.1	2	1.3
Wood and metal	13	7.3	6	3.9	3	1.8	8	5.2
Household utensils	7	3.9	2	1.3	1	0.6	2	1.3
Barbers, surgeons, and dentists	0	0.0	0	0.0	1	0.6	2	1.3
Clerical workers and small managers	0	0.0	0	0.0	0	0.0	0	0.0
Servants, attendants, minor government employees	0	0.0	0	0.0	0	0.0	0	0.0
Porters, warehousemen, heavy laborers	1	0.6	3	2.0	0	0.0	1	0.6
Number identified by profession	90	50.6	50	32.7	45	27.6	61	39.6
Number unidentified by profession	88	49.4	103	67.3	118	72.4	93	60.4
Total sample	178	100.0%	153	100.0%	163	100.0%	154	100.0%

SOURCE: ASV, Scuola Grande di Santa Maria della Valverde, Busta A, Mariegola 3; Scuole Piccole, Buste 726, 24, 57bis.

The fourteenth-century scuole grandi drew from a wide geographic range. The 15 officers of the confraternity of the Carità in 1353 came from 11 parishes scattered about the city. Three came from San Bartolomeo, 2 each from San Zulian and San Giacomo dall'Orio, and 1 each from San Moisè, San Trovaso, San Luca, Santa Maria Formosa, San Vitale, San Gimignano, San Pantalon, and the Giudecca.[99] Table 5.2

TABLE 5.2 Geographic Distribution of *Scuole* Members

Sestiere	Valverde		Celestia		Sant'Anna		Santi Apostoli	
Castello	43	24.2%	85	55.6%	94	57.7%	23	7.8%
San Marco	55	30.9	40	26.1	31	19.0	14	9.1
Cannaregio	68	38.2	14	9.2	22	13.5	99	64.3
Dorsoduro	2	1.1	6	3.9	8	4.9	6	3.9
San Polo	4	2.2	6	3.9	2	1.2	9	5.8
Santa Croce	6	3.4	2	1.3	1	0.6	6	3.9
Other or unidentified	0	0.0	0	0.0	5	3.1	8	5.2
TOTAL	178	100.0%	153	100.0%	163	100.0%	154	100.0%

SOURCE: ASV, Scuola Grande di Santa Maria della Valverde, Busta A, Mariegola 3; Scuole Piccole, Buste 726, 24, 57bis.

lists the residences, by sestiere, of the 178 popolano members of Santa Maria della Valverde sampled (as well as of the members of the scuole piccole, discussed below). As might be expected, the largest number of members came from the sestiere in which the scuola was located, Cannaregio. The parish with the highest representation was San Marziale with 22 members. San Marziale was located near the scuola and was also the site of a house for the poor maintained by the scuola.[100] Members were drawn fairly evenly from the San Marco side of the Grand Canal, but the canal proved a formidable barrier. Less than 7 percent of members came from the Rialto side of the city.

But the scuole grandi represented only one aspect of the Venetian confraternal movement, for there were scores of smaller confraternities—the scuole piccole—with devotional sites (altars and tombs) in parish churches, hospitals, and monasteries throughout the city. In general the goals of the scuole piccole, as expressed in their capitularies, were the same as those of the scuole grandi.[101] Members were expected to attend mass together once a month and to attend the funerals of their brethren. One important difference between the scuole grandi and piccole was that many of the latter admitted female members, a practice discontinued by the scuole grandi after 1327.[102] The capitulary of the scuola of Santa Maria della Celestia stated that when one of the sisters died, the deaconesses of the scuola were to bathe and presumably keep vigil over the body of the deceased and that the gastaldus and deacons of the scuola were to come to the house and accompany the body to burial. The gastaldus and deacons were also required to display the cross and banner of the scuola at the funeral.[103] Women were not admitted to the same membership as men; rather they formed a sort of independent organization of their own under the umbrella of the scuola. The scuola of the Celestia, for example, included only men in its membership list.

A few extant membership lists provide some sense of the geographic range and professional composition of the scuole piccole. The lists examined are those of Santa Maria della Celestia, located at the monastery of the same name; Sant'Anna, adjacent to the episcopal church of San Pietro di Castello; and Santi Apostoli, in the parish of the same name.[104] A sampling has yielded the names of 153 members of the Celestia, 163 members of Sant'Anna, and 154 members of Santi Apostoli.[105] Table 5.2 lists the geographic distribution of members by sestiere. The table shows that the scuole piccole drew by far the largest number of members from the sestieri in which they were located. The parishes with the highest representations were the parishes closest to the scuole: 15 members of the Celestia came from Santa Trinità; 52 members of Sant'Anna came from San Pietro, and 58 members of Santi Apostoli lived in the parish of Santi Apostoli. More than the scuole grandi, the scuole piccole were organs of the local community.

Nevertheless, all parts of the city were represented by membership in the scuole. All three scuole piccole were located on the San Marco side of the Grand Canal, yet all three drew a few members from the other side of the city; indeed, they did so in about the same proportion as the Valverde. For instance, three residents of the parish of San Polo were members of the Celestia; Sant'Anna counted among its members two residents of the distant parish of San Raffaele; and Santi Apostoli had members living in the parishes of Santa Croce and San Simeon Piccolo. Despite their tendency to reinforce to a certain degree sestiere and parish loyalties, the scuole did bring Venetians from distant parts of the city together in a spirit of brotherhood. We should recall that one of the primary responsibilities of the scuole was to take part in processions to the homes of deceased members and accompany their bodies to burial. These processions, with their panoply of flags, candles, and mourners, served as visual reminders that Venetians throughout the city formed a spiritual brotherhood.

Like the scuole grandi, the scuole piccole drew members from a variety of social backgrounds. Nobles belonged to the scuole piccole. Francesco Dalle Boccole and Alban Sagredo were members of the Celestia; Zane Contarini and Alvise Valaresso were members of Sant'Anna. Various popolani grandi also held scuole memberships. The Barbafella, Borsa, and Passamonte families had members in the

Celestia. Yet it is difficult to determine precisely the social composition of the scuole at any particular time since the lists tend to be cumulative. In the sample from the Celestia 50 members (32.7 percent) are identified by profession, as are 45 members (27.6 percent) of Sant'Anna and 61 members (39.6 percent) of Santi Apostoli.

Table 5.1 lists members by occupational groups. Noteworthy is the heavy concentration of members in the textile and nautical trades. This bias is partly attributable to the location of the scuole of the Celestia and Sant'Anna. Both were located near the Arsenal and in an area where cloth production was common.[106] However, this does not explain why the same was true for Santi Apostoli. The Celestia showed a fairly even distribution of members over several categories, even including among its members three binders of bales. Artisans in the luxury trades (notably goldsmiths) were fairly common in the Celestia, less so in Sant'Anna and Santi Apostoli. Santi Apostoli drew fairly heavily on men in the wine and victualling trades and in the wood and metal trades.

Conclusions based on these figures are difficult to determine. All that can be said with certitude is that the scuole piccole, like the scuole grandi, tended to draw from a fairly wide occupational base and that occupational biases often reflected the professions most commonly practiced in the areas where the scuole were located. It is impossible to determine the extent to which the scuole piccole included the popolo minuto, yet it is important to recall that there were scores of these small confraternities throughout the city, providing many opportunities for membership for popolano minuto men and women.

Membership lists provide only one perspective on the scuole. Other sources, notably testaments, show that the scuole piccole often played a significant role in the lives of the popolo minuto. Diambra, a patient at a hospital in Santa Trinità, left 2 soldi di grossi to the scuola of San Teodoro; and a certain Bona who lived in the courtyard of the palace of popolano Duxini Borsa left 12 grossi each to the Celestia and to the scuola of Sant'Anastasio, which was located at the parish church of Santa Trinità.[107] Marco Nigro, who left only 2 ducats to each of his daughters and 3 lire di piccoli to his son Bartolomeo, bequeathed the residuum of his estate to the scuola of Sant'Antonio.[108]

Wealthier popolani sometimes left bequests to several scuole. In some instances they left bequests to a series of scuole that quite literally encircled their place of residence. Lucia Cavazza, from the parish of San Giacomo dall'Orio, left bequests to the scuole of San Giacomo, Sant'Agata (at San Boldo), Sant'Agostin, and Santa Caterina (at San Stae); Caterina of Santa Trinità endowed the scuole of the Celestia, Sant'Anastasio, and San Francesco della Vigna.[109] Giovanni Asapone of San Giacomo remembered the scuole of Santa Croce, San Giacomo, Sant'Agata, San Giovanni Evangelista, and San Francesco.[110]

Because of their great number, the scuole piccole provided many opportunities for popolani, some of whom were popolani minuti, to hold positions of power and authority in them. A wool shearer was gastaldus of a scuola at the Frari, a tailor was gastaldus of the scuola of San Giacomo, a cobbler was gastaldus of the scuola of Sant'Agata, and a schoolmaster (*rector scolarum*) was gastaldus of the scuola of Sant'Angelo.[111] The scuole piccole also offered opportunities for women to hold office. Costanza, widow of a furrier, was deaconess of the scuola of Santi Pietro e Paolo in the parish of San Polo, Maddalena, a gold-thread spinner, was *gastaldatrix* of the scuola of Sant'Angelo, Margarita a Zolonibus was *gastalda* of the scuola of Santa Fosca, and Pasqua was deaconess of the scuola of Santa Clara.[112] The scuole provided opportunities for women to manage money and take an active role in affairs outside the confines of household and convent.

For individuals from a variety of social backgrounds, the scuole provided a sense of identity with a group of people with whom they might otherwise have had little in common. The confraternities brought together people from different backgrounds and from different parts of the city and allowed them—in moments of ritual behavior—to dispel differences of wealth, kinship, and power that in their everyday lives kept them apart. For popolani the scuole provided opportunities to exercise power and enjoy prestige. Devotion to the saints and concern for the dead allowed early Renaissance Venetians to set aside their differences and come together in a spirit of sacred community.

Another way of gauging the religious sensibilities of early Renaissance Venetians is to examine their funeral practices. In their wills, many Venetians set forth instructions about their funerals, tombs, and burial sites. The choices they made provide a useful measure of their solidarities and attachments.[113]

When making funeral arrangements, Venetians tended either to want their funerals to be as elaborate as they could afford or extremely simple. Benevenuta, wife of schoolmaster Antonio de Fontanaruosa of San Moisè, wished to be buried in a tomb at the convent of San Zaccaria. She wanted twelve priests to be present at her funeral and wanted twelve candles used.[114] Cittadino Marco Arian wished for six members of the confraternities of San Marco and Santa Maria della Carità to keep vigil over his body and accompany it to burial. Among other instructions, Arian stated that the officiating priest had to proclaim "with a loud voice, Lord have mercy on me" (con grande boxe [voce] Adio missericordia per mi).[115] Nicolò Arimondo wanted his funeral to be a grand affair. He wanted the great prelates of the diocese of Venice, including patriarchs, bishops, abbots, and priors to be invited, as well as representatives of various monasteries, hospitals, and scuole.[116]

Others wished for the greatest simplicity. Griana of Santa Trinità asked only that she be buried "decently" (decenter).[117] Many artisans and laborers could not afford to spend much on their funerals. They scraped together a bit of savings so that they would receive the same kind of decent burial that Griana desired. Caterina, a former wet nurse, left two ducats for her funeral; her only other bequest was to the sister of her executor so that the recipient might marry or become a nun.[118]

Tombs could also be elaborate or simple, depending on the sensibilities and resources of the testator. Pantaleone, a metal refiner of Santa Fosca, wished to be buried in a stone tomb at the church of the Madonna dell'Orto. Since he had no relatives, he asked that the tomb be sealed and leaded, "so that no one else may be placed in it" (che nesuna altra persona se meta).[119] Bono of the parish of Santa Marina wished to be buried at the Celestia in a tomb located either on the west front or on the side facing the canal. He wanted "a tombstone with an inscription" (unum lapidem cum literis tituli superpositi) to adorn it.[120] Giovanni de Gallipolo feared inundation of his tomb; he asked to be buried "in a tomb in which water cannot seep" (in una archa in qua non aqua sit).[121] And Demetrio Colleto of San Cassian asked to be buried at Santo Stefano. He wanted an altar constructed on the spot with his patron saint (Saint Demetrius) "depicted on an altar cloth" (depicto super unam pallam).[122]

In planning their funerals and tombs, Venetians vacillated between two extremes. Some, like Nicolò Arimondo, wished for their funerals to be final statements of their status in society. It was important for as many distinguished prelates as possible to be in attendance. Others hoped to gain a degree of fame and to earn merit by constructing elaborate tombs adorned with depictions of the saints. Still others saw their funerals as a time for humility. Their funerals were to be held without pomp and their bodies buried in the common cemetery. Perhaps this desire for simplicity reflected the influence of Franciscan ideals of poverty and humility.

The most important consideration, however, was not the cost of the tomb or its decoration but rather its location. Venetians were free to select the site of burial (they were not restricted to the home parish), and so the selection of graves provides a good measure of the solidarities in Venetian society, for people were able to choose the company they would keep in death.[123]

The selection of a site often involved complex negotiations. If one wished to be buried in a particular church, either the testator or one of his executors had to secure the permission of the clergy; and this usually required money. Many Venetians wrote bequests to churches into their wills with the proviso that in return they be granted burial rights. If they were refused burial, the bequests were void. As already noted in chapter 4, the furrier Tiziano wished to be buried under the portico of the church of San Giacomo in the tomb of his relatives. If the priests refused him burial there, then he wished to be buried at the church of Santa Maria della Carità.[124] Plebanus Nicolò Staniario of San Fantin, perhaps familiar with such negotiations, anticipated potential problems. He wished to be buried at the church of San Fantin in front of the altar of San Geronimo—he even included provisions for the annual celebration of masses. But if the chapter refused him burial there, he wanted to be buried at Santa Trinità—the church where he had served earlier in his career. And, if the priests of Santa Trinità refused him burial, he asked to be buried at the convent of the Celestia.[125]

The majority of people did not specify in their wills the site of their graves. In the absence of clear statements, we can assume that they expected and wished to be buried in their parish cemetery. Angelo Odorigo for one stated that he wanted to be buried at Santa Croce, "in the courtyard that is behind the campanile, that is the graveyard" (in la cortesela che xé dintro dal cha[n]panil che xé chanposento).[126]

One of two considerations seems to have figured in the decisions made by the laymen who left explicit instructions about the site of their burial: either they wanted to be buried with kinsmen or they wanted to be buried in a location associated with a religious order or confraternity. The desire to be buried with kinsmen was especially strong among noblemen and is another indication of their consciousness of lineage. Nobleman Nicoleto Moro of San Giacomo wished to be buried in the family tomb at San Marziale; Nicolò Morosini wanted to be buried in the Morosini tomb at the Celestia; and as we saw in an earlier chapter, the Dalle Boccole men wished to be buried together at San Zanipolo.[127]

Noblewomen's choices reflect their ambiguous position as members of both their father's and their husband's families. Some noblewomen chose to be buried in the tombs of their husbands' relatives; other times they acted independently. Donata Badoer wished to be buried in the Badoer family tomb at the Frari, and Caterina Soranzo asked to be buried in her father-in-law's tomb as he had promised.[128] Çaneta, widow of Filippo Orio, asked to be buried in the tomb of her children at the Celestia.[129] Franceschina Dalle Boccole, on the other hand, did not choose the Dalle Boccole tomb at San Zanipolo. She chose instead the Celestia.[130]

Many popolani, like patricians, requested burial with relatives. Aliegra, wife of Nicolò a Olperti of San Giacomo, asked to be buried in her father's tomb at Santa Croce; and Maria, wife of a schoolmaster in San Tomà, wished to be buried at the Frari in the tomb of her brother.[131] Popolano husbands and wives did not always choose to be buried together. Guglielmo, a smith from San Cassian, wanted to be buried at San Giovanni Evangelista; but his wife Çoanna selected Santa Maria dei Servi.[132] Immigrants sometimes chose to have their bodies returned to their homes. Martino de Villa, an immigrant from Treviso living in San Giacomo, asked to be returned to Treviso, and Giacomo, a schoolmaster in San Cassian, asked to be buried in his home town (Solicho) in the church of San Pietro.[133]

Burial beside family members provided solace for the living and reinforced notions of family solidarity. It was with one's kinsmen that one would sleep and with one's kinsmen that one would rise at the Last Judgment. Perhaps members of great families such as the Badoers took comfort in the idea that they would go to judgment not as individuals but as members of ca' Badoer.

For others, religious considerations were paramount in the selection of burial sites. Some hoped to gain spiritual benefit by being buried in the precincts of a monastery or convent. The custom of patrician women entering religious orders in widowhood has already been noted. Yet men and women of both patrician and popolano status selected monasteries as the site of their graves. Giovanni Vallaresso of Santa Trinità asked to be buried at the Benedictine convent of San Lorenzo, and Tommaso Sanuto of Santa Trinità sought burial at the Frari.[134] Maria, wife of nobleman Benedetto Dolfin of Sant'Angelo, wished to be buried at Santo Stefano; and Çaneta, widow of Domenico Dolfin of Santa Trinità, chose the Celestia as the site of her grave.[135] *Magister* Giovanni of Santa Trinità, a physician, wished to be buried at San Zanipolo, as did his fellow parishioner Francesca, wife of a goldbeater.[136] Leonardo, a schoolmaster from San Stin,

MAP 3 Distribution of San Giacomo dall'Orio Burial Sites

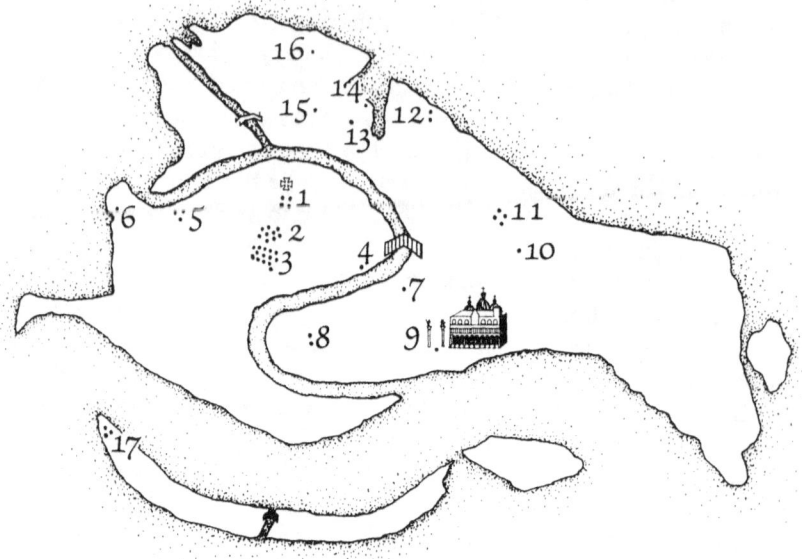

1. San Giacomo dall'Orio
2. San Giovanni Evangelista
3. Santa Maria dei Frari
4. San Silvestro
5. Santa Croce
6. Sant'Andrea de Zirada
7. San Salvador
8. Santo Stefano
9. San Marco
10. San Lorenzo
11. San Zanipolo
12. Santa Maria dei Crociferi
13. San Marziale
14. Santa Maria della Misericordia
15. Santa Maria dei Servi
16. Madonna dell'Orto
17. Santi Biagio e Cataldo
*One unplotted burial in Treviso

chose the cemetery of San Giovanni Evangelista; Benevenuta, wife of another master, selected the convent of San Zaccaria.[137]

Still others sought to replicate in death the sense of belonging they had garnered from the scuole in life. Olda, wife of a notary, wished to be buried in the tomb of the scuola of San Francesco located at the Frari.[138] Nicolò Burdulo of Santa Trinità selected the tomb of the scuola of Sant'Orsola; Luchino de Pergula selected the "archa scole SS. Filippi et Iacobi," and Antonia, a widow from Santi Apostoli, chose to be buried "ex sepulturis scole S. Barbare."[139]

Priests also wanted to be buried in the company of those with

MAP 4 Distribution of Santa Trinità Burial Sites

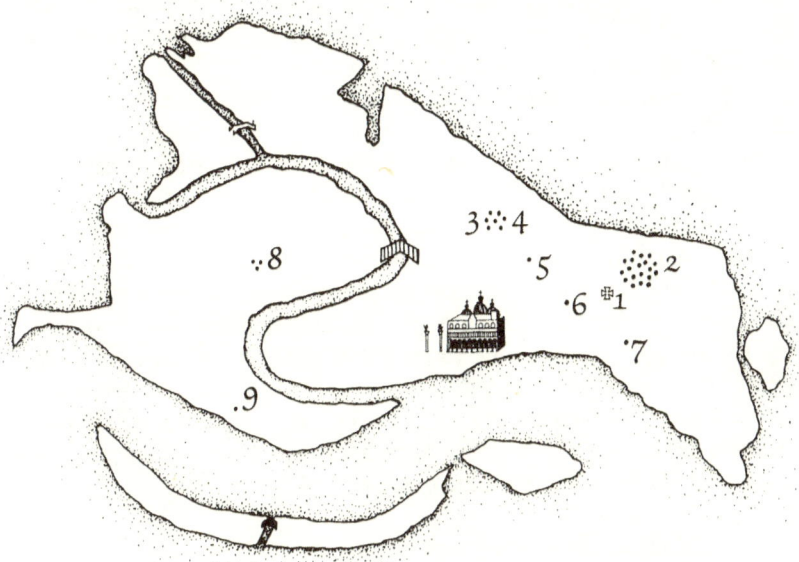

1. Santa Trinità
2. Santa Maria della Celestia
3. San Zanipolo
4. Sant'Orsola
5. San Lorenzo
6. San Giovanni dei Templari
7. San Martino
8. Santa Maria dei Frari
9. Sant'Agnese

whom they shared a corporate identity. Presbyter Marco Venturino, a schoolmaster living in San Basso, wished to be buried in the tomb of the congregation of San Luca—one of the nine congregations of secular clergy.[140] Francesco de Recovratis, a canon of San Marco, stipulated that he wanted to be buried "in arca canonicorum."[141]

Plotting the grave sites of Venetians tells us something about the sacred geography of the city. Fifty-one of the 333 parishioners from San Giacomo dall'Orio whose wills were examined left explicit instructions about their grave sites; 33 of 223 residents of Santa Trinità whose wills were examined also left instructions in their wills. Among the residents of San Giacomo, the church of the Frari was the most popular burial site among those who named one; the hospital and scuola of San Giovanni Evangelista were second with 9, followed by the parish church itself with 4 and San Zanipolo with 4. Some chose other parish or monastic churches such as Santa Croce, San Salvador, and San Silvestro. Among the residents of Santa Trinità, the Celestia was the overwhelming favorite, selected by 19 parishioners; San Zanipolo was second with 6, followed by the Frari with 3.

Maps 3 and 4 plot these grave sites and suggest some conclusions about the geographic range of Venetians' religious activities and their notions concerning the location of the sacred. In both cases, it is clear that the parish stood at the center of a religious zone comprising roughly the neighboring eight to ten parishes. Many of the religious activities engaged in by parishioners took place within those parts of the city. Only two great religious establishments, the Franciscan church of the Frari, and the Dominican church of San Zanipolo, were consistently able to pull Venetians from throughout the city to their doors. Yet for individual Venetians there were sites with special meaning located throughout the city and even into the far reaches of the lagoon. For most Venetians, the sacred was proximate to but not identical with their place of residence.

In very different but complementary ways, religion was a cohesive force in Venetian society, contributing powerfully to a sense of community. The parochial clergy served as social intermediaries, ministering to the spiritual and, in some instances, to the material needs of the flock. Their diversity of background, training, and interests made them ideally suited to perform the cure of souls.

Yet almost by definition, the parish clergy were unable to meet the other great need of their parishioners—the need to experience in special places and at particular times the presence and power of the sacred—the presence and power that could make earthly distinctions among men and women meaningless. For this, Venetians looked to the monasteries and scuole; in those places social barriers tended to disappear as Venetians came together in a sense of community.

Death was a moment to be prepared for, as Venetians' preoccupation with its time, place, and circumstances indicates.[142] No one wished to face death or await the Last Judgment alone. Instead, Venetians chose to meet death in the company of kinsmen, the religious, or their confraternal brothers and sisters. These choices indicate that the most powerful and meaningful solidarities operating in Venetian society were blood ties and ties to ritual brothers. On the threshold of eternity, all other bonds were meaningless.

SIX

Vicinanza and *Amicizia:* Neighborhoods and Patronage in Early Renaissance Venice

In the aftermath of the Querini-Tiepolo conspiracy the Council of Ten, suspecting the complicity of noblemen Angelo Trevisan, Michele Salamon, and Marco Zane, passed a law restricting their movement. The three were forbidden to go to San Marco and Rialto or to use the Merceria or the other "vias magistras" leading to San Marco and Rialto. In 1323 the Ten lifted the restrictions when the three men agreed to swear "loyalty and obedience" (fidelitatem et reverenciam) to the doge.[1]

In March 1389 the state attorneys, the avogadori di comun, placed popolano Marino de Quarteriis on trial for insulting Clara, wife of nobleman Marco Salamon. The incident took place when the Salamons and de Quarteriis were attending wedding celebrations for nobleman Donato Michiel in the parish of San Canciano. Noblemen were sensitive to their wives' reputations, and the avogadori sentenced de Quarteriis to a 100 lire fine and a month in jail. They also ruled,

> And he is banished and prohibited from entering the church of Santa Maria Formosa either the portico of the said church or the campo at ca' Morosini, nor may he cross the stone bridge in campo Santa Maria Formosa or the bridge at ca' da Mezzo that runs toward ca' Salamon, nor may he cross the bridge at ca' Soranzo in San Giovanni Novo, nor enter the church of San Giovanni Novo, running toward ca' da Lezze, nor may he enter the street behind ca' Soranzo that runs toward ca' Faraon; he cannot enter the said neighborhood, on foot or by boat for the next ten years, so long as Clara wife of Marco Salamon is alive and living in the said neighborhood (*contrata*).[2]

At first glance these rulings appear rather arbitrary. The Ten punished Trevisan, Salamon, and Zane by prohibiting them from going to the city's government and commercial centers. And the avogadori protected Clara Salamon by defining an area, roughly corresponding to the parishes of Santa Maria Formosa and San Giovanni Novo, that her tormenter could not enter.[3] In fact, these decisions made perfect sense given prevailing notions of the relationship between gender, space, and power. The Ten and the avogadori identified the centers of male and female power and made their decisions accordingly.

This chapter will show that patrician men and women operated at the helms of two different patronage systems that were closely linked to notions of male and female space. Male patronage was citywide, highly institutionalized, and focused on the councils of government. By forbidding the offending noblemen to go to San Marco, Rialto, or the Merceria, the Ten effectively isolated them from the loci of male power. Female patronage, by contrast, was parochial, private, and highly personal. By restricting the movement of de Quarteriis, the avogadori protected Clara Salamon's center of influence. This chapter will also show that, although different in form, both patronage systems served, like religion, the same end of creating a sense of community among Venetians of varying status, thereby lessening the tension brought on by patrician domination.

Male Patronage: The Development of State-Centered Ties

Neighborhoods in the cities of north Italy often served as power bases for great families. In Florence, Genoa, and other towns patricians lived in close physical proximity to their kinsmen, creating family enclaves in a particular parish or quarter of the city. The houses of the Peruzzi family of Florence were clustered near Santa Croce on the piazza de' Peruzzi, and the Doria of Genoa lived in the parish of San Matteo. Great families also cultivated ties to members of the poorer classes who were their neighbors. The Medici built a clientele in the gonfalon of Lion d'Oro, and the great families of Genoa organized in *alberghi* turned that city into a cluster of fortified, inward-looking cells. Neighborhood life contributed much to the disorder and conflict within the Italian city-states.[4]

The situation in Venice was quite different. Venetian patrician families generally did not cluster their palaces in one particular parish or sestiere. In 1379, for instance, the Badoer family owned property (and presumably had family members living) in the parishes of Santa Giustina, San Marco, San Paternian, San Salvador, San Canciano, San Stin, San Giovanni de Rialto, and San Giacomo dall'Orio.[5] Physical dispersion was characteristic of most patrician families. According to Stanley Chojnacki, in 1379 more than 98 percent of patrician families with more than one male had members living in different sestieri.⁶

Yet the situation was a bit more complicated than that figure seems to indicate. Although patrician families were widely dispersed about the city, sometimes they did have pockets of concentration. The Badoer holdings formed roughly three clusters: Santa Giustina and San Marco; San Salvador, San Canciano, and San Paternian; and San Giacomo dall'Orio and San Stin (including the adjacent San Giovanni Evangelista). We have already seen in chapter 3 how the Badoers of San Giacomo dall'Orio reached an agreement with relatives in Santa Giustina that allowed the Badoers of San Giacomo to consolidate their holdings on the Rialto side of the Grand Canal. Distantly related members of the Donà family had adjoining palaces in the parish of San Marcuola, but the family also maintained a palace across the Grand Canal in San Stin.⁷

Sometimes families viewed one particular palace, known as the *domus magna* or *ca' mazor*, as the familial center.⁸ Many nobles wrote provisions into their wills prohibiting the alienation of these palaces, for they viewed these ancestral strongholds as embodiments of the fortunes and spirit of their families. The government's decision in 1310 to raze the Tiepolo palace in Sant'Agostin in the wake of the Querini-Tiepolo conspiracy is especially revealing. The government decided to destroy a palace that was associated in the popular mind not only with the traitor Baiamonte Tiepolo but also with his grandfather Doge Lorenzo Tiepolo. There Lorenzo's wife the dogaressa had received the artisan guilds. By destroying its palace, the government hoped to exorcise the spirit of the family.⁹

As individuals, patricians sometimes felt attachments to their parish of residence or other sites. Pantaleone Giustiniani, patriarch of Constantinople, left several bequests to his home parish—San Pantalon. He endowed a clerical benefice at the church and arranged for the construction of a chapel there. Giustiniani may have been named for the parish's patron saint. Giovanni Contarini of Santi Apostoli made provision in his will for the construction of an altar dedicated to Santa Lucia in his home parish.¹⁰ In addition, patrician families enjoyed patronage rights over various religious sites. The Moro family enjoyed iuspatronatus over the abbey of Santa Maria della Misericordia.¹¹

In spite of all this, there was a qualitative difference between Venetian attachments to particular palaces or religious establishments and the family enclaves and fortress-like palaces of Genoa and Florence. The palaces of Venetian patrician families did not form defensive cells. Except for the retention of vestigial towers (and Angelo da Pesaro's Fondaco dei Turchi is a good example of this), Venetian patrician palaces were conspicuously lacking in martial characteristics.[12]

Similarly, there is little evidence to suggest that Venetian noble families tried to turn their popolano neighbors into armed retainers. There may have been some movement in that direction during the 1260s. The Great Council passed a law prohibiting any man, either "parvus vel magnus," from bearing the arms or wearing the livery of any "magnus homo."[13] The Querini-Tiepolo conspiracy reawakened such fears. The various police forces conducted frequent arms checks in the months and years following the conspiracy, and the Ten authorized various officials and their assistants to carry weapons.[14] In 1355, when the Ducal Council learned there was a conspiracy afoot led by Doge Falier, it called on nobles to arm themselves and men from the neighborhoods whom they could trust.[15] But the council probably intended to activate the regularly constituted civic militia, the *duodene*. Venice was not plagued with the kind of armed and liveried retainers found in *Romeo and Juliet*.

Nobles as a group also made little effort to serve as the patrons of their popolano neighbors. An extensive reading of notarial registers reveals little to suggest that noblemen actively tried to create a clientele of non-noble neighbors. In three recorded instances in which Marino Dalle Boccole of Santa Trinità made loans to members of the popolo minuto, there was no neighborhood connection. One borrower, Giacomo, was from the area around Treviso; another was a boatman named Giacomino who lived in Santi Apostoli; the third was a woman named Beta, wife of a tailor, who lived in Santa Maria Formosa.[16] A notable exception to this pattern is nobleman Nicolò Venier of San Samuele, who was creditor to various popolani living near him. The notarial records of Domenico, priest of San Maurizio, contain eleven small loans made by Venier: seven to fellow parishioners, two to popolani from the neighboring parish of San Vitale, and two to a cooper who lived across the Grand Canal in San Trovaso.[17] Again the Venetian experience contrasts with that of Florence, where men such as Cosimo de' Medici actively cultivated popular clienteles within their districts through devices such as loans.[18]

The parish-based civic festival of the *Marie* provoked a great deal of discord among the noble families who were responsible for sponsoring the event. Several times the Great Council had to intervene and appoint commissioners whose job it was to apportion the expense of the *Marie* among noble (or popolano grande) families who could afford to pay.[19] And in 1323 a law was passed imposing fines on residents of San Giacomo dall'Orio and San Giovanni Degolà who fled the parishes in order to avoid their duty.[20] Rather than vying for the privilege of sponsoring the event, most noblemen wanted to avoid this onerous and expensive parish responsibility.

What factors account for noblemen's lack of interest in the neighborhood? Why was the Venetian experience so different from that of other Italian cities? We have already considered some of the reasons in our discussion of Venice's urban development. The gradual transformation of the separate island communities into a unified urban core, the shift from landed to mercantile wealth, and the practice of using property as collateral in high-risk transactions all led to a devaluation in noblemen's minds of land and place per se. The increasingly settled nature of Venetian political life after 1172 and the new restrictions on ducal power allowed nobles to abandon arms and the defensive posture that family enclaves afforded. Topography may have played a role as well. As the best property on the Grand Canal was occupied, families had to build new or additional palaces in peripheral areas of the city. In the early seventeenth century, the Donà family chose the commodius Fondamenta Nuova, on the edge of the city, as the site for its new family palace.[21]

More important, however, was the Serrata and the political transformation that it entailed. The redefinition of Venetian politics on family principles tied the fortunes of noble families to those of the government. The welfare and the prestige of the nobility as a whole came to depend on the welfare and prestige of the regime. This provided a powerful incentive for nobles to cooperate and serve the city, although in actual practice their behavior often fell short of the civic responsibilities they preached.[22] For the individual patrician male, his personal prestige and that of his family compared with other patricians came to be measured increasingly by the number of offices he held and his success in securing state-sponsored favors (grazie) for his clients. It depended on his ability to work through the state apparatus, rather than on his control of a particular neighborhood or private clientele.

As part of this new orientation, the securing of grazie became a focus of male patronage. The granting of grazie probably began in the early days of Venetian history as a ducal prerogative. Like other sovereigns, the doge had the power to grant absolution from penalties to criminals and special privileges to others. But as the communal form of government grew and overwhelmed the personal government of the doge, the doge's power to grant grazie was restricted. In 1255 the Great Council passed a law declaring that the doge and his councillors could not grant grazie worth more than 10 lire di piccoli without the consent of the heads and members of the Council of Forty and the Great Council. In order to deter the doge even further, the law stated that he and his councillors had to receive a pledge from those who received grazie that they would not be abused. Although the grazie retained the form of a ducal prerogative, by the thirteenth century, real power to grant them rested with the patricians sitting in council.[23]

The conferral of a grazia required the consent of several of Venice's governing bodies. The process began with a petition to the doge and his councillors. The petition could be presented by the supplicant himself or by a proxy. At this point, the doge and his councillors referred the request to the government body with jurisdiction over the issue for an official opinion. The petition then went to the Signoria (the doge, the Lesser Council, and the heads of the Forty). Upon their approval, it was sent to the Forty. Depending on the nature of the request, it had to receive between 20 and 35 votes in the Forty. It was then forwarded to the Great Council, where passage required the consent of two-thirds of the members. Failure of a petition to get past any of the prescribed steps killed it, but provision was made for a petition to be brought to a vote three times in the Forty and three times in the Great Council. If a petition made its way successfully through the process, word was sent to the body with jurisdiction to grant the request; and a letter granting the petition was presented to the supplicant. Although this was the officially prescribed sequence, there was some flexibility in the procedures.[24]

Grazie fell into two general categories. Some were pardons—that is, they excused or released recipients from fines or jail terms levied on them by the government. Other grazie conferred favors or privileges. They bestowed money, exemptions from the law, or government posts on the recipients. Large areas of public life were controlled by the grazie procedure. In 1317 the Great Council approved a law stating that all raises for government officials, such as notaries, had to be secured through the process.[25]

All groups in Venetian society took advantage of grazie. Patricians made extensive use of them, relying on them to gain exemptions from the burdensome laws governing office-holding. In 1299, for instance, nobleman Marco Falier received a grazia absolving him of a 100 lire fine he incurred for refusing a post in Capodistria. In 1305 Angelo Mudazzo was absolved of a 20 soldi fine imposed on him when he refused to go on an ambassadorial mission to Sardinia.[26]

Noblemen also used the grazie to secure shortened terms of office, delays in departure, and permission to return to Venice to attend to family business.[27]

Impoverished patrician families also made use of grazie. The noble Sagredo family went through hard times in the 1330s and 1340s and looked to the state for assistance. In 1341 Lorenzo Sagredo and his father Francesco petitioned the Great Council for a grazia. Although they did not specify the misfortune that had befallen them, they noted that the family was in trouble. As compensation the Great Council voted to award Lorenzo a government post for one year.[28] A year later the family submitted more petitions. Marco Sagredo received an outright grant of 20 soldi di grossi, "considering his great poverty and illness."[29] Lorenzo Sagredo asked to have a fine levied on him by the capi di sestieri reduced because of his "weak and tenuous condition and poverty." Apparently it did not pass.[30] A year later, however, the Great Council approved a petition allowing Francesco Sagredo to assume the post awarded to his son Lorenzo. This was done since Lorenzo had been offered the opportunity to accompany Giovanni Contarini on his mission as castellan of Modon and Coron.[31] In 1344 another member of the Sagredo family, Francesco, son of Tommaso, petitioned the council to be allowed to export salt pork to Istria. He made the petition on behalf of himself and his sons, pleading poverty. It does not appear to have passed.[32] And in 1345 Giovanni Sagredo brought forward a successful petition for an office, claiming that he was "bereft of his father and other kinsmen" (derelictus a patre et aliis suis propinquis) and in a poor state.[33]

This cluster of Sagredo family petitions calls for comment. First, it is uncertain how financially strapped the family actually was. It was customary to claim poverty in grazie petitions. Nonetheless, the outright grant of money to Marco Sagredo was fairly unusual and may indicate that the family was indeed in serious trouble. Second, it is worth noting that the petitions for financial favors—to be released from a fine of the capi di sestieri and to export salt pork—were apparently denied. Instead, the Great Council preferred to help the family by offering members government posts that tied their fortunes more closely to those of the state. This practice may have prevented disaffected poorer nobles from turning to revolt. Third, within the confines of the patriciate, the grazie process created a legitimate arena for the exercise of patronage. It is likely that Giovanni Contarini served as the patron of Francesco Sagredo and his son Lorenzo.

Patricians were by no means the only ones who received grazie; the city's commoners, both the popolo grande and popolo minuto, sought the favors that grazie conferred. We have already noted that merchant families like the Bedolotos and Reglas and artisans such as furrier Bartolomeo Brocha and draper Francesco Rabia received grazie. The conferral of offices in the bureaucracy and salary increases were of particular importance to the popolo grande. Benintendi de' Ravagnani, who became grand chancellor in 1353, received at least ten grazie during his career. Several of them granted him salary increases; two awarded him 100 ducats to help dower his daughters.[34] Giacomo Zambono, *proto* of the carpenters at the Arsenal, was forced to retire at age eighty, but the Great Council voted to give Zambono a yearly pension of 60 ducats, "because it is a pious act and an honorable thing for our government to do and because it sets a good example for others." Patricians often awarded grazie on the grounds that they set good examples.[35]

The popolo minuto also received grazie. Sometimes they received these favors as recompense for their service to the republic. Ermolao de Lorenzo, who lost use of an eye in the war with Ferrara, received a job with the giustizieri vecchi through a grazia; and Zanino, a barber, had a fine reduced because he fought on the side of the doge during the Querini-Tiepolo revolt.[36] In 1333 the Great Council voted to allow Bona, widow of Pietro, a barber from San Moisè, to maintain her husband's tavern even though the number of taverns already exceeded the limit set by law. The council approved the favor in order to support Bona's children (pro subventione filiorum).[37] In 1347 the council passed a law awarding 2 ducats every year for twenty years to children whose fathers had died in the recent war with Genoa.[38]

The cryptic records of the grazie do not identify the patrons who managed petitions as they made their way through the councils of government. There are hints of how the system worked but no explicit statements. In 1310, for instance, a certain Uzolino received a pardon excusing him from a fine levied by the signori di notte for carrying a weapon. He received a grazia because the night he was caught he was in the service of nobleman Alvise Morosini. It is likely that Morosini intervened on his behalf.[39] Fantino Sancto received a grazia absolving him of a fine imposed by customs officials. According to the act's prologue, Sancto came to Venice in his boyhood and served as the servant of "plurium nobilium de Veneciis." Through "hard work and sweat" he earned money and merchandise valued at 110 ducats, but his trade practices got him in trouble with the customs officials. Undoubtedly it was some of the "plurium nobilium" who secured the favor for him.[40] There are other cryptic references to patronage as well. In his will, physician Giovanni Fantinelli bequeathed 200 ducats to one of the procurators of San Marco as recompense "for the many little services he has performed." And the humanist Bernardo Giustiniani assured Pietro Perleone that his future employer would "mobilize all his means and those of his friends and relatives" to secure Perleone a post in Greece.[41]

Even though the actual operation of the patronage system is obscure, its importance to patricians is unmistakable. In June 1348, during the height of the plague, a bill was introduced in the Great Council proposing a change in procedures. Since so many notaries were dying and could not be replaced at lower salaries, the bill proposed that the ducal councillors and the heads of the Forty be allowed to appoint notaries to offices at the salaries enjoyed by their predecessors in those offices. The bill was designed to keep the government running by circumventing the grazie procedure by which notaries received higher salaries. It was to be a temporary measure, lasting only until the feast of Saint Michael. Yet even during the height of the plague, patricians refused to relinquish their patronage rights. The first vote found 149 in favor of the change, 138 opposed, and 11 abstentions. The bill was defeated on a second vote when 125 voted in favor, 160 against, and 15 abstained. By the mid-fourteenth century the grazie had become so much a part of noblemen's stock-in-trade that not even the Black Death could convince them to make a temporary change.[42]

Grazie were not the only form of state patronage available to patricians. For a time in the first half of the fourteenth century, office-holding carried with it certain patronage rights. In October 1330 the Great Council passed a law that whenever a post became available in the offices of the various magistracies, the noble magistrates could each nominate a candidate for the post. The Council of Forty would then elect one of the three candidates. This new procedure gave nobles a chance to reward popolani with nominations.[43]

Presbyter Felice de Merlis from the parish of San Giacomo dall'Orio was often a nominee. In June 1333 a notarial post with one of Venice's civil courts, the *giudici del proprio*, became vacant. In accordance with the law each of the patrician judges nominated a candidate. Leonardo Mocenigo nominated the priest Avancio of Santa Sofia, Marco Morosini nominated the parish priest of Santa Maria Mater Domini, and Giovanni Sanuto nominated de Merlis. Avancio defeated de Merlis by only two votes.[44] In 1334 a notarial post with the *giudici del procurator* became vacant. De Merlis, now the parish priest of San Simeon Piccolo, was nominated by nobleman Marino

Pasqualigo. His opponents were Barnaba dalla Fontana, nominated by Angelo Bembo, and Giovanni de Ruggiero, nominated by Nicolò Venier. This time de Ruggiero won.[45] Finally in 1337 Andrea Pisani nominated de Merlis for a vacant post with the giudici del proprio, and de Merlis won the election. He defeated his old rivals Barnaba dalla Fontana (nominated by Marco Morosini) and Giovanni de Ruggiero (nominated by Federigo Dandolo).[46]

The fortuitous survival of Nicolò Bon's letter to Felice de Merlis allows us to glimpse the machinations behind patronage. In the letter Bon advised de Merlis to try to secure the favor of their fellow parishioner, nobleman Marino Badoer, by sending him a tapestry (or carpet). If that was not possible, he at least wanted de Merlis to write to Badoer. Bon reminded him that Badoer was the "best of his family" and that he [Badoer] was "interested in your welfare."[47]

Bon's immediate concern was to find a way for de Merlis to remain in Ayas as chaplain to the new governor, but he was not confident of his friend's chances since the parish priests of Sant'Agnese and the Giudecca were interested in the job as well. Nevertheless Bon intended to submit a petition filled with "sweet sounding phrases" (verbis congruis) to the doge in order to try to secure a grazia allowing de Merlis to continue in the post. Bon was confident of nobleman Pietro Barbarigo's support but not that of Enrico Michiel. Yet Bon had one more persuasive technique up his sleeve. He was ready to spend up to 50 lire in bribes. He assured his friend that it would be done "faithfully and discreetly" (fideliter et confidenter). In order to have a petition "read by friends" (per amicos consultum), as Bon put it, it was necessary to grease the palms of noble patrons.[48]

Corruption of this sort became so widespread that in 1340 the Great Council was forced to modify the nominating procedure it had created only ten years before. Noting that the system had led to "uncontrolled bribery" (preces infinite), the council decided that the magistrates themselves had to agree on a candidate who would then be approved by the Forty.[49] Despite these efforts, corruption continued, and grazie continued to grow in popularity.

The devastating War of Chioggia marked a new stage in the grazie process. The destruction and sacrifice caused by the war seem to have led to a greater awareness, especially on the part of popolo minuto, of the benefits to be derived from grazie. The government was flooded with petitions for favors—petitions like that of the sailor Marco Gafaro.

Sometime after 1381 Marco Gafaro of San Nicolò dei Mendicoli submitted a petition for a grazia asking to be named one of the *poveri del pevere*. In 1362 the government decided to use part of a tax on pepper to support aged mariners who had served the republic their entire lives. In his petition Gafaro, age seventy-five, recounted the highlights of his sixty years of service to the republic. He had served in the rebellion of Capodistria, the Third Genoese War, the rebellion of Candia, the war with Trieste, the war with the Carrara of Padua, and the War of Chioggia. He had been wounded many times and imprisoned in Genoa. Now, decrepit and almost blind, he was seeking the subsidy so that he would not have to beg and so that he could support his two nieces or granddaughters (*neze*).[50]

Gafaro's petition was one of many submitted to the government in the years following the war. In August 1382 the Great Council passed a law temporarily easing the voting requirements on grazie. Rather than requiring 35, 30, or 25 votes for approval in the Council of Forty, grazie could be passed with only 30, 25, or 20 votes. The requirements were relaxed again in September and December. The reason behind these changes was that the Forty could not gather a quorum because an epidemic was ravaging the city, and petitions for grazie were backing up. According to the law of September 1382, the change in voting requirements was an act "of piety and mercy in expediting the petitions of poor persons"; and the law of December spoke of the "multe pauperes persone" seeking grazie.[51] Similar changes were approved in September 1388, August 1389, September 1395, and September 1397. The government was being flooded with petitions for favors and was feeling pressure to expedite the petitions of "the large number of people who sought grazie and are seeking them continuously" (multis et infinitis personis qui petierunt gratias et continue petunt).[52]

The sacrifices made by all Venetians during the War of Chioggia led patricians to reward those who served the republic well. We have already noted that thirty popolano grande families were inducted into the nobility as recompense for the financial sacrifices they made. The popolo minuto who had sacrificed now came forward in great numbers to demand of the state some form of recompense as well. In the flood of petitions, we detect a greater reliance by the popolo minuto on the state and the favors it dispensed.

All this suggests that during the early Renaissance the procuring of state-sponsored favors became the crux of male patronage. Any number of factors including *parentado, amicizia,* or *vicinanza* could serve as the bond between patrons and clients. Nicolò Bon and Felice de Merlis, for instance, tried to court the favor of their fellow parishioner Marino Badoer. Yet de Merlis counted several other noblemen as patrons, including Giovanni Sanuto, Marco Pasqualigo, and

Andrea Pisani. Presbyter Barnaba dalla Fontana, member of a noble family, had Angelo Bembo, Nicolò Venier, and Marco Morosini for patrons.[53] Marriage or friendship ties may have linked him to these powerful families. In other cases money may have formed the bond between patrons and clients. Nobles sometimes served as patrons to those who paid the biggest bribes.

Male patronage was also highly flexible. It does not appear that popolani courted the same nobles and nobles served the same clients for years on end. Rather the links between male patrons and clients shifted as rapidly as certain families rose to positions of power and prominence and popolani (and other nobles) detected the shift. Nobles did not proceed to San Marco and Rialto with loyal groups of supporters like the ancient Roman patricians whose clients accompanied them to the forum. Instead they went to the *broglio*, the arcade under the ducal palace, where they sought friends and clients who could do them a favor that day.[54]

The same flexibility was characteristic of the grazie themselves. Some forms of grazie were actually transferable. In May 1339 nobleman Nicolò Briosso received a grazia permitting him to export 500 ducats worth of military outfits. In August of that year Briosso transferred the grazia to nobleman Donato da Lezze. In February 1338 nobleman Marco Manolesso received certain trade privileges through a grazia. He subsequently transferred them to Donato del Conte and Matteo de Porto.[55] Venice's mercantile environment even extended to political favors.

Given the flexibility and variability of patron-client relationships, their essential characteristic was their state-centeredness. Patrons and clients might change as rapidly as the most recent election, but the source of the favors remained constant. In the end, despite the lobbying for votes and bribes, grazie were favors granted by the government, not by individual patricians. This served to tie the interests of patrons and clients alike more closely to those of the state.

With the arena for patronage clearly focused on the government, patrician males turned away from the neighborhoods. Unlike Florentine gonfalons, which remained the loci of fiscal and electoral politics, Venetian parishes had responsibility only for mundane administrative tasks.[56] In order to preserve their power Florentine patricians had to remain attentive to the neighborhood, whereas Venetian patricians had to turn their attention to the city government. According to Marino Sanuto, Francesco Foscari gained the dogeship by dispensing favors through his position as procurator of San Marco. He rewarded friends and clients with grants from the procurators' funds.⁵⁷ Foscari recognized that the road to power in Venetian society lay, in a double sense, along the "vias magistras" leading to Rialto and San Marco.

Neighbors and Friends: Female Patronage

In contrast to men, Venetian patrician women lived in a restricted physical space bounded largely by the confines of the parish and even more so by the walls of the family palace. Patrician women, as the example of Clara Salamon illustrates, found their physical movement and activities restricted by male notions of proper female behavior. While noblewomen had some clout as lenders of money and investors in government bonds, they did not become actively involved in the actual work of commerce and politics. Patrician women seldom left the family palace or the parish except for chaperoned visits to churches, convents, and the homes of friends.⁵⁸

One reason for these restrictions had to do with the desire of patrician men to preserve their own honor by protecting the virtue of their women. In order to protect their wives and daughters from sexual and verbal attacks, males forbade them to leave carefully defined confines where they could be guarded.⁵⁹ This can be seen in Gentile Bellini's famous painting in the San Giovanni Evangelista cycle (Plate 3). While men move about freely in the piazza engaging in business and participating in the religious procession, most women observe the scene from the secure vantage point of balconies and windows.

Another reason had to do with the division of labor in Venetian society. Men viewed the household as women's proper realm. In his 1416 treatise entitled *De re uxoria*, nobleman Francesco Barbaro wrote that it was a woman's responsibility to oversee the operation of the household. "What," he asked, "is the use of bringing home great wealth unless the wife will work at preserving, maintaining, and utilizing it?"⁶⁰ In order to perform this duty properly, it was necessary for a woman to remain at home where she could oversee and instruct the servants. Barbaro admonished wives to "imitate the leaders of bees, who supervise, receive, and preserve whatever comes into their hives, to the end that, unless necessity dictates otherwise, they remain in their honeycombs where they develop and mature beautifully."⁶¹ The proper patrician wife stayed home supervising the household in order to ensure her husband's comfort and peace of mind.

With these male restrictions on their activity, it is not surprising

PLATE 3 Gentile Bellini, *Procession in Piazza San Marco* (Detail). Photo: Osvaldo Böhm.

to find that patrician women developed ties of affection and friendship with other women in their parish. Confinement and simple boredom drew them together. Yet there were many positive aspects to these associations as well. Female networks provided support and assistance during important moments in women's lives. Significant occasions in the female life cycle, notably marriage, childbirth, and death, brought together groups of women, including women of differing social classes. Childbirth brought to the bedside of the patrician woman not only patrician relatives and friends who provided support and comfort, but also midwives and servants of popolano rank who actually assisted with the birth. Similarly, death brought together clusters of women whose job it was to bathe, wrap, and keep vigil over the body of the deceased. These were peculiarly female occasions when status differences were mitigated by the shared female experience.[62]

The closest bonds, actual friendships, developed between women of equal status. The parish of San Giacomo dall'Orio provides several examples of neighborhood-based friendships between patrician women. Cecilia, wife of nobleman Marco Loredan, and the women of ca' Badoer were close. Cecilia selected Querina, widow of nobleman Nicolò Badoer, as one of her executors; and Zana Soranzo (who was born a Badoer but married into the Soranzo family of San Pantalon) remembered Cecilia with a bequest.[63] Beta, wife of Pietro Regla, and Fiordelise, wife of Bernardo Bedoloto, were also friends. They had much in common. Fiordelise was a member of the noble da Riva family, and Beta was probably from a patrician family as well; yet they both married non-nobles. In addition, they were immediate neighbors; the Reglas and Bedolotos owned adjoining properties in San Giacomo dall'Orio.[64] When it came time to draw up her will, Beta chose to remember Fiordelise with a bequest. In her first extant will, dated 1389, she left Fiordelise 10 ducats; in the second, dated 1427, she remembered Fiordelise with a bequest of clothing. Clearly Fiordelise, a wealthy woman, did not need 10 ducats or an article of clothing. Rather it seems that Beta intended these bequests as tokens of a friendship that had lasted almost forty years.[65] Fiordelise Bedoloto was also on good terms with Agnesina, wife of Doge Antonio Venier. In her will dated 1400 she named Agnesina as one of her executors. At first the choice seems surprising. After all, although Fiordelise was herself a patrician, she had married a non-noble. Yet an investigation of their lives shows that the wife of a non-noble merchant and the wife of the doge had reasons to be close. Fiordelise and Agnesina had both been raised across the Grand Canal in the contiguous parishes of San Canciano and Santa Maria Nova; and when they married, they married men who lived in the contiguous parishes of San Giacomo dall'Orio and San Giovanni Degolà.[66] Common status, physical proximity, and a shared move created an atmosphere that may have served to unite these women in friendship.

Parishes were the site of associations and friendships among women of patrician status. On a personal level, these relationships provided support for patrician women at critical moments in their lives and relief from the isolation that resulted from male restrictions on their activities. These friendships had a greater significance as well. In an important study of dowry accumulation, Stanley Chojnacki showed how patrician women helped secure the internal stability of the Venetian patriciate by linking through testamentary bequests their natal and affinal kin.[67] To a lesser degree, friendships between patrician women at the parochial level performed a similar function. Networks of noblewomen grouped around parishes and households provided another thread in the complex web of associations that bound the patriciate together in a kind of great interlocking family.

Yet the world of the parish and the world of the household were not class-bound. Nowhere in Venetian society were the contacts between patricians and popolani as frequent or as intimate as they were in the households of patrician families. The household included servants, slaves, wet nurses, and tutors and could number twenty-five people or more.[68] The patrician woman in her role as overseer of the household was in charge of the staff, and she had constant contact with them. In his treatise on wives, Barbaro included a chapter on the supervision and training of servants.[69]

The frequent contact between patrician women and servants combined with the shared responsibilities of caring for the household and children served to create intimate if not always cordial relations between them. Relations between patrician wives and the wet nurses who cared for their children tended to be cordial. In some cases, wet nurses had to leave their own families and take up residence in the homes of their employers. Under these circumstances a shared sense of separation from kin, coupled with a common concern for the children, helped to create close ties between patrician women and their children's wet nurses.[70] By contrast, relations between patrician women and slave girls were often tense. This was particularly the case when the slave was attractive, for she then became a potential object of the husband's sexual advances.[71] The intimate environment of the patrician household was replete with complex and multi-leveled contacts between patrician and popolano women.

Yet the actual boundaries of the Venetian household were ill-defined. Palaces were sprawling edifices with courtyards and covered passageways. Popolani rented space in mezzanines and attics.[72] Communication between apartments was easy, and the courtyard with its *pozzo* (well) became a social center.[73] Restricted as they were to this narrow geographic area, patrician women became familiar with their neighbors, often knowing the most intimate details of their lives. In some respects, the entire palace complex formed a kind of extended household.

Beyond the immediate courtyard, the parish provided another sphere for female interaction. Both noble and popolano women could safely venture to the parish church for a chat with the priests or to say prayers in a chapel. Veneration of the parish's patron saint and news of parish events united patrician and popolano women in a way that counting-houses, workshops, and taverns, the places where men gathered, could not. For patrician women, unlike patrician men, social contacts were more likely to be based on physical proximity than on other interests and were more likely to cross class lines.

Testamentary evidence shows that patrician women came to look upon their employees and neighbors with special concern. Expanding on the image males assigned them as managers of households and nurturers of children, Venetian patrician women developed their own networks of clientage.

Patrician women filled their testaments with bequests to their servants, slaves, and wet nurses. A few examples will illustrate the practice. When she drew up her will in 1336, Mario Orio of Santa Trinità left 2 soldi di grossi to her servant Caterina; in her will dated 1390, Franceschina Soranzo bequeathed a bed and coverlet to her former servant (*famula*) Margarita; and Donata, widow of Nicoleto Badoer, left money and clothing to her servants Agnes, Maddalena, and Cateruzia. Cecilia, widow of nobleman Marco Loredan, left 2 ducats to Caterina, "who served me in my present infirmity."[74]

Slaves were also the recipients of testamentary largesse. Sometimes a slave received freedom. Cecilia Loredan from the parish of San Giacomo dall'Orio freed her slave Vittore.[75] Other women offered their slaves financial rewards but not manumission. Franceschina, widow of Marino Dalle Boccole, left 2 ducats to each of her slaves but required that they continue in their servitude.[76] Clara

Emo's stipulations concerning her slave Margarita combined the two practices. Clara requested that Margarita be freed, but only after she had served her son for an additional five years.[77]

Some wet nurses received generous legacies. Maria, wife of nobleman Pietro Soranzo, left 30 ducats to her wet nurse Caterina; and Marina, widow of Leonardo Loredan, left 20 ducats to Bartolomea whom she described as, "my servant and the wet nurse of my daughter."[78] Lucia, wife of Marco da Molin, remembered all five of her children's wet nurses; she left them 5 lire each.[79] Beriola Morosini's bequest of 10 soldi di grossi to Caterina, wet nurse of her son Nicoleto, provides evidence of the intense bond between patrician women and their wet nurses. Beriola remembered Caterina and the service she had performed despite the fact that Nicoleto, the object of Caterina's service, had died some time before.[80]

The centrality of the household in women's lives can also be seen in the fact that patrician women remembered not only their own servants with legacies but also the servants of friends and relatives. Marchesina Contarini left 3 lire and a fur garment to Marchesina, servant of her sister-in-law; and Beriola Morosini bequeathed 4 soldi di grossi to Agnes, servant of her daughter Maria Zeno.[81] Household roles and responsibilities bound patrician and popolano women together in networks of association.

Patrician women also left bequests to tenants and neighbors in the courtyard of the family palace. Cateruzia, wife of Nicoleto Badoer, left 1 ducat to "donna Fina who lives in my courtyard"; and Cecilia Loredan left a tunic to donna Zana, "who lives below me."[82] During the autumn of 1350 a number of popolano women described as *vicine* (neighbors) went to the notary Stefano Pianigo to draw up receipts for bequests that noblewoman Maria Dandolo had left them.[83] Sometimes concern for neighbors and tenants extended beyond concern for particular individuals to include them all. Ysabeta da Mosto left 6 grossi to the poor women living in the courtyard in which she lived, and Maria Malipiero left 6 grossi "to the other poor households (casse piçolle) of my courtyard."[84] When she drafted her will in 1331, Zana Querini of Santa Giustina included a bequest of 7 lire to a certain Margarita, "who lives in the parish of San Giacomo dall'Orio at ca' Badoer."[85] Zana was born a Badoer and raised in San Giacomo dall'Orio. Perhaps this bequest commemorated a childhood friendship between her and Margarita.

Finally, the testamentary largesse of noblewomen extended beyond the walls of the family palace to include fellow parishioners. Caterina Soranzo of Santa Trinità left 3 ducats to fellow parishioner donna Margarita, a cobbler; Cecilia Loredan left bequests to her neighbors Beta, a used-clothing dealer, and Zana, widow of a stonecutter; and Donata, widow of Nicoleto Badoer of San Giacomo, left bequests to Humiliana and Azolina, wives of furriers in the parish.[86] Lucia Querini of San Simeon Grande left bequests to at least six popolano women in her parish, including three servants, a female cobbler, and the wives of a boatman and a clothworker.[87]

These bequests show that Venetian patrician women saw themselves as the guardians and protectors of their servants, tenants, and neighbors. When it came time for them to dispose of their worldly possessions, they chose to remember not only their kinsmen and friends of patrician status, but also persons of lesser status, especially women, with whom they shared their physical environment and their concern for household and offspring. Among women there was a sense of familiarity and domesticity extending beyond the strict confines of blood and marriage and beyond the family living quarters.

Some patrician women left bequests to popolano women to help them accumulate a dowry. For instance, Clara Morosini of Santa Trinità left 5 ducats to help dower the daughter of Marco, a ropemaker; and Marchesina Contarini of San Paternian left 6 soldi di grossi to help dower the daughter of her former servant Agnes Derigo. Marchesina stipulated that the money was to be invested until the girl married.[88] Bequests of clothes, linens, and household utensils helped popolano girls assemble a trousseau. By specifically stating that bequests were to be used for dowries, patrician women revealed an active concern for the recipients. These bequests would not only benefit the testators' souls and bring honor to their families, they would also positively affect the lives of the recipients.[89]

Although meagre in comparison to bequests to patrician girls, noblewomen's bequests to popolano girls were welcome and significant contributions to their dowry funds. As we have seen, during the period from 1309 to 1419, the average popolano dowry was 74 ducats. The receipt of 5 ducats or even 1 ducat from a noblewoman was an important increment to the dowry, especially for the poorest girls whose dowries ranged between 10 and 30 ducats. When Beta Regla left Fiordelise Bedoloto 10 ducats, it was a token of their longstanding friendship. A similar bequest to a popolano minuto girl was an important step in ensuring that the girl would marry. Some laboring-class men and women could attribute their marriage, in part at least, to the charitable ministrations of patrician women they knew.[90]

The client's side of these patron-client relationships can be seen in the wills drafted by popolano women. When non-noble women selected executors for their estates, a number turned to patrician women. For instance, in her will dated 1361, Vendramina, widow of tavernkeeper Giovanni of San Giacomo dall'Orio, selected noblewoman and fellow parishioner Cecilia Loredan and nobleman Nicoleto Corner to be her fiduciaries; Agnese, servant of noblewoman Agnesina de Mezzo, chose her employer as her sole executor; Iacobina, a resident (perhaps a servant) in the house of nobleman Dardi Polani, selected Polani and his wife Maria to be her executors; and Diamota, from the parish of Santa Trinità, wanted the procurators of San Marco and noblewoman Beruzia Venier of Santa Trinità to handle her estate.[91] Maria Dandolo of the parish of Santa Trinità served as patron of a number of popolano women in the parish. Both Diambra, a resident at a hospital in the parish, and Beatrice, wife of caulker Ioachino, chose Maria as one of the persons they wanted to handle their affairs.[92] In the artisan wills examined in chapter 3, none of the 50 artisan men selected patricians as executors; but at least 4 of the 70 wives and widows did so. When popolano women ventured beyond kinsmen in the selection of executors for their estates, a number turned to noblewomen in their parish or to former employers. They viewed these women as powerful, responsible persons who could be trusted to fulfill the provisions of their wills. It is difficult to imagine that they would have made such choices unless these women previously had demonstrated an interest in their welfare.

Testamentary evidence indicates that there was a lively system of patronage operating among women in the palaces, courtyards, and parishes of early Renaissance Venice. Drawn together by shared space, duties, and concern for things female, Venetian women of varying status formed patron-client relationships. Patrician women drew on the image of themselves as protectors and nurturers to assist popolano women in any way they could. It is not difficult to imagine that patrician women served as intermediaries between their clients and their husbands as well. Undoubtedly, popolano women asked noblewomen to intercede with their husbands for jobs, loans, and other favors.

The boundaries between men's and women's patronage should not, however, be overdrawn. Patrician males also left bequests to popolani at the neighborhood level. For instance, in his will dated 1413, Doge Michele Steno left numerous bequests to servants, slaves, and neighbors. And there were patrician women who, judging from their testaments, played no role as patrons or intercessors.[93]

Nevertheless there was a quantitative and qualitative difference between patrician men's and women's attitudes toward household and parish. The aggregated evidence of charitable bequests underscores the difference. One hundred wills drafted by Venetian nobles between 1309 and 1422 allow us to compare the incidence of blanket bequests given to provide for the parish poor and to help dower poor girls with the incidence of bequests given to specific non-noble individuals.[94] Blanket bequests were bequests intended for those groups but not assigned to specific individuals. When it was simply a question of leaving money to recipients who were to be chosen by someone else at a later time, giving by noblemen exceeded that of noblewomen. Twenty-three percent of the men left money for the poor of the parish, and 41 percent left money to help dower poor girls. By contrast, only 13 percent of the noblewomen left money to the poor of the parish, and 7 percent left money to help dower poor girls.[95] Under these circumstances, males were more generous, perhaps because they had more wealth to dispense. But when it was a question of leaving bequests to specific non-noble individuals, the roles were reversed. Seventy-four percent of the women testators left at least one bequest to a non-noble; whereas 54 percent of the men did so. In addition, women named more popolani per will than did men.[96] Patrician women who knew the inhabitants of the household and parish as individuals took time to tailor their bequests to fit individual cases.[97] Contemporary Venetians recognized this difference in orientation. On March 13, 1376 nobleman Marco da Mosto from Santi Apostoli drafted his will. In it he left 100 ducats for distribution to the poor of the parish. But he went further, stating that the money was to be entrusted to his wife Maria for dispensation (dadi a mia muier a sua man) since it was "she who knows who the deserving poor of the parish truly are" (perchè ella chognosse li puoueri besognosi).[98] Nobleman Marco da Mosto knew that his wife was more familiar with the parochial community than he was. The parish was her realm.

Patron-client relationships contributed much to the social stability of Venetian society and to the continued domination of that society by patricians. Paternalistic and maternalistic ties that linked men and women in networks of association cut across social boundaries and promoted feelings of community. Ties to powerful patrons helped meliorate the worst aspects of political exclusion and feelings of social inferiority among popolani. By creating ties of dependency between themselves and commoners, patrician women and men lessened the threat of social unrest.[99]

Yet male and female patronage networks contributed in different ways to the furtherance of this stability. Male patronage with its emphasis on procuring offices and favors led patrons and clients alike to look to (and ultimately support) the prevailing regime. Both patrons and clients recognized that in the end, despite all the lobbying by patrons, grazie were favors bestowed by the state. Mercy (*misericordia*) was a prerogative not of individual patrons but of the government itself. Furthermore, the orientation of male patronage promoted cooperation within the ranks of the patriciate. Rather than cultivating neighborhood clienteles and promoting family enclaves that could be mobilized and defended in times of civil strife, noblemen jostled for power within the broadly legal confines of the government. The orientation of patrician men away from neighborhoods and toward the government promoted stability.

Women's patronage promoted harmony by making popolani feel that there were specific individuals who were interested in their welfare. Whereas male patronage was bent on the use of influence to affect the decisions of government councils, female patronage was oriented toward the delivery of tangible benefits such as dowries and clothing.[100] Women were seen (and saw themselves) as intercessors in this world in much the same way that the Virgin Mary was seen as an intercessor in the next. The household and neighborhood orientation of female patronage promoted the sense that there were real places of belonging in an otherwise rather impersonal urban world.

In early Renaissance Venice patronage was closely tied to gender and gender determined notions of physical space. When the Ten and the avogadori di comun meted out punishments to noblemen Angelo Trevisan, Michele Salamon, and Marco Zane and popolano Marino de Quarteriis, they devised punishments designed to isolate Trevisan, Salamon, and Zane from the centers of male power and to prevent de Quarteriis from invading noblewoman Clara Salamon's sphere of influence. Angelo Trevisan recognized the full significance of his punishment. In his petition for clemency, he asked for permission to return to Rialto since his livelihood depended on the trade that took place there. Over time Trevisan, Salamon, and Zane all received grazie from the Ten that allowed them to return to the centers of male power at Rialto and San Marco.[101]

SEVEN 🙵

From Community to Hierarchy: The Transformation of Venetian Social Ties

I want... 500 ducats to be used to buy stones and stakes to reinforce the lido of San Nicolò for the benefit of my soul and for the welfare and fortification of Venice—may God maintain the city always.—Rubric from the testament of the metal refiner Pantaleone, 1398

The poems inscribed below about the deeds, situation and glory of the distinguished city of the Venetians, were composed by me, Bartolomeo de Arcangelis of Venice, a notary in the office of the avogadori di comun—may the most High in his goodness and clemency protect and preserve her most happily for all time.—Scribbling on the cover of Doge Andrea Dandolo's oath of office, mid-fourteenth century

Be careful what you do, for the boy may be the son of a nobleman and things could become very unpleasant for you.—Warning of Franco Mallaza to his friend the sailor Monte, 1356

Mad Venice—you have forgotten your poor.—Graffiti scrawled on the church of San Boldo, 1400

These are sentiments of the Venetian popolani. Preserved in documents maintained by patricians, they resonate across the centuries and return us directly to the central concern of this study, namely how the associative tendencies of early Renaissance Venetians contributed to social stability by influencing and shaping popular attitudes toward the patrician regime. In order to understand how attitudes were formed, this study has focused on the private lives of early Renaissance Venetians, particularly on their family lives, working lives, religious associations, and their ties to patrons, clients, and neighbors. This final chapter weaves these disparate strands together to present a picture of the social world(s) in which

Venetians of the early Renaissance moved. It also explores changes that occurred during the last quarter of the fourteenth century and first quarter of the fifteenth century, which transformed Venetian society from one based on the notion of community to one based on a sense of hierarchy.

Venetian Society in the Early Renaissance

One way to illustrate the subtle interplay of associations and relationships in the lives and attitudes of people is to focus on the experience of particular individuals. In this case, the individuals are a metal refiner named Pantaleone and a worker of unknown trade named Franco Mallaza. The concrete examples of their lives provide a springboard from which to suggest more general conclusions about the Venetian social experience. Although it is risky to argue for the typicality of either man, their experiences do point to some of the more salient features of popolano grande and popolano minuto life. What is more, Pantaleone and Franco have left direct though cryptic indications of their attitudes toward the patrician regime. Hence their experiences are unusually suggestive of how personal experiences may have shaped political and social attitudes.

On the tenth day of October 1398 the metal refiner Pantaleone of the parish of Santa Fosca had the notary Bernardo de Rodulfis draft his will.[1] A surprising amount of information about Pantaleone and his social situation can be gleaned from the will. For one thing, he was a very wealthy man. He had an estate worth more than 6,000 ducats, of which 4,300 was in bullion as might be expected of someone practicing his trade. He also owned his own house. Few other details about his business dealings or financial status can be discerned from his will except to note that he owned at least two slaves (and possibly more), that three of his executors were goldsmiths, and that he left a bequest of 50 ducats to the widow and children of a money changer named Andrea Mora. Goldsmiths and money changers were the sort of people with whom a metal refiner like Pantaleone had contact. In terms of wealth and business interests then, Pantaleone was clearly in the elite of Venetian society; this set him apart from the majority of Venetian popolani.[2]

Pantaleone had no living relatives except his wife Caterucia to whom he seems to have been fairly close. He named her as his fourth executor and bequeathed 1,000 ducats' worth of government bonds for her maintenance. In addition, his will stipulated that she was to have use of an apartment in his house and all the household items she desired. If she remained a widow, she would also have the right to dispose of 500 ducats' worth of the bonds as she saw fit; but if she remarried, she would receive her dowry (100 ducats), an additional 100 ducats, and nothing more. He bequeathed 20 ducats to his godson Lando Grillo and 30 ducats to his goddaughter (or perhaps his adopted daughter) Francesca, a nun at the convent of San Marco Piccolo of Padua.[3] Pantaleone requested that his tomb at the Madonna dell'Orto be sealed, "since I have no relatives."

Perhaps because he had no kinsmen to whom he could bequeath his estate, Pantaleone left a wide variety of bequests to various charitable causes and pious establishments, including the church of the Madonna dell'Orto. He wanted the church to purchase a chalice and other objects worth between 60 and 70 ducats for use when celebrating a monthly mass for his soul. He also left enough government bonds to pay a priest to say the masses and for candles and oil. He left another 70 to 80 ducats for the construction of an altar at which the masses could be said. Pantaleone remembered his home parish with two bequests: he wanted the priests of Santa Fosca to receive 12 ducats as his tithe, and he asked that a *caritade* (love feast) be given in the parish. He also left 1 ducat apiece to the poor of San Lazzaro, the city's leper and plague hospital. In disposing of his properties, Pantaleone stated that he wanted the part of the property that his wife did not use for her personal living quarters to be rented and the profit used to help the poor of the parish. After his wife's death, or in case she remarried, the rent was to go to the scuola grande of San Marco to clothe the poor of the scuola. After ten years, the property was to be sold and the money used to help marry either the daughters and sisters of his brothers in the scuola of San Marco or the daughters and sisters of poor seamen who had died "in honor de la signoria nostra." Finally, Pantaleone requested that another 400 ducats of his estate be used for the same purpose as well.

The will also gives a sense of the social circles in which Pantaleone moved. As noted above, he named three goldsmiths in addition to his wife as his executors. They were ser Giacomo de la Stopa, ser Marco Fassa, and ser Marco Negro. The first, ser Giacomo de la Stopa, lived in the parish of San Vitale. He appears in the estimo with an assessment of 1,000 lire. The second executor was Marco Fassa, who was serving as the guardian of the scuola of San Marco at the time Pantaleone drafted his will. When the notary asked Pantaleone whether he wanted any officers of scuole or monasteries to serve as his executors, he responded no and said that he had named Fassa, "as a private person and not as a deacon or official of the scuola." The third executor was Marco Negro from Santa Marina. In naming Negro, Pantaleone noted that "he is like a brother to me" (sì como mio frar).

While the executors were all goldsmiths from other parishes, the witnesses to the will were all fellow parishioners who worked in professions unrelated to that of Pantaleone. The first was Karolo Petrarca, *comes palatinus*, a notary, the second, Francesco da Poço, a draper, and the third, Petrarca's son Nicolò.

In some ways, Pantaleone was the archetypical popolano grande. He was prosperous and successful. As he himself noted, he had worked hard (ò guadagnato cum grande fadiga), but the benefits had been great; he had earned a large amount of money, even by patrician standards. His position as a property owner gave him standing in the parish, and he patronized his home parish and the monastery of the Madonna dell'Orto. In addition, he belonged to one of the major religious confraternities.

More than anything else, however, Pantaleone's friendship circle reveals his place in Venetian society. He moved in a world of men similar to himself—men who were prosperous and well connected. His friends and associates were goldsmiths, drapers, and notaries—men of social standing. One even held the post of guardian in the scuola grande of San Marco. These were men with a substantial stake in Venetian society.

Herein lies much of the explanation for the popolo grande's acceptance and support of the patrician regime. They were men and women who had arrived. They had respectable if modest fortunes and enjoyed a considerable degree of prestige. They held positions of authority in guilds, scuole, and parishes. Government offices were open to them as secretaries, and clerical careers provided opportunities to advance to powerful positions.

In addition, the personal and professional lives of the popolo grande were closely tied to those of patricians. Some well-to-do commoners were engaged in commercial ventures with patricians, while others shared a mutual interest in overseas trade. Bernardo Bedoloto, for instance, jointly owned a ship with noblemen Lorenzo Foscarini, Lorenzo Erizzo, and others. The well-to-do Regla brothers were active in the grain trade; and a furrier by the name of Fachino Bono engaged in overseas trade, dealing in a variety of commodities including wheat, hemp, tallow, and jewels.[4] Clerics such as Nicolò Bon and Felice de Merlis took advantage of overseas posts to engage in trade as well. The popolo grande shared a community of interest with noble merchants and had a stake in the commercial policies of the city.

This community of interest extended to the home markets as well. As our discussion of guild organization illustrated, nobles had investments in some of the most important Venetian industries, such as glassmaking, textiles, and furs. In some industries nobles owned the industrial equipment, whereas in others they had contracts with guildsmen. Common interests, especially in keeping the costs of labor down, brought nobles and the popolo grande together in opposition to the demands of workers. This helps explain the relatively free hand masters got in running the guilds.

Contact between patricians and the popolo grande extended beyond the world of work to other aspects of their lives as well. They sat together in parish meetings, where as property owners they had the privilege of discussing parish business and perhaps electing the parish clergy. And in the scuole they were ritual brothers. It is often remarked that in the scuole, the cittadini found an outlet for their ambitions and were allowed to exercise authority. It ought also to be remembered that the scuole represented a place of ritual equality. Within the confines of the confraternity, all men were brothers.

Some popolani were related by marriage to patricians. Although the actual rate of intermarriage may not have been very great, the social and psychological impact of intermarriage on the popolo grande was considerable. First, intermarriage provided the only sure (albeit indirect) means of upward social mobility. The children of unions between patrician men and popolano women would themselves be nobles. Second, marriage into patrician families promised the popolo grande tangible benefits such as business partners and intangible ones such as prestige. Finally and perhaps most importantly, intermarriage was a sign that Venetian society as defined by the patricians remained open.

This same sense of openness and accessibility is evident in friendship circles. Patrician and popolano grande men and women formed close friendships and attachments to one another. For instance, the oft-cited Bernardo Bedoloto was placed on trial twice for committing crimes with noble companions. In one incident he assisted noblemen Domenico Dolfin and Antonio Loredan in the commission of a rape. Noblemen Fantino Ghisi and Fantino Contarini were also present. A few years later, Bedoloto went with noblemen Marco Contarini, Moreto Boccassio, Zanino Baseggio, and another popolano, Filippo de Mercadellis, on an escapade to the convent of San Lorenzo.[5] Bernardo's brother Ludovico got into several scrapes with the law when in the company of noblemen from the Bondemiro, Querini, Manolesso, and other families.[6] And as we have seen, popolano Marino de Quarteriis got in trouble for insulting the wife of nobleman Marco Salamon when both were attending wedding celebrations for nobleman Donato Michiel. Boys moved in mixed circles as well. In 1373 youngsters Pietro Giustiniani and Zanino Condulmer and several boys of artisan background were caught throwing rocks at the dormitory of the Friars Minor at San Stin.[7] The humanist Paolo de Bernardo, bastard son of the noble ca' Bernardo, remarked perhaps somewhat rhetorically that he spent his youth in the company of fishermen and butchers.[8] Noble and popolano grande women also moved in friendship circles. Convents, households, and children provided common areas of interest and concern. Among women, friendships were often parish-based.

There were a number of factors, then, that help explain why the popolo grande accepted the political regime and acquiesced to it. They were a solid, substantial class of citizens who recognized that their interests were tied to those of the patricians. They saw avenues of mobility open to them through intermarriage with patricians and through careers in the bureaucracy and the church. Furthermore, they did not perceive a vast gap separating themselves from patricians.

Despite their relatively small size, the popolo grande were the one group that could have provided leadership for the aspirations of all Venetian popolani, for they had the wealth, expertise, and connections needed to lead an organized resistance to the patrician regime. Indeed, in the other cities of northern Italy, it was new men, the *novi cives* or *gente nuova*, who usually were the catalysts for political change. Yet the popolo grande of Venice chose not to do so, and if violence is any indication of disaffection, they were the most contented group in Venetian society.[9]

In his will the metal refiner Pantaleone gave verbal and financial expression to his support of the regime. He bequeathed 500 ducats worth of state bonds to the government for the repair of fortifications on the Lido. In making the bequest, he hoped to earn merit for his soul and protection for his native city. He concluded the bequest by beseeching God to "maintain the city always." The notary Bartolomeo de Arcangelis, friend of humanist Paolo de Bernardo, expressed nearly identical sentiments in the poems he composed.[10] Even the disaffected among the popolo grande revealed their underlying desire to be part of the regime. In his will popolano Antonio Arian enjoined his children not to marry patricians. He forbade his children to have contact with a group that rejected his family's claims to noble status.[11] The popolo grande wanted participation in the system, not a transformation of it.

If the position of well-to-do-commoners and their attitudes toward the regime are fairly clear, those of the popolo minuto are harder to arrive at and, in the end, appear much more ambivalent. On one hand, isolation and exclusion from the centers of power and prestige led to a sense of alienation; on the other, the paternalistic and maternalistic attitude of patricians, especially as demonstrated in patron-client ties and charity, helped meliorate some of the worst aspects of their condition. In order to recapture something of the tenor of working-class lives, let us examine an incident involving Franco Mallaza and his friend Monte.[12]

On Christmas Day 1356, Franco Mallaza of Sant'Antonin and his friend Monte, a sailor, had dinner at the home of Franco's sister Agnesina. After dinner they went to the parish of Santa Maria Formosa where they met two of Monte's kinsmen, including a youngster who was a custodian (zago) at Santa Maria Formosa. The boy was whiling away his time in a game of draughts. Franco and Monte had nowhere to go and no plans and kept asking each other, "What do you want to do?" Franco left for a time, and when he returned, the group proceeded to the home of a gold-thread spinner named Cristina who invited them in for a drink. In the meantime, however, a well-dressed young boy had joined them. Leaving Cristina's, the group proceeded to the campo San Zanipolo where, when asked what he wanted to do, Monte confided to Franco that he wanted to steal the boy's silver-studded belt. At that point Franco warned his friend of the trouble that awaited him if the boy were the son of a noble.[13] Monte did not heed the advice and stole the boy's belt. Monte and Franco then went to the archery range at San Martino where they examined the belt. Monte entrusted it to Franco for safekeeping. From there they went back to Franco's sister's house where they were traced by guards of the signori di notte. Monte escaped and Franco was captured.

The transcript of this case tells us less about the circumstances of Franco's and Monte's lives than does the will of the metal refiner Pantaleone about his life, yet several significant points emerge. First, Monte, Franco, and their friends were people of humble status. Three professions were noted in the transcript. Monte was a sailor, his nephew was a custodian, and Cristina was a gold-thread spinner. None of the professions carried much social status—they were professions of the popolo minuto. Second, it appears that both Franco and Monte were single; at least no mention was made of wives or children. Franco probably lived with his sister. Little is learned about Monte except that he had two kinsmen. The men's physical movement that night was also notable. They wandered through the sestiere of Castello and parts of San Marco as well. Finally, it is clear that on this Christmas night, drinking and gambling were the primary activities in which they and their friends engaged. There was a sense of restlessness and aimlessness in the men's actions. Having nothing better to do, the two wandered about their quarter of the city looking for a bit of excitement and in the end getting more than they bargained for. The well-dressed boy was the son of nobleman Daniele Vitturi of Santa Maria Formosa.

This incident brings into focus some but not all the salient features of laboring-class life. All Venetians were susceptible to the ravages of pestilence and war. Many patrician families, like the Dalle Boccole, became extinct during the course of the fourteenth and fifteenth centuries. But life was even more insecure for the popolo minuto. The poorer classes could not rely on an extended kinship group for comfort and support because their families were small and often physically dispersed. To compensate, the popolo minuto emphasized the importance of the nuclear family and particularly the conjugal bond. Those who were unmarried, like Monte and Franco, faced life in even more difficult circumstances.

The world of work provided little relief for the popolo minuto. As sellers rather than employers of labor, they were especially susceptible to vagaries of the economy. More importantly, the popolo minuto had little or no voice in guild affairs. Only on rare occasions were laborers able to exert enough influence on the giustizieri vecchi to get them to decide in their favor. Most of the time, noble judges sided with the masters who controlled workshops.

Rather than serving as the locus of popolano solidarity, the workshop was the scene of disaffection, tension, and conflict between masters and workers. This did much to shape the political fortunes of the patrician regime, for if the popolo were to form a successful counter to the patricians, they had to be united. Yet the popolo were not united, and the very group that could have provided leadership for the popolo minuto—the popolo grande—refused to assume that role. Disaffection among popolani, coupled with the lack of a viable corporate tradition in Venice, did much to secure the patrician regime from popular opposition.

The alienation of workers from the guild structure points to the more general lack of focal points around which the working-classes could organize. Unlike mercantile Florence with its concentrated textile industries, Venice was first and foremost a trade center. Nonetheless there were several important and fairly large-scale industries in Venice, including the textile industry, in which workers might have organized. Indeed it is in the wool industry with its large concentration of immigrants that there is the most direct evidence of worker discontent. But in Venice, the industries in which there were large concentrations of workers were geographically dispersed. This made it difficult for workers to organize.

This dispersal of work sites was replicated in residential patterns. Although there was some tendency for nobles to live in the central parishes around San Marco and Rialto and for the poor to live on the periphery, there was only one class-exclusive parish in Venice. According to the estimo of 1379, only the parish of San Nicolò dei Mendicoli had no noble property owners. Hence parish churches that might have served as centers of working-class organization were controlled by the property owners (nobles and popolani grandi). Alienated from guilds, workplaces, and neighborhoods, the popolo minuto had no institutional basis for organization. Disenfranchised and, as Franco's words indicate, often discontented, the popolo minuto formed an inchoate, dispersed mass who felt neglected. As the anonymous rebel of San Boldo proclaimed, Venice had forgotten her poor.[14]

From an anthropological point of view, it is possible to argue that Venetian society was extraordinarily stable in the early Renaissance because cross-cutting social networks diffused class tensions. Vertical links between status groups were strong, whereas horizontal links within status groups, especially among the popolo minuto, were weak. Anthropologists note that a number of forms of association, especially patron-client ties, tend to undermine horizontal solidarities (the ties between persons of equal status) and to strengthen vertical links between persons of unequal status. The effect of strong vertical ties is to weaken the cohesion of the lower classes, thereby lessening the possibility of united opposition to the elites. As John Waterbury suggests, patronage may be not "only a manifestation of class domination but crucial to its maintenance."[15] In Venice, as we have seen, patrician men and women created strong patron-client ties to both the popolo grande and popolo minuto through government and parish-based patronage systems. At the same time solidarity among the popolo, at least as manifest in the artisan workshop, was virtually nonexistent. Religious associations provided yet another wide arena for social interaction, cutting across the layers of society. Priests served as social intermediaries, ministering to the spiritual and temporal needs of different groups; and scuole provided sacred locales in which men and women from different backgrounds could come together in a spirit of fraternity. These and other ties served to weaken the solidarity of the popolo.

There were, however, two special groups among the popolo minuto for whom a conjuncture of profession and residence provided the potential at least for creating a strong sense of group identity and therefore some threat to the regime. These were the *Arsenalotti*, the workers at the Arsenal, and the *Nicolotti*, the fishermen of the parish of San Nicolò dei Mendicoli. It is instructive to examine how the government dealt with them.

The Arsenalotti posed a more serious threat since they could easily arm themselves with weapons from the Arsenal and move quickly into San Marco. Accordingly, the government maintained strict supervision of trades at the Arsenal, allowing workers less autonomy than that granted other guildsmen. But special privileges balanced the restrictions. The Arsenalotti were granted special favors, including the right to form an honor guard at the doge's funeral. Thus an attempt was made by the patricians to integrate the Arsenalotti into the regime—to make them feel they belonged.[16]

The Nicolotti lived in one of the few parishes where community feelings ran high. The fishermen of San Nicolò probably posed no real threat to the regime since they were poor and lived on the city's periphery; but as a precaution, the patricians tried to integrate them into the city as well by according them several privileges, including the right to elect their own official who, in turn, was received by the doge.[17] In both instances, the regime recognized the dangerous potential of working-class solidarity and turned that potential to its advantage. The government acknowledged the danger posed by workers who were organized along neighborhood and professional lines and worked to defuse that danger by making the workers feel that they were in some way part of the regime.

At the same time that it tried to link the Arsenalotti and the Nicolotti to itself, the government fostered competition between the two groups—competition that was channeled into fistfights and regattas. The government thus pursued a policy of "divide and conquer" with regard to these two potentially disruptive groups.[18]

The government may have pursued a similar policy when in 1381 it decided to induct several prominent popolano families into the patriciate. Candidates competed with one another for admission. For instance, Pietro Regla of San Giacomo dall'Orio competed against

Bartolomeo Paruta. Paruta, who made large contributions to the war effort, won the right to noble status.[19] By organizing the election in this manner, the patricians were able to direct any ill feelings on the part of losers not against the regime, but against rival popolano candidates, thereby preventing the losers from forming a unified block of resistance. Again vertical solidarities undermined horizontal ones.

Such an analysis helps explain the stability of Venetian society, yet obscures two essential points that also need to be considered when trying to characterize and understand the society of early Renaissance Venice. First, such an interpretation emphasizes patrician action at the expense of popolano action. Second, it does not adequately take into account the prevailing civic ideology, namely the ideal of community.

Venetian history often is written as a hymn of praise to the sagacity and far-sightedness of the patricians. The myth of the wise and beneficent Venetian patriciate is particularly potent and easily reinforced given the biases of the extant sources. It is easy to forget that all social interactions had two sets of actors—patrician and popolano. If patricians sought clients, then popolani sought patrons; if patricians granted posts of authority to notaries and priests, then popolano families sought (and paid bribes) for those honors; if patricians dispensed charity, then popolani went from house to house seeking charity. Part of the explanation for Venetian popular quiescence has to be sought in the context of popular life itself, independent of patrician action. As we have seen, the familial experience of the popolo minuto did much to determine their actions and perspectives. Cut off from a secure kinship network, the popolo minuto lacked the wherewithal and ultimately the confidence needed to resist the regime effectively. Struggling to subsist, they had little time for political organizing. Excluded from participation in the mainstream institutions of Venetian life, they created their own social world in taverns and workshops. The forms that their protest may have taken, including charivaris and carnivalesque behavior, have largely disappeared from the record.[20] Similarly, the popolo grande were determiners of their own fate. This is apparent in the guilds, where they were able to get the patrician giustizieri vecchi to go along with policies favorable to themselves. They used the commercial ties between themselves and patricians to pressure the government.

We also should recall that ideology as well as interests shapes social bonds. The associations described in this study were associations forged in a society in which the prevailing ideal was one of community. The impulse to belong, to be part of a community, shaped the lives of Venetians in the family, the guild, the church, and the neighborhood. This ideal, memorialized in the translation mosaics, led to the creation of surprisingly fluid and open social ties. Even the patricians, the most status-conscious members of society, associated freely and openly with the subordinate classes. This fluidity and openness prevented Venetian society from becoming overly polarized either along factional or class lines. The cry of the discontented in Venice was not for change in the system, but to be part of it. The lambast against mad Venice that had forgotten its poor was also a plea to be remembered and to be accepted as part of the community. During the early Renaissance, the impulse toward community overcame the countervailing impulse toward conflict.

From Community to Hierarchy

Although during the early Renaissance Venetian society showed remarkable stability on account of the fluidity and openness of social ties based on an ideal of community, changes were underway that would transform Venetian society and, during the course of the fifteenth century, substitute a new ideal for that of the old. During the trecento, traditional bonds and associations weakened as Venetians looked to new institutions with a wider focus and orientation. The beneficiary of this new orientation was in the end the patrician regime itself. Patricians began increasingly to equate their own wellbeing with that of the state and to use the government apparatus to protect and promote their interests. As they did so, a new ideology asserted itself. The early years of the fifteenth century witnessed a hardening of social lines and the substitution of hierarchy for community as the organizing principle in Venetian social relations.

There are several indices that show that during the course of the trecento old social bonds loosened as Venetians looked in new directions. The surest index of this change is the reorientation of Venetian men away from the neighborhood and toward the state. The disappearance of armed retainers after the 1260s, the popolo's requests to the state for favors, and the decline and abolition of the festival of the *Marie* all indicate that traditional personal ties based on physical proximity were becoming weaker as Venetians looked to less personal and more institutionalized forms of association.

Another index of this change is a shift in charitable impulses. An examination of some of the charitable bequests contained in the wills of 333 residents of the parish of San Giacomo dall'Orio shows a dramatic shift during the course of the trecento in the sense of com-

TABLE 7.1 Distribution of Charitable Bequests

Period	Total Testators	Bequests to San Giacomo		Bequests to San Lazzaro	
1297–1347	55	13	23.6%	3	5.5%
1348–1381	130	19	14.6	27	20.8
1382–1423	148	7	4.7	34	23.0
Total	333	39	11.7%	64	19.2%

SOURCE: ASV, Cancelleria Inferiore, Notai, Archivio Notarile, Testamenti, Procuratori di San Marco, Commissarie.

munity and identity. Table 7.1 summarizes the data.[21] In the first half of the fourteenth century nearly one in four parishioners left a bequest, usually in the form of a caritade, to his poorer fellow parishioners. By the end of the fourteenth century and first quarter of the fifteenth century that number had dropped to one parishioner in twenty. At the same time, bequests to the poor of San Lazzaro, the city's leper and plague hospital, grew at approximately the same rate that bequests to the poor of the parish declined. These data suggest two conclusions. First, during this period fewer and fewer parishioners viewed their poorer neighbors as worthy of their legacies. The perception of the entire parish as a community of rich and poor united by common residence and physical proximity was declining. Second, at the same time charity to a more broadly based community, namely victims of leprosy and the plague, increased. Institutions that had a city-wide focus were in ascendance.

How do we account for this shift in focus? Partly it was a natural consequence of urbanization. As the city grew in size and complexity, the last vestiges of social relations as experienced in Rialtine days gave way to the newer, less personal ties of city life. The crises of the mid-fourteenth century also disrupted prevailing social ties and accelerated change. The Black Death caused a demographic catastrophe that perhaps reduced the city's population by 60,000. Old bonds were broken as rich and poor, young and old, were struck down. Venice recovered more quickly than most cities from the plague, yet even the temporary interruption of patterns was enough to alter them.[22]

The recovery itself further transformed the city. After the plague, the government adopted a policy of encouraging immigration, which was on the whole quite successful. Yet the influx of immigrants created new problems. Immigrants, like the textile workers from Tuscany, came with different political traditions that may have exacerbated at least temporarily the tensions and problems within the Venetian community. It took time for immigrants to adapt to Venice's peculiar traditions and institutions.[23]

The War of Chioggia caused tremendous changes in Venetian society. The demands of the war affected patricians and popolani alike. For their part, patricians and well-to-do commoners were forced to make financial sacrifices for the war effort; and the popolo minuto had to serve in the fleet. One effect of the war was financial and personal dislocation. The financial burdens of the war left many patrician and popolano grande families in serious financial trouble. For instance, the Pesaro family was forced to sell its "possession grande," the Fondaco dei Turchi. Another victim of the government's fiscal demands was Marino Carlo. According to the estimo, Carlo was one of the wealthiest popolani in the city, with an assessment of 30,000 lire. Yet the financial burdens of the war and other reverses left Marino's son Pietro bankrupt in 1392.[24] Others profited from misfortunes brought on by the war. Future doge Michele Morosini speculated in real estate during the conflict. In a few short years he was able to quadruple his investment. Another who profited from the problems wrought by the war was Pietro Regla; when nobleman Giacomo da Molin of San Stae was forced by financial exigencies to sell some property in San Giacomo dall'Orio, Regla purchased it.[25]

By making and destroying fortunes, the war caused a reshuffling of power in Venetian society at both the civic and parochial levels. At the civic level the war ended the domination of ducal elections by certain patrician families known as the *lunghi*. No member of these families, which had dominated ducal elections for centuries, was elected doge again until 1612. And the induction of the thirty popolano families into the patriciate was the last major infusion of new blood until the seventeenth century. At the local level, as prominent families lost their property, they lost their right to a voice in parochial affairs. The shift in property ownership also disrupted landlord-tenant relations and, among women, patron-client ties.[26]

Perhaps the most dramatic consequence of the war was the increased intrusion of the state into the private lives of individuals. The heavy fiscal and personal demands made by the state raised the political awareness of the popolo and led them to demand something from the state in return.[27] As we have seen, the years following the War of Chioggia saw a rise in the volume of petitions for grazie. The war made Venetians more fully aware of the power and possibilities inherent in control of the state apparatus. Hence patricians wrapped themselves in the mantle of the state and tried to use their influence in government councils to win favors for their friends and clients, which in turn increased their own power. If the Serrata initiated the process by which certain families and the state were amalgamated, the War of Chioggia sealed the bond.

In this respect, the experience of Venice diverged significantly from that of other Italian republics. In most Italian cities, the state and the family stood in opposition to one another; the power of the state was used to harness or quell the power of families. Florence's anti-magnatial legislation comes to mind. In the end the Florentine government was unable to control the power of families and was overwhelmed by the Medici.[28] In Venice kinship became the basis of political participation and the interests of family and state became to a surprising degree inextricably linked. Indeed, by the sixteenth century, according to the diarist Girolamo Priuli, three-fourths of patricians depended on state offices for their livelihood.[29]

The identity of family and state, cemented by the war, did much to recast Venetian social relations in the latter part of the fourteenth century and first part of the fifteenth century. Venetians began to draw sharper distinctions among themselves. This shift away from the freewheeling, unstructured associations of the trecento was evident everywhere.

The trend was first apparent among the patricians. Inklings of a swing toward greater status-consciousness were already visible in 1365 in the squabbles that accompanied the election of the new doge. One of the objections raised to Marco Corner's candidacy was that his wife was from a large popolano family that would try to insinuate itself into the government. Corner responded to the attack by noting that he hardly stood alone in having a non-noble wife, and he was elected.[30] A further step was taken in 1376 when the rules governing the entry of illegitimate children into the Great Council were tightened.[31] The trend continued until 1403 when the government made what Frederic Lane has termed a "definitive change." The ducal council rejected a proposal that would have allowed one popolano family to enter the nobility every time a noble family became extinct. Lane argues that this decision marked the development of the patriciate into a "closed caste." This trend toward aristocratic self-identification reached its apogee in the early sixteenth century with the compilation of the *Libro d'Oro*, the official register of noble births.[32]

This accelerating sense of social exclusivity was manifest in other aspects of patrician life as well. The early years of the fifteenth century saw the development of special youth groups known as the *compagnie delle calze*. Composed of patrician youths, these companies put on carnival pageants and other celebrations. Closely supervised by the Council of Ten, the companies "gave valuable experience in management and planning to young nobles, [and] harnessed youthful energies to a socially useful end."[33] Unlike the fourteenth century, when patrician youths moved about freely with popolano youths, the fifteenth century witnessed a conscious attempt to distinguish young nobles from their popolano counterparts and to create a sense of exclusivity among patricians. Increasingly the government discouraged freewheeling associations with non-nobles.[34]

Patricians were not the only ones exhibiting a greater sense of exclusivity. The fifteenth century witnessed the same trend toward hierarchy and stratification in popolano life. The trend was most apparent among the cittadini, who came increasingly to see themselves as a separate, distinct, and privileged group. The year in which the ducal council made its momentous decision not to allow additions to the patriciate also saw new legislation designed to tighten eligibility requirements for cittadino status. The cittadini's tendency to see themselves as a second aristocracy and to become themselves a closed caste came to fruition in the early sixteenth century when, as a counterpart to the *Libro d'Oro*, Venetians began to register citizen births in the *Libro d'Argento*.[35]

Even in the artisan community the trend was toward differentiation and stratification. By the sixteenth century at the latest, a hierarchy of trades had developed. The tendency in the trecento for the wealthiest men in every trade to associate with one another and to form a largely undifferentiated class of popolani grandi gave way to a new ordering of professions, in which men engaged in certain trades gained prestige over their fellow artisans.[36] This tendency was even apparent in artisan family life, where the conjugal equality of the nuclear family characteristic of the trecento succumbed to an increasingly virulent (and at times brutal) patriarchy. Artisan fathers now ruled their families as patricians ruled their subjects.[37]

The realm of religion was not immune. Both the ecclesiastical and secular authorities sought increasingly to distinguish their spheres of influence. In 1433 Pope Eugenio IV issued a bull forbidding priests to serve as notaries in the Venetian chancery. Throughout the Middle Ages and early Renaissance, priests formed the backbone of the Venetian writing office. Now the pope hoped to untangle this relationship so that priests would not neglect their primary duty, the cure of souls.[38] This was part of a larger process by which Venetian society was abandoning the close association of church and state, which was a legacy of its Byzantine past. According to Paolo Prodi, "this process of disassociation . . . accelerated rapidly from the first

PLATE 4 *Venice as Justice*. Ducal Palace. Photo: Osvaldo Böhm.

half of the fifteenth century" and led in the end to "an irremediable rift in the social fabric of Venice."[39] The change in social relations was even apparent in the scuole grandi, where equality among ritual brothers was abandoned for an ordering of rich and poor.[40]

In this regard 1423, the end point of this study, had special significance. Not only was it the year of Francesco Foscari's election, it was also the year in which the *Arengo*, the popular assembly that in Rialtine days elected the doge, was formally abolished. The patricians abandoned the myth that the populace had a voice in decisions.[41]

Visual images expressed the change in ideology. The translation mosaics erected over the portals of San Marco captured the ideals of the thirteenth and fourteenth centuries. Recorded forever was the moment when God smiled on the city as Venetians came together as a community to welcome their new patron. During the later years of the fourteenth century and the first decade of the fifteenth century, a number of modifications were made to the ducal palace. Among the decorations were two prominent figures of Justice and Venice as Justice. The latter, placed in a quadrifoil on the western façade of the palace, shows an imposing female figure sitting on a throne and wielding a sword. At her feet cower two figures interpreted as symbols of discord and sedition. The inscription reads, "Fortis iusta trono furias mare sub pede pono." This decoration can also be taken as an expression of the new ideology of the fifteenth century. Immortalized in stone is the power of the rulers and the subordination of the ruled (Plate 4).[42]

The popolo were aware of the changes taking place. In 1414 discontent among the city's artisans came to the attention of the Great Council. It had always been the custom at the time of a ducal election for the newly elected doge and his wife to host a meal for the guilds. Martino da Canal's description of the reception given by Dogaressa Marchesina Tiepolo to the guilds records such a ceremony. In 1414, however, newly elected Doge Tommaso Mocenigo did not have a wife; and the government decided not to hold the meal. When news reached the artisans of the government's decision, they were, in the words of the Great Council deliberations, "stupified and discontented." At that point the Great Council voted to hold the meal, "for the joy and contentment of the people and the city (totius populi et urbis) and so that it will not *appear* that we are abandoning ancient customs" (ut non videatur quod desistamus ab antiquis moribus) [emphasis mine].[43] In these years, the patricians were abandoning ancient customs and the popolo knew it. Traditions such as the communal meal were being abandoned in the wake of a new sense of hierarchy.

The processes that led to stratification and hierarchy can be seen as part of the general trend toward aristocratization that swept Italy in the later Renaissance.[44] By the second quarter of the fifteenth century a new political and social order had begun to emerge in Venice. Gone were the days of loosely formed associations that cut across social strata, drawing Venetians together in a myriad of contrasting and complementary ways and providing stability through a sense of belonging. Now Venetians were assigned a place in society and were expected to adhere to that place. The stability of the Venetian Republic in its days of grandeur was assured when the old sense of community was replaced by a new and equally compelling sense of place. In 1423 the government officially abandoned the traditional appellation *comune* and became instead the *dominio o signoria*.[45] *Auctoritas* had replaced *caritas*.

Notes

List of Abbreviations

ASV   Archivio di Stato di Venezia
BNM   Biblioteca Nazionale Marciana
CI   Cancelleria Inferiore, Notai
mv   *more veneziano* (The Venetian year began on March 1)
NT   Archivio Notarile, Testamenti
PSM   Procuratori di San Marco

ONE   Community and Conflict in Early Renaissance Venice

1. The mosaics are discussed in detail in Demus, *Mosaics of San Marco*, pt. 2, 1:199–206.

2. Geary, *Furta Sacra*, 107–15.

3. P. Brown, *Cult of the Saints*, 93. Brown is speaking in this instance of Constantinople, but the same model can be applied to other cities.

4. Demus, *Mosaics of San Marco*, pt. 2, 1:201.

5. Cessi, ed., *Deliberazioni del Maggior Consiglio* 2:3; for the ruling of the giudici del piovego, see Archivio di Stato di Venezia (hereafter ASV), Giudici del Piovego, Busta 3, Codex Publicorum, Sentenza LVII, 426–28. The phrase reads, "quod inter eos debeat esse amor et dilectio fructuosa tamquam inter bonos convicinos et caros amicos." For the statement of the *scuola* of San Giovanni Evangelista, see Pullan, *Rich and Poor*, 41. The capitulary of the stonecutters' guild is in Monticolo, *I capitolari* 3:249. It reads, "bonum et utilitatem omnium dicte artis et fruencium ea." For the arbitration between brothers, see Sebellico, *Felice de Merlis*, doc. 1039. Marino Lando wished that his sons "se podhesse acordar." See his will in Stussi, ed., *Testi veneziani*, 97–98.

6. da Canal, *Les Estoires de Venise*, 3. See also the discussion of da Canal's chronicle in Cracco, *Società e stato*, 265–90.

7. For the importance of the love feast, see Romano, "Charity and Community," 63–82. For the ideal of concord in Italian cities, see Waley, *Italian City-Republics*, 218–20.

8. Rolandino is quoted in Bouwsma, *Defense of Republican Liberty*, 65; Bishop, trans., *Letters from Petrarch*, 234; and Origo, *World of San Bernardino*, 155.

9. According to Andrea Dandolo's chronicle, "Tunc, populari vociferacione, plebs ad palacium venit, et erga ducem, eos ad quietem suadentem, lapides proiciunt; et postea domos aliquorum nobilium invadentes, illas depredati sunt." Danduli, *Chronica per extensum descripta* 12, pt. 1, p. 314. See also Monticolo, *I capitolari* 2:xxvi, cxxiv.

For some comments on the Boccono conspiracy, see Cappelletti, *Storia della Repubblica* 3:173–82; and Romanin, *Storia documentata* 3:7–8. For the Querini-Tiepolo conspiracy, see ibid. 3:21–39.

10. For the Falier conspiracy, see V. Lazzarini, *Marino Faliero*; and Pillinini, "Marino Falier," 45–71. For a recent discussion of the Querini-Tiepolo and Falier conspiracies, see Ruggiero, *Violence*, 3–9.

11. "E robar tute le chaxe dei zentilomeni et alzader [uccidere] tuti quelli li fosse contrarii E vergogner tute le sue done." Biblioteca Nazionale Marciana (hereafter BNM), Ital. VII, 2051 (8271) *Cronica di Venezia dalle origini al 1396*, fol. 51v.

12. "Excogitaverunt novam malitiam, nam sub profunda nocte dividebant ex se aliquos per contratas penes habitationes ipsorum fidelium popularium, pulsabantque graviter ad ostium eorum, et vociferabantur. O talis ego cum uxore tua aut cum filia tua adulterabor, cum aliis inhonestissimis verbis. Cumque existimarent se auditos, sibilabunt ad invicem quasi se vellent in unum colligere, clamosis vocibus se appellantes nominibus domorum nobilium, ut populares inclusi crederent eos esse nobiles, et irascerentur contra universam nobilitatem." See de Monacis, *Chronicon de rebus venetis*, 317.

13. Monticolo, *I capitolari* 3:399–400. chap. 86.

14. " . . . in danno et in preçudixio de li homeni de la predicta arte et de tutta la comunança de la cittade." Ibid. 3:396.

15. ASV, Scuole Piccole, Busta 726, Scuola di Santa Maria della Celestia, capitulary, chap. II, no pagination.

16. Francastel, "Une peinture anti-hérétique," 1–17.

17. For examples of the kind of enmities listed, see ASV, Giudici del Piovego, Busta 3, Codex Publicorum, Sentenza CXXIX, 770–78; Sebellico, *Felice de Merlis*, docs. 1051–55; and Stussi, *Testi veneziani*, 59–60, 68, 70, 88.

18. In his study of Florentine confraternities, Ronald Weissman argues that the "essential feature of the Florentine social bond was . . . its agonistic character." This characterization can be extended with qualifications to the Italian city-states in general. See Weissman, *Ritual Brotherhood*, 26–35.

19. See Pullan, "Significance of Venice," 443–62.

The political quietude of the Venetian popolo is accepted by virtually all historians. See Cohn, Review of Ruggiero, *Violence*, 300.

20. Martines, *Power and Imagination*, 131.

21. Tenenti, "Sense of Space," 32.

22. Botero, *Reason of State*, 109.

23. Lane, *Venice*, 114–17.

24. Luzzatto, *Storia economica*, 117; Lane, *Venice*, 104.

25. Martines, *Power and Imagination*, 132. On the rise of new men, see Becker, "'Novi Cives' and Florentine Politics," 35–82.

26. Pullan, *Rich and Poor*, esp. 99–131, 157–87.

27. Neff, "Zaccaria de' Freschi," 33–61.

28. For the subordination of the guilds, see Monticolo, *L'ufficio della Giustizia Vecchia*.
29. Rapp, *Industry and Economic Decline*.
30. Mackenney, "Arti e stato," 127–43; idem, "In Place of Strife," 17–22.
31. Lane, *Venice*, 11–17, 98, 109, 271; Mumford, *City in History*, 321–25. Other works adopting this view include Muir, *Civic Ritual*, 3–8, 146, 298–301; and Pavan, "Recherches sur la nuit," 342–43.
32. Lane, *Venice*, 109.
33. Chojnacki, "Crime, Punishment," 184–228. For a different view see Ruggiero, *Violence*.
34. Muir, *Civic Ritual*, 135–81.
35. Najemy, Review of Bowsky, *Medieval Italian Commune*, 1031.
36. Ruggiero, *Violence*, 1–53; idem, "The Ten," 156–68, 238; idem, "Sexual Criminality," 18–37.
37. Cracco, *Società e stato*, 454.
38. Writing of the conspiracies in the fourteenth century, Cessi says, "Il popolo, in nome del quale gli audaci capi erano scesi in piazza, stette muto o soltanto curioso dell'insolito avvenimento, e soltanto come spettatore non quale attore." Cessi, *Storia della Repubblica*, 270. Alberto Tenenti has accused the popolo of being "hardly more than a spineless multitude." Tenenti, "Sense of Space," 19.
39. My methodology has been much influenced by Diane Owen Hughes's work with the notarial records of Genoa and Christiane Klapisch's work on Florence. As Hughes suggests, notarial records "let us start with the individual and construct a network of social relationships, some familial, others not, which will shape his life and give form to the community in which he lives." See Hughes's work, "Toward Historical Ethnography," 61–71. See also Klapisch, "Parenti, amici e vicini," 953–82. Also helpful has been the formulation of Paul Craven and Barry Wellman of the city as a "network of networks." See Craven and Wellman, "Network City," 57–88.

For Venice, several of the studies of Stanley Chojnacki adopt a broadly similar approach; however, his studies are confined to the patriciate. See his "Dowries and Kinsmen," 571–600; and his "Patrician Women," 176–203; and his "Kinship Ties and Young Patricians," 240–70.

40. Two useful surveys of Italian communal politics are Hyde, *Society and Politics*; and Waley, *Italian City-Republics*.
41. Najemy, *Corporatism and Consensus*.
42. Bowsky, "Impact of the Black Death," 1–34; Brucker, *Renaissance Florence*, 169.
43. For the shift in policy accompanying Foscari's election, see Romanin, *Storia documentata* 4:68–88; Lane, *Venice*, 228–29.

TWO Urban Form and Social Stratification: The *Civitas Venetiarum*

1. For factors affecting social networks and definitions of community, see Craven and Wellman, "Network City," 57–88; Effrat, "Approaches to Community," 1–32; and Hillery, "Definitions of Community," 111–23.

2. For Villani, see Brucker, *Renaissance Florence*, 51–52, 223. In his chronicle *Les Estoires de Venise*, Martino da Canal did write of Venice's greatness in terms of the abundance of its foods, the greatness of its men, and the beauty of its women, 4–7.

3. For descriptions of the city, see Sansovino, *Venetia città nobilissima*. Two important modern guides are Lorenzetti, *Venezia e il suo estuario;* and Tassini, *Curiosità*.

For San Marco as Venice's center, see Muir, *Civic Ritual*, 209–11. In his description of victory celebrations held in Venice in 1364, Petrarch noted, "Both performances were held in that great square, which I doubt has any match in this world, in front of the marble and gold façade of the temple." Bishop, *Letters from Petrarch*, 237.

4. On the early history of Venice, see Romanin, *Storia documentata* 1; Cessi, *Storia della Repubblica;* and Maranini, *La costituzione* 1.

For Venice's urban development, see the works cited above and Lanfranchi and Zille, "Il territorio," 3–65; Trincanato, "Venezia nella storia urbanistica," 7–69; Muratori, *Studi per una operante;* Maretto, *L'edilizia;* Cecchetti, *La vita dei Veneziani*, pt. 1, pp. 3–162; and Bellavitis and Romanelli, *Venezia*.

5. Romanin, *Storia documentata* 1:32–34.

6. Muratori, *Studi per una operante*, 29.

7. Ibid.; Lanfranchi and Zille, "Il territorio," 53. For a different interpretation of the course of early development, see Bellavitis and Romanelli, *Venezia*, 32–36. They suggest that the city developed from the entrance of the Grand Canal near Santa Lucia. I wish to thank Paolo Polledri for bringing this point to my attention.

8. Muratori, *Studi per una operante*, 29–30; Maretto, *L'edilizia*, 23. However, much of this remains hypothetical.

9. According to Maretto the area around San Giovanni Grisostomo and Santi Apostoli was "uno dei centri della Venezia pre-dogale, roccaforte della potente famiglia dei Partecipazi." Ibid., 24.

10. Iuspatronatus was the right, enjoyed by certain laymen, to have a voice in the administration of parish churches. According to the city's civil statutes, those who enjoyed the right of iuspatronatus were known as *vicini* (neighbors). Vicini were defined as "qui possessiones habent in parochia ubicunque habitarent." Some historians see iuspatronatus as a vestige of the feudal rights that the founding families enjoyed over the churches they established. See *Volumen statutorum*, bk. 6, chap. 3, 87v–88v; and Muratori, *Studi per una operante*, 30.

11. For the character of these properties, see Robbert, "L'inventario," 287. According to Juergen Schulz, the Ziani family developed their complex in the parish of Santa Giustina "like a medieval manor." It even included a *palacium*. Yet in the period it was created, this family complex may already have been something of an anachronism. See Schulz, "Wealth in Mediaeval Venice," 33–34.

The extent to which feudalistic ties penetrated the Venetian lagoon is very problematic. Lanfranchi and Zille ("Il territorio," 58) note that Dorsoduro for a long time remained a backward part of the Rialtine settlement where "la presenza di un gastaldo di Dorsoduro; la permanenza degli *excusati* nella residenza precipua dei pescatori, ancora vincolati all'autorità ducale da legame regalistico di servizi personali, sono sintomi di una situazione politica e sociale, che certo nelle altre parti era superata." Gina Fasoli, however, doubts that, except for some terms such as *feudum, senior, milites,* and *fideles,* feudalism had an impact in the lagoon. See Fasoli, "Comune veneciarum," 80–81.

12. The parish is considered in detail in Cessi and Alberti, *Rialto,* 21–25. The Orio donation is published in Romanin, *Storia documentata* 1:284–85.

13. Luzzatto, *Storia economica,* 16–29.

14. Maranini, *La costituzione* 1:172–207. For the Michiel family, see Lane, *Venice,* 92.

15. Muratori, *Studi per una operante,* 30; Cessi and Alberti, *Rialto,* 163–64; Mazzi, "Note per una definizione," 5–31.

16. In an excellent study of the powerful Ziani family Silvano Borsari notes, "Non vi è assolutamente nulla che faccia pensare all'esercizio in un potere su altri uomini." Borsari, "Una famiglia," 35.

17. Ibid. For an analysis of the use of property as collateral, see Schulz, "Wealth in Mediaeval Venice," 32.

18. See Cessi, *La politica dei lavori pubblici,* 14–17.

19. The original division may have been into 30 units known as *trentacie.* Martino da Canal writes, "Sachés que monsignor li dus a departie les contrees de Venise en .xxx. parties, c'est .ij. contrees a une feste." da Canal, *Les Estoires de Venise,* 252. Cecchetti argues that the capi were instituted in the twelfth century. Cecchetti, *La vita dei Veneziani,* pt. 1, p. 139. See also F. Zago, ed., *Consiglio dei Dieci* 1, register 2, doc. 31.

20. Roberti, *Le magistrature* 2:278–79, esp. chap. 47. The oath of the capi, in which they swear to distribute grain fairly, is printed in Molmenti, *La storia di Venezia* 1:507.

21. Roberti, *Le magistrature* 3:96; F. Zago, *Consiglio dei Dieci* 1, register 2, doc. 31. For foreigners as troublemakers, see Chojnacki, "Crime, Punishment," 214–18.

22. Lane, *Venice,* 49; for the oath of the capi concerning the militia, see Molmenti, *La storia di Venezia* 1:506–8. In 1346 Taldo Bartholi was fined by the *capi di sestieri* for not registering for the militia. The Great Council reduced his fine on account of his poverty. See ASV, Maggior Consiglio, Grazie, Register 11, fol. 90r.

23. Cessi, *Deliberazioni del Maggior Consiglio,* 3:54, 180.

24. This description is taken from Muir, *Civic Ritual,* 135–56.

25. Tradition assigns the date 1171 for the establishment of the sestieri. See Contento, "Il censimento" 19:231–32.

26. Lanfranchi and Zille suggest that the sestieri corresponded to "talune vecchie caratteristiche insulari." Lanfranchi and Zille, "Il territorio," 54. See also Bellavitis and Romanelli, *Venezia,* 25–26.

The division does not even appear to have been very efficient administratively. The assignation of the parish of Santa Lucia to the sestiere of Santa Croce was very inconvenient. As a result, in 1315 the Great Council assigned the task of patrolling the parish to the *signore di notte* of Cannaregio rather than that of Santa Croce. This was done because it was more convenient (comodius) for him to do so. See ASV, Maggior Consiglio, Deliberazioni, Register 12 (Clericus/Civicus), fol. 50v.

27. F. Zago, *Consiglio dei Dieci* I, register 2, doc. 31; Ruggiero, *Violence*, 12–13.

28. For the capitulary of the signori di notte, see Roberti, *Le magistrature* 3:25.

29. Ibid., 25, nn. 2, 3. See also Ruggiero, *Violence*, 6, 12–17.

30. For the cobblers, see Monticolo, *I capitolari* 2:163, chap. 86; for the jacketmakers, 1:52–53, chap. 46.

31. Lane, *Venice*, 12.

32. Mueller, "Procurators of San Marco," 111–12.

33. Wirobisz, "L'attività edilizia," 307–19. See also Schulz, "Titian, Arentino, and Sansovino," 81.

34. It is perhaps appropriate to view the lagoon as Venice's *contado*. See Crouzet-Pavan, "Murano," 45–92.

35. Maretto, *L'edilizia*, map facing page 26.

36. Spada, "Leggi veneziane," 126.

37. Fasoli notes that *"comune è una vecchia parola che in età romana era usata per indicare come sostantivo il complesso degli abitanti di un municipio."* Fasoli, "Comune veneciarum," 93.

38. For the piovego, see da Mosto, *L'Archivio* 1:95; and Ferro, *Dizionario* 2:442.

The *Codex Publicorum* is now being published in the series Fonti per la Storia di Venezia. See Strina, ed., *Codex Publicorum*.

39. ASV, Giudici del Piovego, Busta 3, Codex Publicorum, Sentenza LX, 436–55.

40. Ibid., 454: "via publica et comunis perpetuo aperta et disocupata ad honorem et proficuum iste ecclesie S. Mauricii et totius comunis veneciarum et omnium circumastancium eidem terre vacue et totius illius contrate S. Mauricii et omnium volentium exinde ire et transire die noctuque debeat sic existere et permanere."

41. Ibid., Sentenza LXII, 468–77.

42. Ibid., 476: "publica et comunis et debeat in publico et comuni perpetuo conservari."

43. Ibid., 468–69: "ad publicam utilitatem omnium volentium per eam transire ire et redire die noctuque."

44. Ibid., Sentenza LXXXVI, 616–19.

45. Ibid., 618: "quod omnia kanalia rivi piscine calles vie palludis kaneta barreni et terre publica sunt et comunia et in publico et comuni sunt conservanda et detinenda nisi publicis instrumentis aut legitimis probationibus contrarium constet deum pre occulis habentes."

46. Doge Jacopo Tiepolo's redaction of Venetian statutes composed in 1242 is very ambiguous on this question. Book 3, chapter 60 states that if anyone closes a canal, street, pond, or bridge so that others cannot use it and a protest is lodged, the person who closed the site must open it again until the case can be heard by judges. Yet the law goes on to state that if anyone closed the site in order to make improvements that will be beneficial to all (ita quod sit comunis utilitas), then no one can lodge a protest. The law is ambiguous

and also revealing for what it does not say. There is no attempt to determine whether the property is publicly or privately owned or what its status will be once the improvements are completed. See Cessi, ed., *Gli statuti*, 169–70.

47. ASV, Maggior Consiglio, Deliberazioni, Register 19 (Novella), fol. 53r.

48. Ibid., Register 15 (Fronesis), fol. 61r; Register 17 (Spiritus), fols. 67r–67v; Register 21 (Leona), fol. 227r.

49. Ibid., Register 21 (Leona), fol. 169v: "civitates sunt tantum divites et potentes quantum sunt populo copiose."

50. Ibid., Register 17 (Spiritus), fol. 95r; Register 19 (Novella), fol. 127v; for the law regarding construction at the Ducal Palace, see Pincus, *Arco Foscari*, 439.

51. Fasoli, "Comune veneciarum," 93; Roberto Cessi believes that this new process took place in the fifteenth century when "ogni spesa sostenuta dallo Stato, non è fatta a vantaggio di questo o quel gruppo, ma a beneficio, direttamente od indirettamente, di tutta la collettività." He believes that this was largely a consequence of Venice's expansion onto the terraferma. Cessi, *La politica dei lavori pubblici*, 23.

52. Ibid., 18; Cecchetti, *La vita dei Veneziani*, pt. 1, p. 39. Another example is a ruling of the Great Council passed in 1303 that declared that all earth collected from the dredging of canals was to be taken to Sant'Elena—the easternmost part of the city where anyone who wanted it for land reclamation could have it. The law stipulated, however, that the residents of the parish whence it came had first claim to it. It reads in part, "Salvo quod si quis rivus cavaretur in aliqua contrata, homines ipsius contrate possint accipere de terra ipsius pro suo usu in dicta contrata tantum." The law is printed in Favaro, ed., *Cassiere della bolla ducale*, 231.

53. Trincanato, "Venezia nella storia urbanistica," 10; for the transition from the *civitas Rivoalti* to the *civitas Venetiarum*, see Lanfranchi and Zille, "Il territorio," 52–53.

54. For modern views of the Serrata, see Lane, "Enlargement of the Great Council," 236–74; Chojnacki, "In Search," 47–90; and Ruggiero, "Modernization and the Mythic State," 245–56.

55. All remarks about the population of the city and the number of nobles must be merely approximate. For the population of the city in general, see Beloch, *Bevölkerungsgeschichte Italiens*, 3:1–5; Lane, *Venice*, 18–20; Mueller, "Peste e demografia"; and Beltrami, *Storia della popolazione*.

For the number of nobles, see Chojnacki, "In Search." Pullan gives the figure of 1,017 members of the council in 1310. See Pullan, *Rich and Poor*, 21.

56. For the position of the church and clergy in Venice, see Prodi, "Church in Renaissance Venice," 409–30.

Molmenti suggests that Venice had about 360 parochial clergymen. I believe the number may have been as high as 450. See Molmenti, "Venezia e il clero," 679.

For the regular clergy of Florence, see Richard C. Trexler, "Le célibat," 1337, 1348.

57. For *cittadini*, see Pullan, *Rich and Poor*, 100–105; Neff, "Zaccaria de' Freschi, 33–61; and Ell, "Citizenship and Immigration."

58. At the turn of this century Giovanni Monticolo published the capitu-

laries of fifty-two guilds that were under the jurisdiction of the giustizieri vecchi. Although incomplete, Monticolo's list gives a good sense of the trades that formed an important part of the city's economy. Monticolo, *I capitolari*. The number of guilds continued to increase so that in the seventeenth century it had grown significantly beyond the sixty or so of the medieval period. Rapp, *Industry and Economic Decline*, 171–75.

59. Fano, "Arte della lana," 73–213; Delort, "Un aspect du commerce," 29–70, 247–73.

60. For the figure of 6,000 carpenters and caulkers, see Luzzatto, *Storia economica*, 67. See also Lane, *Venetian Ships*, 72–87.

61. Wirobisz, "L'attività edilizia," 319–20.

62. On notaries, see Cracco, "Relinquere laicis que laicorum sunt," 179–89. For teachers, see Bertanza, ed., *Documenti* 1.

63. For physicians, Ruggiero, "Status of Physicians," 168–84.

64. For the composition of one Venetian household, see Luzzatto, "Il costo della vita," 288–89.

65. For some remarks on the Venetian underground, see Ruggiero, *Violence*, 95–121.

66. One of the traditional divisions within the nobility was that between the *case vecchie* and the *case nuove*. See Chojnacki, "In Search," 49–50. On the representation of various families in the *estimo*, ibid., 59.

67. On the recruitment of clergy, see chap. 5 below.

68. For Pignol Zucchello, see Morozzo della Rocca, ed., *Lettere di mercanti*, vii.

69. The records of Venice's criminal courts contain many notices of slavery and slaves. See, among others, ASV, Signori di Notte al Criminal, Processi, Register 8, fols. 84r–84v, fols. 87v–91v.

70. Most of this material is taken from Luzzatto, *Storia economica*, 129–33. The estimo is published in Luzzatto, *I prestiti*, doc. 165, pp. 138–95.

71. Chojnacki, "In Search," 61.

72. For Regla's grain dealings, see ASV, Maggior Consiglio, Grazie, Register 18, fol. 32r; for Lunardo dall'Agnella, Molmenti, *La storia di Venezia* 1:71.

73. Luzzatto notes that there were fifteen druggists. Luzzatto, *Storia economica*, 130. He found nine furriers, but my own investigation has revealed four other men who, though not identified as such in the estimo, were furriers.

74. As Luzzatto notes, "Niente dunque di più assurdo di considerare il regime politico consolidatosi a Venezia nel Trecento come una aristocrazia «plutocratica»." Luzzatto, *Storia economica*, 132.

75. ASV, Cancelleria Inferiore, Notai (hereafter CI), Busta 104, notary Tommaso Luciano, protocol, fol. 9r., 20 March 1414; ASV, CI, Busta 38, notary Francesco Cavazza, protocol, 10 February 1369mv; Sebellico, *Felice de Merlis*, doc. 516. It should be noted that dowries involving intermarriage between nobles and popolani were not included.

76. An act of the Great Council indicates that there were women without dowries. See Cessi, *Deliberazioni del Maggior Consiglio* 3:220.

77. ASV, CI, Busta 187, notary Nicolò Saiabianca, protocol dated 1365, 23 December 1365; ASV, CI, Busta 34, notary Giacomo Cavalier, protocol 41, fol. 23v, 15 June 1392.

78. For a breakdown of wealth among patrician families, see Chojnacki, "In Search," 65; for Florence, see Herlihy, "Family and Property," 7–9. For Venice's recovery from the plague, see Mueller, "Peste e demografia," 93–95.

79. I have deliberately chosen to use the term *popolo grande*, since for most Italian communes the term *popolo grasso* indicates a class of politically active new men. See Hyde, *Society and Politics*, 104–18; Waley, *Italian City-Republics*, 182–97; and Lane, *Venice*, 103–4. The idea of an intermediate group is also suggested in Ruggiero, *Violence*, 59–61.

80. Kedar, *Merchants in Crisis*, 90–92. I want to thank Guido Ruggiero for first bringing this point to my attention.

81. For the use of *dominus* to describe Bedoloto, see ASV, CI, Busta 93, notary Giovanni Gazo, protocol, 18 July 1383. In this particular instance, nobles were referred to as *nobili viri domini*, whereas Bedoloto was only called a *dominus*. For Giacomo, ASV, Archivio Notarile, Testamenti (hereafter NT), Busta 1226, notary Fantin Rizzo, protocol, 17 September 1377. For Natalia, Sebellico, *Felice de Merlis*, doc. 1103.

82. Mueller, "Catalogo," 80.

83. For various instances of the use of *nobiles et populares*, see ASV, Maggior Consiglio, Deliberazioni, Register 15 (Fronesis), fol. 106v; Register 19 (Novella), fol. 81v; Register 21 (Leona), fols. 143r, 179v.

84. Ibid., Register 21 (Leona), fol. 79v; see also fol. 85v.

85. ASV, Cinque Savi alla Mercanzia, Capitolare degli Estraordinari, Register 22 ter (formerly Miscellanea Codice 132), fol. 45 right. A grazia to build a scuola at San Fantin stated that the request was made "ad supplicationem capituli ecclesiae Sancti Fantini, et nobilium et convincinorum dicte contrate." ASV, Maggior Consiglio, Grazie, Register 9, fol. 46v.

THREE Family Structure and Marriage Ties

1. Tiepolo, *Domenico prete*, doc. 204.
2. Sebellico, *Felice de Merlis*, doc. 971.
3. Quoted in Sapegno, ed., *Poeti minori*, 356.
4. This point is made in King, "Caldiera and the Barbaros," 19–20.
5. Lane, *Andrea Barbarigo*; and his study, "Family Partnerships," 36–55; J. Davis, *Venetian Family*.
6. Finlay, *Politics in Renaissance Venice*, 89; Chojnacki, "In Search"; idem, "Patrician Women"; and Betto, "Linee di politica matrimoniale," 3–64.
7. F. W. Kent, *Household and Lineage*.
8. Tassini, *Curiosità*, 288; see also Pozza, *I Badoer*.
9. For the genealogy of the Badoer family (males only) see BNM, Ital. VII, 925 (8594), Marco Barbaro, *Genealogie delle famiglie patrizie venete*, fols. 36v–37r. For the fourteenth century Barbaro is not always reliable, but most points in the succeeding discussion have been confirmed independently.
10. Sebellico, *Felice de Merlis*, doc. 862. For the Ghisi family, see Loenertz, *Les Ghisi*.
11. Sebellico, *Felice de Merlis*, docs. 56, 58, 764.
12. Ibid., doc. 1206. Zana's will, dated 17 April 1331, is doc. 1088.
13. See Tommasina's will in ASV, Procuratori di San Marco (hereafter PSM),

de Ultra, Commissarie, Busta 20, Commissaria of Tommasina Badoer, will dated 2 August 1312. Tommasina may have been a member of the branch of the Querinis, known as the Querini of ca' Grande, with whom the Badoers conspired in 1310 to overthrow the government.

14. Sebellico, *Felice de Merlis*, doc. 1010.

15. Ibid., doc. 1206. There is a very slight possibility that Eufemia was nicknamed Sclava (although it does not appear anywhere in the documents). Absolute confirmation of the double marriage is hampered by a lacuna in the text where the name of Pietro Contarini's son should appear. See ibid., doc. 1010.

16. Ibid., doc. 1206.

17. The connection of Beriola Soranzo to Marino can be found in ASV, PSM, de Ultra, Commissarie, Busta 19, Commissaria of Marino Badoer, parchment, 3 March 1320. Beriola remarried (Michaleto Contarini of Santi Apostoli) and on so doing sold her properties in San Giacomo, which she held as surety for her dowry, to Sofia, wife of Marco. One of the properties was the "domus maior seu pars domus maioris." In turn Sofia sold them to Marino. Ibid., 2 parchments, 16 November 1316, 14 June 1317.

18. For the connection of the Badoers with San Giovanni Evangelista, see Cornelio, *Notizie storiche*, 371; Tassini, *Curiosità*, 293.

19. "... pro bono pacis et omni scandallo evitando." ASV, PSM, de Ultra, Commissarie, Busta 19, Commissaria of Marino Badoer, parchment, 3 March 1320.

20. Sebellico, *Felice de Merlis*, doc. 1045.

21. Ibid., doc. 1206.

22. Ibid.

23. Maffeo Badoer's will is in ASV, CI, Busta 34, notary Pietro de Compostellis, protocol, fols. 26r-26v, 14 November 1370.

24. The inscription reads in part, "MCCCXLVIIII fo fato questo lavorier per misier lo vardian de la scola de miser Sen Giovane Vangelista e per li soi conpagni e de li beni de la scola e con l'aida de li nostri frari." Quoted in Mueller, "Catalogo," 81–82. For another example of patrician attachment to a religious site (the Pesaro family and the church of the Frari), see Goffen, *Piety and Patronage*. Joint undertakings by noble families were common occurrences in other Italian cities. See, for example, F. W. Kent, "The Rucellai Family," 397–401.

25. For Pesaro, ASV, PSM, de Ultra, Miscellanea Testamenti, Busta 1–2, testament 58, 15 June 1309; for Loredan, ASV, NT, Busta 1115, notary Lucianus Zeno, protocol, fol. 47r, 17 August 1360; for Barbaro, ASV, NT, Busta 545, notary Lorenzo Buscareno, protocol B, testament 57, 25 February 1418mv.

26. Chojnacki, "In Search," 73.

27. The will is printed in Bernardi, *Antichi testamenti*, fasc. 12 (1893): 21–26. There was a hospital Dalle Boccole in the parish; I have been unable to determine if they were one and the same.

28. ASV, PSM, Misti, Commissarie, Busta 119, Commissaria of Giovanni Dalle Boccole of Santa Trinità, will dated 5 October 1321.

29. For Francesca's marriage, see ASV, CI, Busta 141, notary Antonius Polo, protocol, 20 May 1341; for Beatrice, see ibid., 25 July 1341; for Beriola's marriage, see her father's will (note 28).

30. ASV, CI, Busta 141, notary Antonius Polo, protocol, 1 April 1339, 24 December 1339.

31. The two brothers and their sister Francesca appear repeatedly in the notarial records of notary Antonius Polo cited above. See, among others, acts dated 26 July 1328, 24 April 1338; 27 July 1339, 24 December 1339, 17 February 1339mv, 24 October 1340, passim.

32. Lombardo, ed., *Consiglio del XL* 2, docs. 102-8. The act states that the festival of the *Marie* is to be sponsored by the sons of Marco Dalle Boccole. In my extensive examination of the family, I have found only one other reference to a Marco Dalle Boccole and no references to his children. See Sebellico, *Felice de Merlis*, doc. 232.

33. Tassini, *Curiosità*, 649.

34. According to a property division dated 1359mv, Poluzia was the sole heir of Pietro, brother of Marino. ASV, PSM, Misti, Busta 119, Commissaria of Giovanni Dalle Boccole of Santa Trinità, parchment dated 25 February 1359mv. The four sons of Marino are all mentioned in the same document. For Nicoleto's will see ASV, NT, Busta 982, notary Nicolaus Verde, protocol, testament 2, October 1357; for Andreolo's will, see ASV, CI, Busta 20, notary Bartolomeo di Sant'Angelo, parchment, 15 November 1373.

35. Luzzatto, *I prestiti*, doc. 165, p. 141.

36. ASV, Avogaria di Comun, Raspe, Register 3642, fols. 160v-161r, 162v.

37. Ibid., fol. 286r.

38. For noble criminality, see Ruggiero, *Violence*, 65-81.

39. Marino's will is in ASV, NT, Busta 982, notary Andrea presbiter Santa Trinità, protocol, will 17, 5 November 1341.

40. For Nicolò's will, see ASV, CI, Miscellanea Testamenti, Notai Diversi, Busta 22, testament 730, 6 March 1383.

41. ASV, NT, Busta 573, notary Giorgio de Gibellino, unbound paper testament 472, 17 October 1384; ASV, NT, Busta 55, notary Bartolomeo de Arcangelis, unbound paper testament 46, 3 September 1395. His wife Gratiahumana Zane's will is testament 45 of Busta 55, also dated 3 September 1395.

42. Ibid., testament 3, 12 October 1403.

43. On the extinction of the family, see BNM, Ital. VII, 15 (8304), Girolamo Alessandro Capellari Vivaro, *Il campidoglio veneto*, fol. 164r. Capellari is not always reliable. For instance, he incorrectly lists Antonio as the son of Paolo rather than as the son of Francesco. The problem of family extinction grew more real over the centuries. See J. Davis, *Decline of Venetian Nobility*, 54-74, 81.

For Antonio's many granddaughters and their marriages, see BNM, Ital. VII, 156 (8492), Marco Barbaro, *Libro di nozze patrizie*, fol. 11 left and right (hereafter cited as Barbaro, *Libro di nozze*).

44. The point is made in Chojnacki, "In Search," 70.

45. The phrase is J. Davis's. See *Venetian Family*, 8.

46. The information in this section comes from the will and account books of Marco Disenove's estate found in ASV, PSM, de Ultra, Commissarie, Busta 117A, Commissaria of Marco Disenove (Dixenove), notebook 1 with testament, 3 October 1350.

47. Ibid., parchment 14, dated 18 June 1354.

48. ASV, Maggior Consiglio, Grazie, Register 14, fol. 49v; see also the receipt in his father's will dated September 1361.
49. ASV, PSM, de Ultra, Busta 117A, parchment 8, 27 August 1358.
50. Ibid., receipt written into her father's will dated 8 February 1361mv.
51. Ibid., parchment 31, 15 May 1376.
52. The average size of noble dowries between 1346 and 1366 was 650 ducats. Chojnacki, "Dowries and Kinsmen," 571.
53. For Nardi, ASV, CI, Busta 186, notary Simeon, protocol C, fol. 3r, testament dated January 1371; for Guorro, ASV, CI, Busta 34, notary Giacomo Cavalier, protocol 41, fol. 2r, 11 January 1394mv; for Ravagnani, Bellemo, "Benintendi de' Ravagnani," 268 (see also the will of Zaneta Orio in ASV, PSM, Misti, Commissarie, Busta 103A, Commissaria of Zaneta Orio relicta Filipo, will dated 2 July 1383); for Soranzo, see ASV, NT, Busta 545, notary Lorenzo Buscareno, protocol, testament 50, 7 February 1390mv; for Civran, see ASV, CI, Busta 140, notary Pietro Pino, protocol, 5 December 1332; for Garzoni, Barbaro, *Libro di nozze*, fol. 11 right.

The daughter of noble Maffeo Venier married Lorenzo Ziera. See ASV, NT, Busta 947, notary Henricus Salamon, protocol, 16 September 1418. In 1375 the son of a fustian producer married the adopted (bastard?) daughter of dominus Pietro Orio. See ASV, CI, Busta 93, notary Bartolomeus de Gilberto, protocol, 21 May 1375. See also King, *Venetian Humanism*, 62–63.
54. I would like to thank Stanley Chojnacki for this information.
55. For this Marco Bedoloto, see ASV, PSM, de Ultra, Commissarie, Busta 211, Commissaria of Pietro Navagero da Negroponte, notebook, page dated August 1293; and ASV, Avogaria di Comun, Raspe, Register 3641, fol. 33r.
56. For the marriages see their wills: Ludovico (Alvise), ASV, NT, Busta 1226, notary Fantin Rizzo, protocol, 2 dates, 8 March 1373 (Ferrara), 16 October 1377 (Venice); Bernardo, ASV, CI, Busta 34, notary Giacomo Cavalier, protocol 41, fol. 44v, 28 July 1395.
57. In 1422 a cutler named Antonio Nigro was tried for having sexual relations with Caterucia Bedoloto, abbess of San Giacomo de Palude. ASV, Avogaria di Comun, Raspe, Register 3647, fol. 145v. See the will of Bernardo's son (who mentions his brothers-in-law) and the will of Bernardo's daughter Agnesina: ASV, NT, Busta 467, notary Giacomo Cavalier, unbound testament, 6 March 1396; unbound testament, 17 September 1392. The bastard daughter of Ludovico married Vittore a Stuppa of San Luca. ASV, PSM, de Ultra, Commissarie, Busta 36, Commissaria of Ludovico Bedoloto, parchment dated 30 April 1382.
58. The information on Girolamo's marriage is in Barbaro, *Libro di nozze*, fol. 305 right. I would like to thank Stanley Chojnacki for this information.
59. Sebellico, *Felice de Merlis*, docs. 865, 866, 991. ASV, CI, Busta 143, notary Stefano Pianigo, protocol, fol. 7r, 30 October 1349. In this last act Marina, wife of Francesco Regla, refers both to her husband and her brother as *domini*. For the extinction of the Marango family, see Chojnacki, "In Search," 73.
60. For Leonarda's marriage, ASV, CI, Busta 166, notary Fantin Rizzo, protocol x, fols. 76r and 76v, 2 acts dated 28 June 1379, 20 October 1379. She is included in the estimo with an assessment of 1,000 lire. Luzzatto, *I prestiti*, doc. 165, p. 192 (dona Lunarda Degla). For the connections with the Morosini family,

see the will of Pietro Regla, ASV, NT, Busta 572, notary Giorgio de Gibellino, unbound testament 224, 8 January 1403mv.

61. ASV, NT, Busta 858, notary Marco Raphenellis, unbound testament 129, 1 May 1409; ASV, NT, Busta 54, notary Cechinus Albertus, testament dated 22 June 1421.

62. ASV, NT, Busta 947, notary Henricus Salamon, protocol, testament 202, 10 October 1427.

63. ASV, PSM, de Ultra, Commissarie, Busta 243, Commissaria of Pietro Regla, parchment 9, 16 March 1416 and parchment 19, dated 1 August 1413.

64. ASV, CI, Busta 210, notary Prospero de Tomasi, protocol 1416, fol. 18v, 6 March 1417.

65. See, for example, Stone, *Family, Sex and Marriage*, 72–73; however, recent work on Tuscany suggests that women tended to marry down. Herlihy and Klapisch, *Les Toscans*, 418.

66. For the connection between the marriage of daughters and family honor, see Kirshner, "Pursuing Honor," 2–15; for spinsters, see Ruggiero, *Boundaries of Eros*, 162–63.

67. In his will nobleman Giovanni Basadona left 1,000 lire for each of his daughters to marry, but if they chose to enter convents, they were to receive only 400 lire and a yearly allowance of 10 lire. His will is printed in Bertanza and Lazzarini, eds., *Il dialetto veneziano*, doc. 148, p. 67.

68. The Bedoloto brothers had business connections at Tana, and Bernardo Bedoloto was joint owner of a ship with several nobles. For the property in Tana, see the brothers' wills cited in n. 56 above. For the ship, see ASV, Signori di Notte al Criminal, Processi, Register 9, fols. 80r–82v.

69. The youthful Bedoloto brothers engaged in criminal activity with members of the Contarini, Baseggio, Dolfin, Ghisi, and Loredan families. ASV, Avogaria di Comun, Raspe, Register 3642, fols. 227v–228r, 119v, 316r–316v; see also Lombardo, *Consiglio del XL* 2, doc. 244, p. 72. For patronage and clientage among patricians and popolani, see chap. 6.

70. For the receipt of grazie by popolani grandi, including the Bedolotos and Reglas, see Romano, "*Quod sibi fiat gratia*," 261–66. Franceschino Disenove also received a grazia after he had fulfilled the larger part of a heavy penalty. ASV, Maggior Consiglio, Grazie, Register 14, fol. 49v.

71. Pietro Regla tried to enter the nobility during the mass induction of 1381. He lost his bid to Bartolomeo Paruta. Bini, *I Lucchesi* 1:239. For Girolamo Bedoloto's attempt, see ASV, Avogaria di Comun, Raspe, Register 3647, fols. 190v–191r. Stanley Chojnacki is preparing a study based on this and similar cases.

72. King, "Caldiera and the Barbaros," 22–31.

73. ASV, NT, Busta 573, notary Giorgio de Gibellino, testament 322, 4 July 1375. Francesco Bedoloto does not appear to have been related to the other Bedolotos discussed.

74. Klapisch and Demonet, "A uno pane e uno vino," 874–75; Herlihy, "Population of Verona," 104–5.

75. See the evidence of furriers' wills in chap. 4 below.

76. Monticolo, *I capitolari* 2:482, chap. 16.

77. For the age of marriage in Florence, see Herlihy and Klapisch, *Les*

Toscans, 412–13. For coparentage, see Lynch, *Godparents and Kinship*. I would like to thank Donald Queller for calling this important work to my attention.

78. The wills are taken from Loenertz, *Les Ghisi*, 397–421.

79. Diane Hughes has made the point that in Genoa it was the household, "rather than any ties of kinship that might extend beyond it, that was central to the artisan's concept of family life." Hughes, "Domestic Ideals," 126.

80. For the coopers, Monticolo, *I capitolari*, 2:454, chap. 86. For the experience of artisans in Genoa, Hughes, "Domestic Ideals," 132–36.

81. See Tiepolo, *Domenico prete*, docs. 434–38. The rock crystal carvers prohibited unemancipated sons from taking apprentices and from sharing in the rights of masters. Monticolo, *I capitolari* 3:133–34, chap. 42.

82. Tiepolo, *Domenico prete*, docs. 512–14.

83. In her will a certain Gisla left the residuum of her estate to her grandson and sole executor Marcopaxe. But he was not to receive the legacy until he was emancipated from his father (Gisla's former son-in-law). ASV, NT, Busta 982, notary Andrea presbiter, protocol, testament 68, 6 December 1325. On emancipatory practices in Florence, see Kuehn, *Emancipation*.

84. For examples of women breaking legal ties to their kin, see Tiepolo, *Domenico prete*, docs. 361–62, 366–67.

85. Ibid., docs. 366, 476–77.

86. Sebellico, *Felice de Merlis*, doc. 319; ASV, CI, Busta 143, notary Stefano Pianigo, protocol, fol. 7v, 26 December 1349.

87. Apprenticeship may have further diminished the significance of the kin tie by removing children at a young age from the household. See Hughes, "Domestic Ideals," 132–33. Surprisingly few apprenticeship contracts appear in the notarial records. For two examples, see ASV, CI, Busta 34, notary Giacomo Cavalier, protocol 40, fol. 5v, 30 December 1378; fol. 6r, 11 January 1378mv.

88. ASV, Signori di Notte al Criminal, Processi, Register 7, fols. 89r–89v; Register 9, fols. 43r–43v, fol. 85v.

89. ASV, CI, Busta 185, notary Nicolò Staniero, protocol, 11 May 1367. The father was dead at the time of the act. For the Moro brothers, ASV, NT, Busta 447, notary Petrus Foscolo, testament 45, 17 September 1333. Furrier brothers Giacomo and Pietro Zuchato lived in the parishes of San Giacomo dall'Orio and San Severo. See ASV, CI, Busta 34, notary Pietro de Compostellis, protocol, fol. 9r. See also the residential patterns of the Bono family, Sebellico, *Felice de Merlis*, docs. 1236, 1247, 1293.

Some artisans lived very near one another. The three sons of Leonardo de Spercanigo were all smiths. Two lived in San Barnaba, the third in the neighboring parish of Santa Margarita. ASV, CI, Busta 34, notary Giacomo Cavalier, protocol 40, fols. 9r–9v, 19 March 1379.

90. See chap. 4 below.

91. For instance, parents and sons and brothers-in-law could be called on for loans and to act as proctors. See Tamba, *Bernardo de Rodulfis*, docs. 335, 363; and Sebellico, *Felice de Merlis*, docs. 343, 396, 1236, 1265, 1293.

92. This discussion has been influenced by Hufton's article, "Women and the Family Economy," 1–22. The idea of the Venetian working-class family

as an economic unit is discussed in Lane, *Venice*, 155–56; and Ruggiero, *Boundaries of Eros*, 13, 167.

In 1393 a widow named Simona had to cancel a property purchase made by her late husband. She noted she could not make the payments because of her poverty (paupertatem meam). See Tamba, *Bernardo de Rodulfis*, doc. 53. A certain Mucia, widow of a worker who died from a fall while working on the ducal palace, got a grazia worth 10 lire de piccoli. See ASV, Maggior Consiglio, Grazie, Register 15, fol. 102v. For other examples of destitute widows and wives of prisoners (whose husbands were unable to earn a living), see ASV, Maggior Consiglio, Grazie, Register 7, fols. 22r, 44r, 85r; Register 15, fol. 28r.

93. The rock crystal carvers, for example, allowed masters to hire apprentices of either sex; the coopers allowed widows to maintain their husbands' workshops until their sons reached age 17. Monticolo, *I capitolari* 3:141, chap. 15; 3:146, chap. 37; 2:454, chap. 86. See also J. Brown, "A Woman's Place," 206–24.

94. Tamba, *Bernardo de Rodulfis*, docs. 23–25. In her will Belanesina of Santa Trinità noted that Francesca Grini (?) owed her six grossi "pro filo quod sibi vendidi." ASV, CI, Busta 14, notary Gregorio Bruno, protocol, 18 April 1337. For women selling gold thread, see ASV, Maggior Consiglio, Grazie, Register 8, fol. 27r. In his will nobleman Enrico Dolfin noted that he owed money to two women who had dyed and bleached cloth for him. The will reads, "Item voio ch'el sia pagado una femena, che sta a-san Çane Grisostomo, de la tentura de braça XLIII de uellexio çallo; item voio ch'el sia satisfato ad una femena, che sta a san Çane Pollo, la qual me blanchiça braça C de tella." See Stussi, *Testi veneziani*, doc. 158, p. 75.

95. For women as food sellers, see ASV, Maggior Consiglio, Deliberazioni, Register 8 (Magnus/Capricornus), fols. 143v, 150v. The sisters Zanina and Lucia Nigro were tailors (*sartorese*). ASV, CI, Busta 143, notary Stefano Pianigo, protocol, fol. 8r, acts dated 3 March 1350. Finally, see the interesting case in which a certain Leonardo from Chioggia drew up an agreement with nobleman Giacomello Corner for his wife Gasdia to nurse Corner's son. Lombardo, *Nicola de Boateriis*, doc. 294.

96. It reads in part, "Iacobina uxor mea timeas ipsam peciam terre non posse libere habere, tenere, possidere, afficatare et disfictare, vendere, alienare et pro anima iudicare et de ipsa facere tamquam de tua re propria, volens te exinde securam reddere perpetuo pariter et quietam." Sebellico, *Felice de Merlis*, doc. 164.

97. Ibid., doc. 572.

98. For Biagio, Tiepolo, *Domenico prete*, doc. 256. For other examples, see ibid., docs. 321, 340, 516; ASV, CI, Busta 186, notary Simeon, protocol B, fol. 5v, 26 July 1361; ASV, CI, Busta 34, notary Giacomo Cavalier, protocol 41, fol. 8r, 29 January 1380mv; ASV, CI, Busta 130, notary Nicolò Nadal, protocol A, fol. 22v, 23 March 1380. On the joint ownership of property by spouses in Venice, see Zordan, "I vari aspetti," 144–59.

99. ASV, NT, Busta 335, notary Bortolo da Venezia, unbound testament, 8 July 1379.

100. Ibid., 8 May 1382. Another example is the will of Nicolò de Fontebon, a

furrier, who left most of his estate to his wife if she remained a widow. ASV, NT, Busta 380, notary Nicolò Benedetto, unbound testament, 18 June 1356.

101. Some men realized that their wives would in all likelihood remarry. See the will of Antonio Chavaleto, ASV, NT, Busta 467, notary Giacomo Cavalier, unbound testament 29 November 1384.

102. Diane Hughes has noted that in Genoa, "only in widowhood did aristocratic wives come of age." Hughes, "Domestic Ideals," 138–40, quotation p. 139.

103. In return, Michele agreed to feed, clothe, and house the boy to age eighteen. Tiepolo, *Domenico prete*, docs. 421–23. When Domenico de Are married Agnes, widow of Simeone Berengo, he apparently got the use of his stepdaughter's funds. Sebellico, *Felice de Merlis*, doc. 983. It could also work the opposite way—to the benefit of the stepchild. When Helena, wife of Leonardo Albizzo, drafted her will, she named her stepdaughter Lucia her sole executor and heir. ASV, NT, Busta 447, notary Petrus Foscolo, testament 36, 25 August 1330.

104. The ambivalent attitude of men toward women can be seen in a statute of the potters' guild. The rule required masters to register their wives in the guild's scuola or confraternity and required them to pay one grosso in dues for themselves and their wives. In return, wives received the benefits of membership, including the attendance by the scuola at their funerals. However, if the husband died first, the wife was to be stricken from the rolls. This reveals an interesting set of attitudes: women were accepted as partners to their husbands, but the partnership and the respect due to wives ended with the death of their husbands. Monticolo, *I capitolari* 3:213, chap. 27.

105. Margarita's will is in ASV, NT, Busta 467, notary Giacomo Cavalier, unbound testament, 29 September 1399.

FOUR The World of Work: Guild Structure and Artisan Networks

1. da Canal, *Les Estoires de Venise*, 284–305.

2. For some attempts to limit competition, see the regulations of the rock crystal workers' guild in Monticolo, *I capitolari* 3:124–25, 131, chaps. 6, 7, 33. For charitable and scuole activities, see Lane, *Venetian Ships*, 76–77; and Monticolo, *I capitolari*, 2:260, chap. 64; 2:482–83, chaps. 16, 17; for dowry distribution among guilds, see Museo Civico Correr, Mariegole, Mariegola 17, *Veluderi*, chap. 57, fol. 21r, 21 December 1438.

3. "Nella corporazione artigiana di Venezia mancava un vero contrasto di classe tra maestri e salariati per quanto gli interessi degli uni e degli altri fossero opposti; gli intenti egoistici dei capi di bottega e dei lavoranti non impedirono che lo stato normale dell'associazione fosse la concordia tra i suoi elementi costitutivi rafforzata dalla beneficenza sociale, dalle pratiche devote e dall'azione stessa dello Stato." Monticolo, *I capitolari* 2:cxxxviii.

4. Lane, *Venice*, 103–9; Brunello, *Arti e mestieri*, 11–16; Luzzatto, *Storia economica*, 116–17.

Perhaps in making his claims, Monticolo placed too much faith in the guilds' own professions of equality and fraternity. Unfortunately, we will never know his final thoughts on guild solidarity because he died before writing the preface to the third volume of his edition of Venetian guild statutes, in which he intended to treat guild structure. See Monticolo, *I capitolari* 2:cxxxiv.

5. Lane, *Venice*, 164–65.

6. Goldthwaite, *Building of Renaissance Florence*, 115–17; Lane, *Venice*, 164–65. Any generalization on this matter, however, is perilous. As André Wirobisz has noted, in the Venetian building trades often there was a group of men called "patroni" who directed projects and hired up to fifteen workers. But he adds, "È degno di attenzione il fatto che questo sistema di «patronato» esisteva proprio nelle fornaci e nei laboratori di scalpellini, vale a dire negli artigianati legati coll'edilizia che domandavano degli investimenti relativamente alti per l'avvio della produzione." See Wirobisz, "L'attività edilizia," 326.

7. Brunello, *Arti e mestieri*, 17–30; Lane, *Venice*, 156–61. The capitulary of the glassmakers (*fioleri*) is in Monticolo, *I capitolari* 2:61–98.

8. For a discussion of the fur trade and techniques used by merchants, see Delort, "Un aspect du commerce," 29–70, 247–73, esp. 69.

9. The *varotarii* worked the skins of wild animals, such as vair. The *peliparii* worked the skins of domesticated animals (notably sheepskins). The *glirarii* worked the skins of dormice. Ibid., 46.

10. Ibid., 45–46.

11. Delort uses the phrase "strawmen" (*hommes de paille*). On the various arrangements between merchants and furriers, see ibid., 43–46. For example, during the 1430s Andrea Barbarigo, the noble merchant studied by Delort, had arrangements with about twenty different furriers. Although some were men from whom Barbarigo bought garments for his own use, most served as his agents. Nicoletto Gatta, a furrier of Venetian origin, served as the agent at Tana for several Venetian merchants including Pignol Zucchello, a cittadino. At Tana, Nicoletto purchased and shipped furs for merchants and fellow furriers at home in Venice. For instance, in 1341 he wrote to Pignol, "You know, *compare*, that I received 132 marten skins and 26 ferrets for ser Andriol Pelegrin." See Morozzo della Rocca, *Lettere di mercanti*, 20. For information on Gatta, see pp. x–xi.

In his account book, nobleman Giacomo Badoer recorded dealings with a "Maistro Piero varoter." See Dorini and Bertelè, eds., *Il libro dei conti*, 162–63.

For examples of furriers themselves trading in furs, see ASV, Maggior Consiglio, Grazie, Register 8, fol. 61r; Register 9, fol. 65v.

12. Lane, *Venice*, 161; Fano, "Arte della lana"; Monticolo, *I capitolari* 2:535–81 (*fustagnarii*).

13. Lane, *Andrea Barbarigo*, 30.

14. For the connection between goldsmiths and patrician merchants, see Luzzatto, *Storia economica*, 68. Speaking more generally of the ties between patricians and guildsmen, Luzzatto notes, "Gli stessi elementi del patriziato o—in minor numero—della borghesia ricca, che esercitano il grande commercio . . . si incontrano spesso come finanziatori di piccole e medie imprese industriali." Ibid., p. 72.

15. Monticolo, *I capitolari* 3:374, chap. 1. (In 1265 the Great Council passed a law limiting the gastaldi of all guilds to a one-year term. Ibid., 2:22, chap. 47.)

16. Ibid. 3:378, chap. 18.

17. For the location of various guild halls, see the catalogue prepared by the Comune di Venezia, *Arti e mestieri*.

18. Monticolo, *I capitolari* 3:374-75, chaps. 3-4; Fano, "Arte della lana," 164-65.

19. Monticolo, *I capitolari* 3:376-77, chap. 11. The fustian guild officers could only levy fines up to thirty soldi. Ibid. 2:537, chap. 3.

20. The rock crystal workers' guild was very explicit about the products that could legitimately be produced. See ibid. 3:133, chaps. 40-41. The glirarii included in their capitulary detailed regulations about the number of pelts that had to be included in certain types of garments. Ibid. 3:267, chaps. 5-9.

21. Ibid. 3:137, chap. 50; 3:145, chap. 28; 3:411, chap. 6.

22. Fano, "Arte della lana," 164-68.

23. The *consoli dei mercanti* used the phrase "comunità dell'arte." Ibid., 161.

24. Monticolo, *I capitolari* 3:395-97, chap. 82. The records of the grazie contain many examples of infractions of guild rules. To give one example: furrier Bartolomeo Brocha was charged with having a light in his shop at night. The inspectors of Rialto suspected that he was working at night; that was considered an unfair advantage over his competitors. See ASV, Maggior Consiglio, Grazie, Register 13, fol. 15r. A number of questionable trading practices are documented in Delort, "Un aspect du commerce," 257-58.

25. Monticolo, *I capitolari* 3:127, chap. 13. See also 3:133, chap. 41; 3:134, chap. 43; 2:253, chap. 49; 2:265-66, chap. 71.

26. ASV, Maggior Consiglio, Deliberazioni, Register 21, fol. 13v.

27. Monticolo, *I capitolari* 2:cxxxv.

28. For the smiths, ibid. 2:355-56, chap. 79; for the cobblers, 2:156-57, chap. 70; for the fustian workers, 2:571, chap. 85; for the bellfounders, 3:120, chap. 32.

29. Fano, "Arte della lana," 109, 168-69, chaps. 72-73.

30. Ibid., 207, chap. 260. In 1399 only twenty-three men attended the meeting. Ibid., 208, chap. 267.

31. See, for example, the statutes of the fustian guild, Monticolo, *I capitolari* 2:545, chap. 16; the rock crystal carvers, 3:124, chap. 5; and the drapers' guild, Fano, "Arte della lana," 195, chap. 187.

32. Monticolo, *I capitolari* 2:266, chap. 72; 2:191, chap. 58.

33. Ibid. 2:546, chap. 21.

34. See, for example, the rock crystal carvers. Ibid. 3:130, chap. 32.

35. Fano, "Arte della lana," 199, chaps. 206-9. It reads, "pro evitandis multis questionibus, rissis et impedimentis que cotidie commictuntur et occurunt." Chap. 209 is worth quoting in full: "Preterea volumus et ordinamus quod non sit licitum illis laboratoribus facere aliquam assunatiam laboratorum vel magistrorum artis lane ad octo super extra domos quas habitant nec in terra nec in navigio vel aliquo in loco modo aliquo vel ingenio sub pena librarum III parvorum pro quolibet et qualibet vice et si fuerit accusator habeat medietatem et teneatur de credentia et reliqua medietas camere artis lane et

aliquis illorum, qui fuerint in dicta societate accusabit alios, ille talis accusans sit absolutus a pena et habeat partem sic accusator."

36. Molho, "Cosimo de' Medici," 17.

37. For the large number of immigrants engaged in the textile industry, see Bini, *I Lucchesi*, and Ell, "Citizenship and Immigration," 150. Ell notes that 40 percent of the immigrants from Florence were in the wool or related trades.

38. This point is made in Wirobisz, "L'attività edilizia," 323.

39. For examples, see the capitularies of the glassmakers, Monticolo, *I capitolari* 2:70, chap. 22; the cobblers, ibid., 2:138, chap. 3; the carpenters, 2:206, chap. 21; the dyers, 3:224, chap. 1; and others, passim.

40. Ibid. 2:22, chap. 47.

41. Ibid. 2:46, chap. 30; 2:55–56, chap. 65; 2:58, chap. 72. For some other examples, see the caulkers, 2:260–61, chap. 65; the cobblers, 2:156–57, chap. 70.

42. Ibid. 2:80, chap. 54.

43. The phrase reads, "perchè el va in election persone, le qual cum debita reverentia non cognosce i patroni nè etiam i maestri de sto mestier" and "che 'l mestier non vadi in ruina cum detrimento et danno de tutti." Ibid. 3:251, n. 1.

44. Fano, "Arte della lana," 92, 164–65, chap. 68.

45. Monticolo, *I capitolari* 2:158, chap. 72; 2:279, chap. 43; 2:347, chap. 48.

46. ". . . sufficiens sit et doctus in arte." Ibid. 3:226, chap. 12.

47. The capitulary of the varotarii stated that the guild officers were to assign shops to each master who asked for one, "in good conscience, as seems best to them" (et che puo' el dicto gastaldo e conpagni sian tegnudi de dar staçon o luogo a chadaun del mestier, che la domanderà, a bona consientia chomo a lor meio parerà). Ibid. 3:411, chap. 6.

48. Ibid. 2:163, chap. 87.

49. Ibid. 3:120, chap. 32.

50. "Conciosiachè fosse fatto notitia alli signori iustitieri che la gastaldia di calafadi toccava solamente a qualchuni quasi de anno in anno i quali si feva tuor gastaldi per preghiere e per subornamenti, la qual cosa era tanto dishonesta che questo iera uno atto che havev'a indur più tosto discordia che pace tra gli huomeni dell'Arte di calafadi." Ibid. 2:649, chap. 72. This measure, coming as it did after the institution of elections by lot, indicates that ways were being found to manipulate elections. Clearly the patricians understood the potential abuses as their own attempts to stop corruption in ducal elections indicate. See Lane, *Venice*, 109–11.

51. In his work, *The Laboring Classes in Renaissance Florence*, Samuel Kline Cohn, Jr. uses marriage data as the central criterion by which to judge the strength of social ties in Florence. See pp. 16–18.

52. See Sebellico, *Felice de Merlis*, docs. 41, 531; ASV, CI, Busta 166, notary Fantin Rizzo, protocol IV, 2 June 1375; ASV, CI, Busta 143, notary Stefano Pianigo, protocol, fol. 5r, 23 June 1349. One might also cite the case of Biachino de Gaffa, a former slave, who married a certain Lucia, also a former slave. ASV, CI, Busta 93, notary Giuliano fu Nicolò, protocol, fol. 11r, 9 March 1378.

53. Sebellico, *Felice de Merlis*, doc. 171; ASV, CI, Busta 189, notary Antonio Spinello, protocol, fol. 54r, 14 August 1403; ASV, CI, Busta 166, notary Fantin Rizzo, protocol IV, 30 January 1374mv.

54. ASV, CI, Busta 34, notary Giacomo Cavalier, protocol 40, fol. 11v, 17 October 1379; ASV, CI, Busta 186, notary Simeon, protocol C, fol. 4v, 24 December 1371; ASV, CI, Busta 119, notary Servodio Mazor, protocol, 22 May 1387.

55. Tools were among the most valuable objects that artisans had to bequeath. See the will of Nicolò, a painter of San Luca, who left his materials to his son Geronimo, printed in Fulin, "Cinque testamenti," 147.

56. Sjoberg, *Preindustrial City*, 100–103.

57. For the feast of San Donato, see Monticolo, *I capitolari* 2:86, chap. 75.

58. Ibid. 2:527, chap. 86.

59. Cecchetti, *La vita dei Veneziani*, pt. 2, p. 65, n. 4.

60. Tassini, *Curiosità*, 92. For coopers in other parts of the city, see ASV, CI, Busta 104, notary Tommaso Luciano fu Agostino, protocol. fol. 10r, 13 December 1414; ASV, Scuola Grande di Santa Maria della Valverde, Busta A, Mariegola 3, fol. 82v.

61. Monticolo, *I capitolari* 1:109, chap. 32. There were ropemakers living in San Martino; see 1:255.

62. In 1371 furrier Palanudes got a grazia to make improvements on his property "pro comodo sue artis." See ASV, Maggior Consiglio, Grazie, Register 16, fol. 122v. In 1322 the Great Council passed a law forbidding anyone not from the parish of Sant'Agostin from washing skins "ad ripam Sancti Augustini." ASV, Maggior Consiglio, Deliberazioni, Register 15 (Fronesis), fol. 97v.

In the references to furriers in the commercial documents of the twelfth and thirteenth centuries published by Morozzo della Rocca and Lombardo, the furriers lived on the Rialto side of the Grand Canal. See their work, *Documenti del commercio*, docs. 445, 448, 477, 703, 710. The same is true of the furriers listed in the late thirteenth-century *Liber Forbannitorum*. See Roberti, "Di un *Liber Forbannitorum*," 145–58.

63. ASV, Signori di Notte al Criminal, Processi, Register 7, fol. 86v–88v.

64. ASV, Signori di Notte al Criminal, Processi, Register 7, fol. 33r–34v; Register 9, fols. 72v–73r. In 1356 Guido Adelende, *proto* at the hemp warehouse, requested a grazia increasing his salary. He noted that he lived in Santa Croce with his mother and that it was very inconvenient for him to get to work at the Arsenal. The government granted the raise with the proviso that he find a place to live in San Pietro di Castello, San Martino, or San Biagio. ASV, Maggior Consiglio, Grazie, Register 13, fol. 79r.

65. For the ruga of the varotarii, see ASV, Maggior Consiglio, Deliberazioni, Register 8 (Magnus/Capricornus), fol. 101r. For the peliparii, see Morozzo della Rocca, *Lettere di mercanti*, 94.

66. Monticolo, *I capitolari* 2:112, chap. 52; 3:389, chap. 67.

67. Ibid. 3:405, chap. 96. For the location of the scuola, see 2:lxxvii. In the eighteenth century the varotarii built their new guild hall in the parish of Santa Margarita, near the fourteenth-century residential concentration of furriers. Comune di Venezia, *Arti e mestieri*, 94.

68. Monticolo, *I capitolari* 2:630, chap. 38.

69. Diane Owen Hughes has found that the same was true in Genoa. In Genoa artisan districts were "usually no more than a few houses on a short street, and even these often contained people pursuing other trades." She suggests that their "lack of a geographic base" helps explain the political impo-

tence of the Genoese guilds. See Hughes, "Kinsmen and Neighbors," 105. Similar conclusions are reached by Benjamin Kedar in his study of Genoese notaries in the same volume. See his "Genoese Notaries of 1382," 73–94. See also Grossi Bianchi and Poleggi, *Una città portuale.*

70. ASV, NT, Busta 335, notary Bortolo da Venezia, unbound testament (Petrus Segomator), 8 January 1385mv; ASV, NT, Busta 447, notary Petrus Foscolo, protocol, fol. 23r, 17 September 1333.

71. Sebellico, *Felice de Merlis,* doc. 1087; ASV, NT, Busta 335, notary Bortolo da Venezia, unbound testament, 14 November 1379; ASV, NT, Busta 645, notary Conte di Bertoldi, unbound testament 343, 20 December 1383; ASV, NT, Busta 1063, notary Bertucius Pandin, protocol, testament 132, 3 December 1343; ASV, NT, Busta 925, notary Lotus, protocol, fols. 93r–93v, 7 August 1311.

72. The guildsmen stated, "Conzosiachè in la dicta arte sia puochi maistri e homeni e hogni dì sia plu per manchar cha per multiplichar." Monticolo, *I capitolari* 3:407, chap. 98.

These estimates are not purely hypothetical. In 1595, 42 tanners employed 128 persons, an average of 3 persons per shop. In 1690, 109 persons worked as varotarii: 42 masters, 28 workers, and 37 apprentices. See Rapp, *Industry and Economic Decline,* 92, 122.

73. The wealthiest furrier in the estimo was Agustin de Pelegrin of Sant'Aponal, who was assessed at 4,500 lire a grossi; he was followed by Marco Rosso of Santa Croce assessed at 4,000 lire. Seven furriers had assessments between 500 and 1,500 lire. They were: Nicolò Panciera, Santa Marina (1,300 lire); Bartolamio de Ugolin, San Pantalon (1,000 lire); Nicolò de Francesco, pelizer, San Pantalon (1,000); Zuan da Vanezo, pelizer, San Pantalon (500); Luca da Canal, varoter, San Boldo (500); Zanin Saiben, San Simeon Profete (1,000). Four furriers were assessed at 300 lire each: Donado, varoter, Santa Maria Formosa; Francesco Rizo, varoter, Santa Sofia; Lorenzo Rosso, pelizer, Sant'Aponal; Palamide, pelizer, Santa Croce. Luzzatto, *I prestiti,* doc. 165, pp. 138–95.

74. For the evidence of his *stacione* (workshop) at Rialto, see ASV, Maggior Consiglio, Grazie, Register 13, fol. 15r; for his *volta* (storage space), see ASV, CI, Busta 16-I, notary Suriano Belli, protocol, 1 April 1364.

75. This figure is based on 25 observed cases. In 13 cases sons took up the same profession; in 11 they had different professions; and in one case, one son followed his father, whereas a second son took up a different trade.

In his work Giorgio Cracco suggested that sons followed in their fathers' footsteps in a "specie di schiavitù dell'arte." However, that seems an overstatement. See Cracco, *Società e stato,* 330.

In his will a painter named Nicolò entrusted decisions concerning the future of his son and daughter to *miser* Andrea Zuffo. He stated that his son ought to learn the painters' trade, "if my son wishes, if he does not wish to learn my trade, let him learn one that seems best to *miser* Andrea Zuffo and my executors." Fulin, "Cinque testamenti," 149.

Testimony to the desire for mobility among artisans of trecento Italy can be found in a poem by the Sienese Bindo Bonichi, who wrote,

El calzolai' fa 'l suo figliuol barbiere,
così 'l barbier fa 'l figliuol calzolaio;
el mercatante fa 'l figliuol notaio,
così 'l notaio fa 'l figliuol drapiere.
Mal contento è ciascun de suo mestiere.

Quoted in Sapegno, *Poeti minori*, 291.

76. ASV, Signori di Notte al Criminal, Processi, Register 9, fol. 105r–105v; ASV, CI, Busta 187, notary Nicolò Saiabianca, protocol dated 1365, 25 October 1366; ASV, CI, Busta 87, notary Nicolò Grimanis, protocol, 17 April 1330. In most of the observable cases, men from other professions—barbers, boatmen, smiths, stonecutters, and others—had their sons become furriers.

77. The evidence of Margarita's marriage is from her will in ASV, NT, Busta 567, notary Bartolomeo fu Benvenuto, loose sheet, dated 1385.

78. For Fantina's will, see ASV, CI, Busta 16–1, notary Suriano Belli, protocol, testament 173, 29 May 1355. A number of sources other than dowry receipts reveal professionally endogamous marriages. My impression is that endogamy was more common among the popolo grande than among the popolo minuto.

79. At this date, 1372, Brocha was a resident of San Simeon Grande. ASV, CI, Busta 17, notary Antonio de Belanzinis, protocol, 23 February 1371mv; ASV, CI, Busta 186, notary Simeon, protocol A, fol. 14v, 29 December 1364.

80. These cases are discussed fully in Romano, "Quod sibi fiat gratia," 262–63, 266–68.

81. ASV, Scuola Grande di San Giovanni Evangelista, Mariegole, Mariegola 3, fols. 29r–29v.

82. For Tiziano's will, see ASV, NT, Busta 1226, notary Fantinus Rizzo, protocol, 12 March 1374. For Trevisan as a slave owner, see ASV, CI, Busta 166, notary Fantin Rizzo, protocol IV, 8 June 1376. For his dealings with butchers, see ASV, CI, Busta 201, notary Tomaso de Tomasi, protocol, 30 May 1375, and his grant of cittadinanza in ASV, Senato, Deliberazioni Miste, Register 39, fol. 6v.

83. In her will, Tiziano's mother-in-law is described as "Lene peliparie." This almost certainly indicates that her husband was a furrier. ASV, NT, Busta 335, notary Simeon, unbound testament 146, 16 July 1367.

84. ASV, CI, Busta 130, notary Nicolò Nadal, protocol E, fol. 49v, 19 August 1404.

85. ASV, CI, Busta 335, notary Bortolo da Venezia, unbound testament, 18 October 1377.

86. ASV, Scuola Grande di Santa Maria della Carità, Tome 234, fol. 61v.

87. ASV, CI, Busta 34, notary Giacomo Cavalier, protocol 41, fol. 33r, 5 May 1388. This identification is made on the basis of the name only.

88. For Merlo, ASV, Scuola Grande di San Giovanni Evangelista, Mariegole, vol. 7, fol. 37r; for Nicoleto, see Lombardo, *Nicola de Boateriis*, doc. 235; for Saimben, ASV, CI, Busta 166, notary Fantin Rizzo, protocol IV, 13 March 1376; for Datale, ASV, CI, Busta 166, notary Fantin Rizzo, protocol IV, 14 April 1374. Another furrier, Vendrame, also held the post of guardian of San Giovanni Evangelista. See V. Lazzarini, *Marino Faliero*, 163–64.

89. For Canciano's dowry, see Sebellico, *Felice de Merlis*, doc. 168; for Gia-

como's see, ASV, CI, Busta 199, notary Pietro Torre, protocol II, 19 February 1347mv. For Marco Rosso's bequest to his slave, see ASV, NT, Busta 915, notary Constantino di Cison, protocol, testament 40, 24 May 1378.

90. This conclusion is based on the evidence of 110 testaments. In 71 wills of furrier wives and widows, the average number of children mentioned is 0.66. In 39 men's wills, the number of children mentioned is 1.10. While testaments surely underreport the number of children, they do give some indication that furriers were probably not reproducing themselves.

91. ASV, Signori di Notte al Criminal, Processi, Register 11, fols. 1r–1v.

92. Ibid., fols. 95r–96r.

93. Sebellico, *Felice de Merlis*, doc. 170. Melio's poor standing seems assured since his daughter's dowry of 30 ducats was exactly one-half the value of the average popolano dowry during that decade. ASV, CI, Busta 130, notary Nicolò Nadal, protocol E, fol. 68v, 6 December 1413.

94. ASV, Avogaria di Comun, Raspe, Register 3646, fols. 121r–122r. For a case of furriers acting together, see ASV, Signori di Notte al Criminal, Processi, Register 9, fols. 105r–105v.

95. See Cecchetti, *La vita dei Veneziani*, pt. 2, pp. 136–72, esp. 169. For examples of artisans meeting in taverns, see ASV, Signori di Notte al Criminal, Processi, Register 8, fols. 78v–79r, 73r–73v, 9v–10v; Register 7, fols. 49v–51v, 70r–72v; Register 11, fols. 1r–1v. For taverns as centers of Florentine laboring-class life, see Cohn, *Laboring Classes*, 88–89.

96. For Zanino's marriage, see ASV, CI, Busta 186, notary Simeon, protocol A, fol. 16v, 10 February 1365mv (the woman's dowry was 190 ducats). In the case of goldsmith Matteo Simiteculo, he received permission to work in his shop at night through the intercession of Michele Zancani's son. ASV, Maggior Consiglio, Deliberazioni, Register 8 (Magnus/Capricornus), fol. 178v. For the dowry that Andrea received, see ASV, CI, Busta 143, notary Stefano Pianigo, protocol, fol. 18r, 2 April 1348.

97. Fano, "Arte della lana," 203; Barbaro, *Libro di nozze*, fols. 16 left, 403 left; Museo Civico Correr, Codice Cicogna 3063, fasc. 10, *Serie delli Guardiani Grandi della Scuola Grande di San Giovanni Evangelista*, see 1430.

98. ASV, Senato, Deliberazioni Miste, Register 52, fol. 189v. Noblemen Antonio Foscarini and Marco Barbo and cittadino Simeon Faxolo received similar grants.

99. ASV, Signori di Notte al Criminal, Processi, Register 12, fol. 69v.

100. Fulin, "Cinque testamenti," 146–47.

101. ASV, Signori di Notte al Criminal, Processi, Register 10, fols. 35r–35v. Guido Ruggiero has found a similarly high level of tension between the intermediate group he labels "important people" and workers. See Ruggiero, *Violence*, 91–93.

102. ASV, Signori di Notte al Criminal, Processi, Register 9, fols. 70r–71r.

103. ASV, Avogaria di Comun, Raspe, Register 3647, fol. 7v.

104. Alvise was an official with the *giustizieri novi*. ASV, Signori di Notte al Criminal, Register 10, fols. 95r–96r. I have accepted that the two workers were immigrants on the basis of their names. For a consideration of this issue in Venice, see Ruggiero, "Status of Physicians," 183–84.

105. The nature of the sources makes it difficult to evaluate the extent to

which certain families developed into a "dynastic" guild elite. For instance, Tiziano, whose father had been a furrier, had no sons, only daughters. Hence the family's influence in the fur trade ended with him. In another case, Franceschino Vendelino wrote into his will special incentives for his son to maintain the family workshop, as if he feared that he would not do so. ASV, NT, Busta 335, notary Bortolo da Venezia, 14 November 1379.

In his study of the building trades in Florence, Richard Goldthwaite notes that the "consular elite appears not to have been an oligarchy that perpetuated itself on a familial principle, and indeed this is not surprising, since artisan families lacked the kind of solidarity and stability one might expect to find in the upper classes of society." Goldthwaite, *Building of Renaissance Florence*, 275. Guido Ruggiero has found that dynasties did develop among the physicians of Venice. Yet the need to procure a government license (and the specialized training required to become a physician) may have encouraged this tendency more among physicians than among persons practicing other trades. See Ruggiero, "Status of Physicians," 168–84.

106. Najemy, *Corporatism and Consensus*. As Gene Brucker has noted, during the Ciompi Revolt the main thrust of the workers' demands was to be accepted into the system. See Brucker, "Ciompi Revolution," 314–56.

FIVE The Parochial Clergy and Communities of the Sacred

1. For the position of the church in Venice, see among others, Cecchetti, *La Republica di Venezia*; and Piva, *Il Patriarcato*.

2. Prodi, "Church in Renaissance Venice," 409–30.

3. The lists of parish priests are scattered throughout the work. I have not included in the count monastic churches that enjoyed parochial rights. Cornelio, *Ecclesiae venetae*.

4. Rosada, ed., *S. Maria Formosa*, xliii; Cornelio, *Ecclesiae venetae* 2, decade 5, p. 312.

5. Tiepolo, *Domenico prete*, doc. 375; Cornelio, *Ecclesiae venetae* 2, decade 6, p. 334; ASV, CI, Busta 156, notary Giovanni Rizzo, protocol, 10 January 1355mv. Some of the identifications of priests as members of noble families are based on the evidence of surnames alone.

6. ASV, CI, Busta 143, notary Stefano Pianigo, protocol, fol. 11v, 20 July 1350; ASV, CI, Busta 219, notary Vettore, protocol, 18 July 1325; Cessi, *Deliberazioni del Maggior Consiglio* 3:347; ASV, NT, Busta 447, notary Ludovico Falcon, unbound testament 57, 11 July 1359.

7. ASV, CI, Busta 141, notary Antonius Polo, protocol, 31 July 1340; ASV, CI, Busta 14, notary Gregorio Bruno, unbound parchment, 17 May 1335.

8. For examples from later centuries, see J. Davis, *Venetian Family*, 104–5.

9. Tassini, "D'una lapide mortuaria," 389.

10. ASV, CI, Busta 156, notary Giovanni Rizzo, protocol, 7 March 1353; ASV, NT, Busta 447, notary Victor presbiter San Canciano, parchment, testament 75, 2 April 1340; ASV, Maggior Consiglio, *Grazie*, Register 14, fols. 1v, 69r.

11. Sebellico, *Felice de Merlis*, p. vii, n. 1.

12. ASV, NT, Busta 850, notary Nicolò Bon, protocol C, testament 29, 13 Feb-

ruary 1326mv; ASV, NT, Busta 573, notary Giorgio de Gibellino, testament 322, 4 July 1375.

13. ASV, CI, Busta 190, notary Stefano, protocol, 17 November 1392; for Cristoforo as procurator, see ASV, CI, Busta 34, notary Giacomo Cavalier, protocol 41, fol. 14r, 9 November 1382.

14. Tamba, *Bernardo de Rodulfis,* doc. 27; ASV, NT, Busta 545, notary Lorenzo Buscareno, protocol B, testament 55, 11 April 1420.

15. ASV, NT, Busta 467, notary Giacomo Cavalier, unbound testament, 2 June 1388; ASV, NT, Busta 1062, notary Lorenzo della Torre, protocol, fols. 59v–60r, 19 January 1347mv.

16. Rosada, *S. Maria Formosa,* xliii.

17. ASV, CI, Busta 17, notary Giovanni Barbafella, unbound parchment, 8 August 1370; for the poverty of the parish, see the estimo in Luzzatto, *I prestiti,* doc. 165, pp. 164, 173.

18. ASV, CI, Busta 143, notary Stefano Pianigo, protocol, fol. 9r, 11 March 1350; ibid., fol. 17r, 19 February 1347mv; ASV, NT, Busta 982, notary Andrea presbiter, protocol, testament 14, 9 June 1341; ibid., testament 41, 24 October 1321.

19. ASV, CI, Busta 79, notary Gasparino Favaccio, protocol, acts dated 3 October 1359.

20. For the Staniario, see ASV, CI, Busta 156, notary Giovanni Rizzo, protocol, 28 August 1350; for the Favaccio, see ASV, CI, Busta 166, notary Fantin Rizzo, protocol II, 31 October 1368.

21. ASV, CI, Busta 141, notary Antonius Polo, protocol, acts dated 5 September 1339, 22 June 1346.

22. Ibid., acts dated 22 June 1346, 22 March 1347.

23. ASV, CI, Busta 186, notary Simeon, protocol A, fol. 17r, 6 April 1366.

24. ASV, NT, Busta 447, notary Victor presbiter San Canciano, parchment, testament 75, 2 April 1340; Cornelio, *Ecclesiae venetae* I, decade 2, p. 219.

25. Cornelio, *Ecclesiae venetae* I, decade 3, p. 320.

26. For Felice, see Sebellico, *Felice de Merlis,* xi; for Dartico, ASV, CI, Busta 186, notary Simeon, protocol A, fol. 18v, 2 December 1366; ASV, CI, Busta 93, notary Giovanni Gazo, protocol, 28 August 1377.

27. ASV, NT, Busta 982, notary Andrea presbiter, protocol, testament 73, 15 September 1335; for Baccariis' earlier career in San Martino, see Bernardi, *Antichi testamenti,* fasc. 12 (1893): 26.

28. Cornelio, *Ecclesiae venetae* I, decade 3, p. 377.

29. See his will in ASV, PSM, de Ultra, Commissarie, Busta 32, Commissaria of Bartolomeus plebanus.

30. L. Lazzarini, "Amici del Petrarca," 4.

31. For the position of procurator, see the discussion in Rosada, *S. Maria Formosa,* xxiv, n. 3.

32. ASV, CI, Busta 79, notary Gasparino Favaccio, protocol, 10 May 1359.

33. ASV, CI, Busta 79, notary Ludovico Falcon, protocol, 5 April 1359; ASV, CI, Busta 141, notary Antonius Polo, protocol, 22 March 1347.

34. ASV, CI, Busta 114, notary Marino San Tomà, protocol 1335–1350, 5 November 1346; ASV, CI, Busta 93, notary Giovanni Gazo, protocol, 26 August 1377 (in the act Martino is also called Marino); ASV, Giudici del Piovego, Busta 3, Codex Publicorum, 685–90; ASV, CI, Busta 143, notary Stefano Pianigo, protocol,

fol. 1r, 12 February 1348mv; ASV, CI, Busta 180, notary Vivianus, protocol, 8 September 1349. Some of the identifications are made on the basis of surnames.

35. ASV, PSM, de Ultra, Commissarie, Busta 211, Commissaria of Pietro Navagero da Negroponte, notebook, page dated August 1293.

36. For Tranquillo, see ASV, NT, Busta 645, notary Conte di Bertoldi, unbound testament 323, 30 September 1385; for Giovanni, see ASV, CI, Busta 70, notary Basilius Darvasio, protocol, 2 March 1406; for Nicolaus de Zane, see ASV, CI, Busta 20, notary Bartolomeo fu Benvenuto, protocol, 19 December 1381; for Benedetto, ASV, CI, Busta 69, notary Damiano fu Cristoforo, protocol beginning 30 March 1378, act dated 29 October 1378.

37. For instances of procurators defending the interests of their churches in court, see ASV, Giudici del Piovego, Busta 3, Codex Publicorum, 483–93, 685–90.

38. Sebellico, *Felice de Merlis*, doc. 130.

39. The eighteenth-century scholar Giovanni Battista Gallicciolli believed that five mother churches had baptistries and that on appointed days parish clergy went to those churches to baptize their parishioners. See Gallicciolli, *Delle memorie venete* 3, bk. 2, chap. 6, pp. 156–85. For a judicious summary of the problem, see Rosada, *S. Maria Formosa*, xx, n. 2.

40. "... secundum ritum et formam ecclesie Romane."

41. In his will, Lorenzo de Tomasi left a bequest to Giacomello de Gusmer, "perchè l'è stato et è al presente mio compagno e mio congiunto, perchè Io gli ò battezati tutti i so *fioli* e *fiole* infin a questo dì." See Bernardi, *Antichi testamenti*, fasc. 5 (1886): 11.

42. ASV, CI, Busta 34, notary Giacomo Cavalier, protocol 41, fol. 40r, 20 July 1389. Margarita, wife of Nicolò Dalle Boccole of San Martino, left a bequest to her "patrino de penetentia." ASV, NT, Busta 1062, notary Lorenzo della Torre, testament 362, 22 October 1397. The term *patrinus* was used in medieval Europe to denote a godfather. In Venice, as the additional words *de penetentia* indicate, it was most commonly used to indicate a priest. See Lynch, *Godparents and Kinship*, 170–71.

43. ASV, NT, Busta 982, notary Nicolaus Verde, protocol, testament 25, 18 June 1348; Bernardi, *Antichi testamenti*, fasc. 10 (1891): 17.

44. Romano, "Charity and Community," 67.

45. ASV, NT, Busta 1226, notary Fantin Rizzo, protocol, 12 March 1374.

46. Sebellico, *Felice de Merlis*, docs., 1266, 1289.

47. ASV, CI, Busta 143, notary Stefano Pianigo, protocol, fol. 17v, 21 March 1348; ASV, CI, Busta 14, notary Bertuccio Sant'Angelo, protocol, 5 January 1336mv.

48. Sebellico, *Felice de Merlis*, docs. 1285, 1216, 1236, 1247.

49. For an exception, see an act in which Marino Signolo of Sant'Agnese gave power of attorney to Pantaleone Cavazza, a *clericus* of San Trovaso. ASV, CI, Busta 143, notary Stefano Pianigo, protocol, fol. 6r, 1 September 1349.

50. ASV, CI, Busta 93, notary Giovanni Gazo, protocol, 28 August 1377; ASV, CI, Busta 79, notary Ludovico Falcon, protocol, 11 July 1359.

51. See pt. 3 of Pullan's *Rich and Poor* for a discussion of the Jews in Venice and the *Monte di Pietà*. For the medieval background, see especially pp. 431–75. For a discussion of free loans, see Lopez and Raymond, *Medieval Trade*, 157–58.

52. Sebellico, *Felice de Merlis*, doc. 19.
53. Ibid., docs. 18, 250.
54. Ibid., doc. 405; Tiepolo, *Domenico prete*, doc. 495; ASV, CI, Busta 143, notary Stefano Pianigo, protocol, fol. 22v, 17 October 1348.
55. ASV, NT, Busta 545, notary Lorenzo Buscareno, protocol, testament 25, 14 February 1410mv.
56. For a discussion of the local colleganza, see Mueller, "Procurators of San Marco," 156–65; also Luzzatto, "La commenda nella vita" 59–79; and Arcangeli, "La commenda a Venezia," 107–64.
57. ASV, CI, Busta 219, notary Vettore, protocol, 11 January 1329mv.
58. Ibid., 29 September 1329; ASV, CI, Busta 156, notary Giovanni Rizzo, protocol, 7 March 1353.
59. ASV, PSM, de Ultra, Commissarie, Busta 117A, Commissaria of Marco Disenove, parchment 8, 27 September 1348.
60. Sebellico, *Felice de Merlis*, docs. 322, 410, 890.
61. Arcangeli, "La commenda a Venezia," 152, doc. 17.
62. ASV, NT, Busta 982, notary Nicolaus Verde, protocol, testament 13, 20 May 1348.
63. " . . . dedi amite tue soldos .IIII ÷ . grossorum et Bogatinus soldos III. grossorum. De reliquis soldis .III. grossorum, duos soldos grossorum dedi Tasso pilipario, reliquos .XII. grossos posui in mea racione de grossis .XXXII. quos michi debebas, sic quod michi restares ad dandum grossos .XX., de quibus plebanus noster pridie accepit suam coppam et dedit michi soldos .II. grossorum. Restant michi grossos .IIII. quos restituam plebano, aut dabo amite tue, quia de racione antiqua prescripta nunquam tibi amplius faciam racionem. Modo perveniamus ad alia. Dedi amite tue soldos .III. grossorum. Item grossos .XII.. Mee intencionis est alio viatico satisfacere Marco Tervisano de grossis .XV., quis peciit, dicens quod tibi pro me dedit." Sebellico, *Felice de Merlis*, xxxvi.
64. ASV, CI, Busta 93, notary Bartolomeus de Gilberto, protocol, 24 July 1378.
65. " . . . de meis propriis denariis, sumptibus, et exspensis." ASV, PSM, de Ultra, Commissarie, Busta 32, Commissaria of Bartolomeus plebanus, testament. For other examples of priests as property owners, see Sebellico, *Felice de Merlis*, docs. 337, 647; Tiepolo, *Domenico prete*, doc. 299.
66. ASV, Giudici di Petizion, Sentenze e Interdetti, Register 3, fol. 88r.
67. Prodi, "Church in Renaissance Venice," 422.
68. V. Turner and E. Turner, *Image and Pilgrimage*, esp. 1–39.
69. For an interesting attempt to locate the sacred in an urban context, see N. Z. Davis, "Sacred and the Body Social," 40–70. The importance of the parish is considered in chap. 6.
70. The history of Venetian monasteries and convents remains largely unwritten, but see the recent work of Goffen, *Piety and Patronage*.
71. Ruggiero, *Boundaries of Eros*, 70–88.
72. ASV, NT, Busta 447, notary Ludovico Falcon, parchment pages, fols. 8r–8v, 8 October 1358; ASV, NT, Busta 819, notary Antonio Polo, protocol, 12 August 1336.
73. See Bertanza and Lazzarini, *Il dialetto veneziano*, doc. 148, p. 67. Some women of artisanal background did enter convents, but they tended to enter

convents distant from the city, perhaps because entry fees were lower. For an example see Tamba, *Bernardo de Rodulfis*, doc. 378.

74. ASV, CI, Busta 70, notary Basilius Davasio, protocol, act dated 21 February 1406mv. For lists of the members of the convents of Santa Maria delle Vergini and Santa Maria della Celestia, which read like a "Who's Who" of the Venetian patriciate, see Cornelio, *Ecclesiae venetae* 2, decade 6, p. 61; 6, decade 13, pt. 2, pp. 257-58.

75. For church-going among women, see Newett, "Sumptuary Laws of Venice," 268. Convents could also represent places of confinement. The widow of conspirator Nicolò Querini was allowed to return to Venice after the death of her husband, provided she remained confined to a convent. Romanin, *Storia documentata* 3:36.

76. ASV, NT, Busta 335, notary Bortolo da Venezia, testament, 2 March 1389; ASV, NT, Busta 947, notary Henricus Salamon, protocol, testament 202, 10 October 1427. I would like to thank Sharon Strocchia for explaining some of these practices to me.

77. ASV, CI, Busta 34, notary Giacomo Cavalier, protocol 41, fol. 5v, 5 November 1397.

78. ASV, CI, Busta 69, notary Damiano fu Cristoforo, protocol, testament 141, 20 January 1383mv.

79. ASV, PSM, Misti, Commissarie, Busta 119, Commissaria of Giovanni Dalle Boccole of Santa Trinità, testament dated 5 October 1321; ibid., Busta 74A, Commissaria of Tommaso Sanuto qd. Nicolò, testament dated 23 January 1374mv; ASV, NT, Busta 1226, notary Fantinus Rizzo, protocol, 2 dates: 12 January 1376mv, 10 July 1378; Sebellico, *Felice de Merlis*, doc. 1206.

80. ASV, NT, Busta 447, notary Ludovico Falcon, parchment pages, fols. 1r-1v, 21 May 1356; ASV, NT, Busta 1226, notary Fantinus Rizzo, protocol, 12 March 1374.

81. ASV, NT, Busta 335, notary Bortolo da Venezia, unbound testament, 7 August 1385; ASV, NT, Busta 447, notary Victor presbiter S. Canciano, testament 75, 2 April 1340.

82. The ninety wills are drawn from 223 wills of parishioners of Santa Trinità I have gathered for the period 1297 to 1423.

83. ASV, NT, Busta 850, notary Nicolò Bon, protocol C, testament 31, 18 September 1328; ASV, NT, Busta 335, notary Bortolo da Venezia, unbound testament, 16 September 1373.

84. ASV, NT, Busta 1226, notary Fantin Rizzo, protocol, 21 January 1374mv.

85. ASV, NT, Busta 447, notary Ludovico Falcon, parchment pages, fols. 8r-8v, 8 October 1358; ASV, NT, Busta 1062, notary Lorenzo della Torre, protocol, fols. 59v-60r, 19 January 1347mv.

86. ASV, NT, Busta 567, notary Bartolomeo fu Benvenuto, unbound testament, 1 July 1396; ASV, NT, Busta 364, notary Basilio Darvasio, protocol, fol. 87r, 13 November 1405.

87. ASV, NT, Busta 819, notary Nicolaus Pelegrino, unbound testament 43, 27 September 1406.

88. Ibid., unbound testament 15, 20 August 1373.

89. ASV, NT, Busta 567, notary Bartolomeo fu Benvenuto, unbound testament, 17 March 1380 (will of Franceschina Dalle Boccole); ibid., will dated 20

November 1396 of Dona Antonia de ser Michiel da Lorto; ibid., will dated 8 April 1394 of Agnese femena che fo de Madona Marchesin Valentin. For the potter Daniele, see ASV, NT, Busta 335, notary Bortolo da Venezia, unbound testament, 16 September 1373.

90. ASV, PSM, Misti, Commissarie, Busta 119, Commissaria of Giovanni Dalle Boccole, testament dated 5 October 1321.

91. Pullan, *Rich and Poor*, 40–42.

92. "... viva honestamente in paxe et in caritate, senza fraudo et senza soperbia et senza mormoracion, toiando senpre ananti li soi ogli lo semplo deli santi apostoli che Christo li comanda ame paxe e karitate et ame lo proximo sicome vui medemi." Cited in Cecchetti, *La Republica di Venezia* 1:252.

93. Ibid. 1:247–48, 250. See also Weissman, *Ritual Brotherhood*, esp. 43–105.

94. See Sbriziolo, "Per la storia delle confraternite," 406.

95. According to Brian Pullan, in the sixteenth century, 7 or 8 percent of adult males were members of the scuole grandi. He also notes that they drew their members from "a wide social range, and from a great variety of trades and professions." Pullan, *Rich and Poor*, 94–98.

96. ASV, Scuola Grande di Santa Maria della Carità, Tomes 233, 233bis, 234. I have also examined the following mariegole and lists: ASV, Scuola di Santa Maria della Valverde, Busta A, Mariegole 1, 2, 3; ASV, Scuola Grande di San Giovanni Evangelista, Tomes 3, 5, 6, 7. Some of the lists for San Giovanni Evangelista are arranged by parish.

97. ASV, Scuola Grande di Santa Maria della Valverde, Busta A, Mariegola 3. The capitulary (apparently an updated version of Mariegola 1) begins with the prologue dated 1308; the last addition to the capitulary is dated 1390. The capitulary lists noble and popolano members separately and alphabetically. The sample was made by taking the first ten names of each letter of the alphabet (if there were ten names listed). This was done for the popolano members only and yielded 178 names. The total number of popolani inscribed is 1279, so the sample represents 13.9 percent of popolano members.

98. It should be noted that the Carità list includes 80 men in the category of the moon (the category corresponding to traghetto operators, laborers, and porters). ASV, Scuola Grande di Santa Maria della Carità, Tome 234, fols. 56r–57v. This again suggests how tentative any conclusions must remain.

99. Ibid., fol. 3r.

100. ASV, Scuola di Santa Maria della Valverde, Busta A, Mariegola 3, fols. 21v–22r.

101. For remarks on the scuole piccole, see Mackenney, "Arti e stato"; idem, "Devotional Confraternities," 85–96.

102. Pullan, *Rich and Poor*, 49.

103. ASV, Scuole Piccole, Busta 726, Santa Maria della Celestia, chap. 39.

104. Ibid.; ASV, Scuole Piccole, Busta 24, Sant'Anna di Castello; Busta 57 bis, Santi Apostoli. For a more complete statistical analysis of these lists and of another extant trecento list, see Mackenney, *Tradesmen and Traders*. I would like to thank Professor Mackenney for allowing me to read his discussion of the scuole piccole prior to publication. The published volume reached me too late to incorporate its many other findings into this study.

105. The lists are arranged alphabetically according to members' first

names. The sample was compiled by taking the first ten names in each letter of the alphabet if the handwriting indicated that the name was from the fourteenth century (there are later additions to the lists). Only lists of popolani were analyzed.

106. The open spaces in this distant part of the city provided opportunities to construct mills and other facilities essential to the production of cloth. See ASV, Giudici del Piovego, Busta 3, Codex Publicorum, 480-82. This act gives permission to a fustagnarius from San Biagio to construct equipment for blanching cloth.

107. ASV, NT, Busta 982, notary Andrea presbiter, protocol, testament 45, 15 April 1320 (the scuola of San Teodoro was raised in 1552 to the status of a scuola grande); ASV, NT, Busta 567, notary Bartolomeo fu Benvenuto, unbound testament, 11 March 1367.

108. ASV, NT, Busta 567, notary Bartolomeo fu Benvenuto, unbound testament, 21 June 1398.

109. ASV, NT, Busta 467, notary Giacomo Cavalier, unbound testament, 28 July 1392; ASV, NT, Busta 568, notary Bartolomeo fu Benvenuto, unbound testament, 2 March 1381.

110. ASV, CI, Busta 130, notary Nicolò Nadal, protocol B, fol. 2v, 13 March 1383.

111. Lombardo, *Nicola de Boateriis*, doc. 299; ASV, CI, Busta 241, notary Petrus Zane, protocol dated 1388-1418, fol. 6IV, act dated July 1404; ASV, CI, Busta 166, notary Fantin Rizzo, protocol IV, 20 October 1374; Bertanza, *Documenti*, 58.

112. ASV, CI, Busta 114, notary Marino di San Tomà, protocol 1335-50, 22 February 1339mv; ASV, CI, Busta 199, notary Pietro Torre, protocol beginning January 1332mv, 25 April 1340; ASV, CI, Busta 190, notary Enrico Salamon, protocol dated 1417-21, 16 January 1420mv; ASV, PSM, Misti, Commissarie, Busta 179, Commissaria of Lucia dell'Agnella, relicta Donato, act dated 30 April 1382.

113. A useful survey of Venetian funeral and burial practices is found in B. Cecchetti, "Funerali," 265-84.

114. Bertanza, *Documenti*, 193.

115. Cecchetti, "Funerali," 270.

116. Ibid., 276-77.

117. ASV, NT, Busta 567, notary Bartolomeo fu Benvenuto, unbound testament, 20 July 1390.

118. ASV, CI, Busta 189, notary Antonio Spinello, protocol, fol. 4v, testament 8, 13 November 1397.

119. Tamba, *Bernardo de Rodulfis*, doc. 378.

120. Bertanza, *Documenti*, 114.

121. Cecchetti, "Funerali," 269. This request is dated 1497.

122. Bertanza, *Documenti*, 337. His will is dated 1488.

123. Cecchetti, *La Republica di Venezia* 1:110.

124. ASV, NT, Busta 1226, notary Fantin Rizzo, protocol, 12 March 1374.

125. ASV, NT, Busta 447, notary Ludovico Falcon, unbound testament 57, 11 July 1359.

126. Stussi, *Testi veneziani*, 131.

127. ASV, NT, Busta 1226, notary Fantin Rizzo, protocol, 2 dates: 12 January 1376mv, 10 July 1378; ASV, NT, Busta 364, notary Basilio Darvasio, testament 278, 18 March 1411; for the Dalle Boccole, see chap. 3.
128. ASV, NT, Busta 827, notary Stefano Pianigo, protocol, 3 April 1349; ASV, NT, Busta 1023, notary Ariano Passamonte, testament 30, 4 September 1391.
129. ASV, PSM, Misti, Commissarie, Busta 103A, Commissaria of Zanetta Orio, will dated 2 July 1383.
130. ASV, NT, Busta 567, notary Bartolomeo fu Benvenuto, unbound testament, 17 November 1384.
131. ASV, NT, Busta 915, notary Constantino di Cison, testament 1, 23 August 1379; Bertanza, *Documenti,* 309.
132. Lombardo, *Nicola de Boateriis,* docs. 308, 309.
133. ASV, NT, Busta 1226, notary Fantin Rizzo, protocol, 17 November 1378; Bertanza, *Documenti,* 169.
134. ASV, NT, Busta 982, notary Andrea presbiter Santa Trinità, testament 92, 13 January 1337mv; ASV, PSM, Misti, Busta 74A, Commissaria of Tommaso Sanuto qd. Nicolò, testament dated 23 January 1374mv.
135. ASV, NT, Busta 568, notary Bartolomeo fu Benvenuto, unbound testament, 10 December 1382; ibid., 2 April 1396.
136. Ibid., testament 38, 7 January 1383mv, 20 May 1361.
137. Bertanza, *Documenti,* 142, 193.
138. ASV, NT, Busta 335, notary Simeon, testament 199, 29 January 1366mv.
139. ASV, NT, Busta 982, notary Andrea presbiter Santa Trinità, testament 27, 22 August 1334; Bertanza, *Documenti,* 276, 314.
For the arrangements between the scuola grande of the Carità and the convent of the Carità for the tomb, see Rosand, *Painting in Cinquecento Venice,* 133.
140. Bertanza, *Documenti,* 302.
141. ASV, NT, Busta 1063, notary Bertucius Pandin, unbound testament 5, 20 May 1348.
142. Cecchetti cites numerous examples in which Venetians left explicit instructions about the number of hours they wanted their bodies to remain above ground and other concerns. See Cecchetti, "Funerali," esp. 265–67.

SIX *Vicinanza* and *Amicizia:* Neighborhoods and Patronage in Early Renaissance Venice

1. F. Zago, *Consiglio dei Dieci* I, register 2, docs. 384, 385, 386, 449, 548. See also V. Lazzarini, "Aneddoti," 81–83.
2. ASV, Avogaria di Comun, Raspe, Register 3644, fol. 127r. It reads, "Et baniatur et confinetur quod non possit ire in ecclesiam Sancte Marie Formose, neque sub porticalibus dictae ecclesiae neque super campedelo de cha mauraceno, neque super ponte lapideo, posito in contrata predicta Sancte Marie Formose, neque transire pontem de cha da mezo, pro veniendo versus cha salamone, nec transire pontem de cha superamcio Sancti Iohannis Novi, neque ecclesiam Sancti Iohannis Novi, pro veniendo versus ca delege, nec intrare calem post ca superamcio, per quam itur ad ca faraon, non possendo preterire dicta confinia, per terram neque per aquam usque ad annos .x. proximos,

vivente domina clara uxore ser Marci salamon et stante in dicta contrata."

3. Guido Ruggiero cites a case in which a girl's reputation had to be publicly exonerated by proclamation. The announcement was made in the girl's home parish—Sant'Agnese—and the nearby parish of San Nicolò dei Mendicoli. This provides further evidence that a woman's world was considered to encompass a restricted area. See Ruggiero, *Boundaries of Eros*, 38.

4. See Kent and Kent, "Self-Disciplining Pact," 347–48; Heers, *Family Clans*, 158–59; D. Kent, *The Rise of the Medici*, 64–71; and Heers, "Urbanisme," 384–88, 412. See also Klapisch, "'Parenti, amici e vicini.'"

5. See Luzzatto, *I prestiti*. For other examples of the geographic dispersion of nobles, see Gallo, "Una famiglia patrizia," 65–73; and Howard, *Jacopo Sansovino*, 134–38.

6. Chojnacki, "In Search," 60.

7. J. Davis, *Venetian Family*, 3–4. I would like to thank Donald Queller for suggesting the clustering of residences to me.

8. Schulz, "Titian, Arentino, and Sansovino," 83.

9. For the decision to raze the Tiepolo palace, see Romanin, *Storia documentata*, 3:30. On the totemic significance of houses, see Heers, *Family Clans*, 104–5; and LeRoy Ladurie, *Montaillou*, 31–37.

10. V. Lazzarini, "Il testamento," 80–88; and Cecchetti, "Nomi di pittori," 49, n. 2.

11. Tassini, *Curiosità*, 4.

12. Howard, *Jacopo Sansovino*, 123. A Senate deliberation from 1324 refers to the "Domus et turris de ca Zane." See Cessi and Sambin, eds., *Consiglio dei Rogati (Senato)*, 288.

13. Cessi, *Deliberazioni del Maggior Consiglio* 2:212–13.

14. Zago, ed., *Consiglio dei Dieci* 2, register 3, doc. 143, passim. See also Ruggiero, *Violence*, 15, 139.

15. V. Lazzarini, *Marino Faliero*, 176.

16. ASV, CI, Busta 141, notary Antonius Polo, protocol, paper insert dated 5 June 1340, act dated 26 December 1340; act dated 14 January 1340mv. For other examples, see Lombardo, *Nicola de Boateriis*, docs. 238, 269, 321.

17. Tiepolo, *Domenico prete*, docs. 108, 109, 132, 134, 147, 178, 179, 233, 344, 352, 359.

18. Molho, "Cosimo de' Medici."

19. For deliberations concerning the *Marie*, see ASV, Maggior Consiglio, Deliberazioni, Register 19 (Novella), fols. 76v, 92r, 104r, 116r, 119v, 136r, passim.

20. ASV, Cinque Savi alla Mercanzia, Capitolare degli Estraordinari, Register 22 ter (formerly Miscellanea Codice 132), fols. 41right–42left.

21. J. Davis, *Venetian Family*, 4–6.

22. Queller, "Civic Irresponsibility," 223–35; idem, *Venetian Patriciate*; and V. Lazzarini, "Obbligo di assumere pubblici uffici," 184–98. See also Ruggiero, *Violence*, 65–66.

23. For the position of the doge, see Maranini, *La costituzione* 1:73–79, 109–55. For the law restricting the doge's grazie powers, see Favaro, *Cassiere della bolla ducale*, Appendix, doc. 1, pp. 189–90.

24. This discussion of the procedures follows that outlined by Elena Favaro and Luigi Lanfranchi in the preface to the printed edition of the first register

of grazie, the *Novus Liber*. See Favaro, *Cassiere della bolla ducale*, lxix–lxxviii.

25. ASV, Maggior Consiglio, Deliberazioni, Register 12 (Clericus/Civicus), fol. 165r.

26. Favaro, *Cassiere della bolla ducale*, docs. 7, 508.

27. Ibid., docs. 21, 22, 32, 64, 124, 158, passim.

28. ASV, Maggior Consiglio, Grazie, Register 9, fol. 16r.

29. Ibid., fol. 37v. It reads, "considerata eius magna paupertate et infirmitate."

30. Ibid., fol. 39v. It is very difficult to determine whether all the grazie recorded in the registers were approved or only the ones with a cross. This one does not contain a cross.

31. Ibid., fol. 57v.

32. Ibid., Register 10, fol. 53r.

33. Ibid., Register 11, fol. 1v.

34. Bellemo, "Benintendi de' Ravagnani," n.s., 24:77–95 (docs. I, IV, X, XII, XV, XVII, XXI, XXII, XXIII, XXV).

35. ASV, Maggior Consiglio, Deliberazioni, Register 21 (Leona), fol. 155v; Bertanza, *Documenti*, 61.

36. ASV, Maggior Consiglio, Deliberazioni, Register 10 (Presbiter), fols. 17r, 25v.

37. Ibid., Register 17 (Spiritus), fol. 65r.

38. Ibid., fol. 152r.

39. Ibid., Register 10 (Presbiter), fol. 30v.

40. Ibid., Register 12 (Clericus/Civicus), fol. 75r.

41. Ruggiero, "Status of Physicians," 181; Labalme, *Bernardo Giustiniani*, 66. For some insights into patron-client relationships, see King, *Venetian Humanism*, 49–58.

42. ASV, Maggior Consiglio, Deliberazioni, Register 17 (Spiritus), fol. 157v.

43. Ibid., fol. 43v. See also Trebbi, "La cancelleria," 89.

Office-holding also provided opportunities to pressure others into granting favors. In 1421 the Council of Ten passed a law allowing a caulker named Paolo Gruato to join the scuola grande of San Marco, although at the time of the election he would be out of the city in the service of nobleman Stefano Contarini. The statutes of the scuola prohibited election of anyone not present in the city. In the following February, the Ten passed a law forbidding its members from interfering in scuola elections. See ASV, Consiglio dei Dieci, Deliberazioni Miste, Register 10, fols. 39r, 40v.

44. ASV, Senato, Deliberazioni Miste, Register 16, fol. 16r.

45. Ibid., fol. 83v.

46. Ibid., Register 17, fol. 69r. Some of these deliberations have been published in Cessi and Brunetti, eds., *Consiglio dei Rogati (Senato)*.

47. Sebellico, *Felice de Merlis*, xxxvi.

48. Ibid.

49. ASV, Maggior Consiglio, Deliberazioni, Register 17 (Spiritus), fol. 111v. The change is reflected in the records of the Senate. See, for example, ASV, Senato, Deliberazioni Miste, Register 20, fols. 85r, 90r.

50. Printed in Archivio di Stato di Venezia, *Dalla Guerra di Chioggia*," 84–

85. For the poveri del pevere, see Pullan, *Rich and Poor*, 214–15.

51. ASV, Maggior Consiglio, Deliberazioni, Register 19 (Novella), fols. 190r–190v, 191v, 198v.

52. Ibid., Register 21 (Leona), fols. 24v, 35r, 86r, 100v. The quotation is on fol. 86r.

53. ASV, Senato, Deliberazioni Miste, Register 16, fols. 83v, 99v; Register 17, fol. 69r.

54. Hence the derivation of "imbroglio." See Finlay, *Politics in Renaissance Venice*, 22–29. For the fluidity of patron-client ties in complex societies, see Wolf, "Patron-Client Relations," 18.

55. ASV, Senato, Deliberazioni Miste, Register 18, fols. 37v, 48r, 73v, 87v; Register 20, fol. 4v. For another example, see Bertanza, *Documenti*, 61.

56. D. V. Kent and F. W. Kent, *Neighbors and Neighborhood*.

57. Cited in Hazlitt, *Venetian Republic* 1: 847–48.

58. See Chojnacki, "Patrician Women"; and Cecchetti, "La donna nel medioevo," 33–69, 307–49. For women investors, see Lane, "Investment and Usury," 59; and Arcangeli, "La commenda a Venezia," 136.

59. See Hughes, Review of Ruggiero, *Violence*, 225. For a discussion of honor in Venetian society, see Ruggiero, *Boundaries of Eros*, 17–22.

60. Part of this treatise, which was written to celebrate the marriage of Lorenzo de' Medici and Ginevra Cavalcanti, can be found in Kohl and Witt, eds., *Earthly Republic*, 179–228. Citation on 216.

61. Ibid., 217.

62. For a discussion of the customs surrounding births in Venice, see Martin, "Out of the Shadow," 27–28. A mid-fifteenth-century Florentine *desco da parto* (birth salver) shows a group of women going to visit a mother and her newborn child. It is reproduced in Wohl, *Paintings of Domenico Veneziano*, plate 176.

For an instance of women caring for the dead, see ASV, Signori di Notte al Criminal, *Processi*, Register 7, fols. 60v–62r. In her will, Lucia, wife of Andreolo Corner, left four soldi di piccoli for each of six "mulieribus que vigilabunt corpus meum." See ASV, CI, Busta 20, notary Bartolomeo fu Benvenuto, parchment, 1 July 1382.

63. For Cecilia's will, see ASV, CI, Busta 34, notary Giacomo Cavalier, protocol 41, fol. 36r, 28 December 1388. Zana's will is in ASV, CI, Busta 186, notary Simeon, protocol C, fol. 4v, 21 December 1371.

64. For Fiordelise's family background, see ASV, CI, Busta 34, notary Giacomo Cavalier, protocol 41, fol. 44v, 28 July 1395; for the adjoining properties, see ibid., unbound parchment 25, 12 August 1390.

65. ASV, NT, Busta 335, notary Bortolo da Venezia, testament, 2 March 1389; ASV, NT, Busta 947, notary Henricus Salamon, protocol, testament 202, 10 October 1427.

66. ASV, NT, Busta 467, notary Giacomo Cavalier, unbound testament, 17 July 1400. For Agnesina's history, see da Mosto, *I dogi*, 147.

67. Chojnacki, "Dowries and Kinsmen." Richard Trexler has identified a similar role for women and girls in Florence. He notes that they "served in a sense as the liminal bridges between different powers, serving to disarm visitors and permit communication between males." Trexler, *Public Life*, 236.

68. The Procurator of San Marco Pietro Mocenigo had twenty-six people in his household; Procurator Andrea Morosini, twenty-five. See ASV, Maggior Consiglio, Deliberazioni, Register 21 (Leona), fols. 45v–46r; Register 17 (Spiritus), fol. IIIv. Not much work has been done on the patrician household. See, however, the remarks in Luzzatto, "Il costo della vita," 288–89; J. Davis, *Venetian Family*, 2–8; and Lane, *Andrea Barbarigo*, 11–44.

69. Kohl and Witt, *Earthly Republic*, 215–220.

70. It was common practice in Tuscany for children to be sent out of the city to wet nurses. See Ross, "Middle-Class Child," 184–96. However, a contract in the acts of notary Nicola de Boateriis indicates that in at least some instances, wet nurses in Venice took up residence in the houses of their employers. See Lombardo, *Nicola de Boateriis*, doc. 294.

Evidence of the close ties to wet nurses is found in the will of presbyter Giovanni Foscarini. He left eight ducats to the son of his wet nurse Maria whom he described as "fratri meo de lacte." ASV, NT, Busta 447, notary Ludovico Falcon, unbound testament 42, 8 November 1360.

71. See Origo, "Domestic Enemy," 321–66; and Stuard, "Slavery in Medieval Ragusa," 155–71.

72. A good example of the variety of people living in one patrician palace is the *palazzo* Morosini at San Samuele. Tenants included a sailor, a shoemaker, a tailor, a textile worker, and others. See ASV, Signori di Notte al Criminal, Processi, Register 7, fols. 86v–88v.

73. An excellent example of the feelings of loyalty engendered in the courtyards of Venice is an incident that occurred in 1365 when a schoolmaster named Egidio told a certain Giacoma, who lived at the Morosini palace, not to draw water from the well of the Mocenigo palace ("in ipsa curte"). See ASV, Signori di Notte al Criminal, Processi, Register 9, fols. 47v–48r.

74. ASV, NT, Busta 819, notary Antonio Polo, protocol, fols. 3v–4r, 11 October 1336; ASV, NT, Busta 545, notary Lorenzo Buscareno, protocol, testament 50, 7 February 1390mv; ASV, NT, Busta 827, notary Stefano Pianigo, protocol, 3 April 1349; ASV, NT, Busta 645, notary Conte di Bertoldi, unbound testament 137, 10 August 1392.

75. ASV, NT, Busta 645, notary Conte di Bertoldi, unbound testament 137, 10 August 1392.

76. ASV, NT, Busta 567, notary Bartolomeo fu Benvenuto, unbound parchment, 17 November 1384.

77. ASV, NT, Busta 545, notary Lorenzo Buscareno, protocol, testament 6, 16 August 1404.

78. Sebellico, *Felice de Merlis* doc. 1102; ASV, NT, Busta 467, notary Giacomo Cavalier, unbound testament, 2 dates: 8 September 1395, 27 April 1400.

79. Sebellico, *Felice de Merlis*, doc. 1100.

80. ASV, CI, Busta 156, notary Giovanni Rizzo, unbound parchment, 13 August 1342.

81. Ibid. (Beriola Morosini); ibid., 29 August 1343 (Marchesina Contarini).

82. ASV, CI, Busta 128, notary Nicolò Sant'Angelo, protocol B, fols. 2r–2v, 17 December 1368; ASV, CI, Busta 34, notary Giacomo Cavalier, protocol 41, fol. 36r, 28 December 1388.

83. ASV, CI, Busta 143, notary Stefano Pianigo, protocol, fol. 12v, 27 September 1350, 18 October 1350.

84. ASV, NT, Busta 447, notary Ludovico Falcon, protocol, fols. 8r-8v, 8 October 1358; ASV, CI, Busta 69, notary Damiano fu Cristoforo, protocol, testament 141, 20 January 1383mv. Noblewoman Maria Falier asked that her property be converted into a hospital for poor women after her death. See ASV, NT, Busta 364, notary Basilius Darvasio, protocol, fol. 34r, 21 May 1405.

85. Sebellico, *Felice de Merlis*, doc. 1088.

86. ASV, NT, Busta 447, notary Ludovico Falcon, protocol, fol. 7v, 10 September 1358; ASV, NT, Busta 645, notary Conte di Bertoldi, unbound testament 137, 10 August 1392; ASV, NT, Busta 827, notary Stefano Pianigo, protocol, 3 April 1349.

87. ASV, CI, Busta 166, notary Fantin Rizzo, protocol IV, acts dated 7 November 1375. The wills of patrician women contain bequests to popolano women who are not described in any way that allows us to identify the ties between them and the testators. To cite just one example: Ysabeta da Mosto left bequests to donna Caterina Turlon, to donna Tota Bono, and to Caterina Tanoligo. If one considers these bequests, then the incidence of patrician women patronizing popolano women is even greater. For da Mosto's will, see ASV, NT, Busta 447, notary Ludovico Falcon, protocol, fols. 8r-8v, 8 October 1358.

88. ASV, NT 567, notary Bartolomeo fu Benvenuto, unbound parchment, 4 September 1398; ASV, CI, Busta 156, notary Giovanni Rizzo, unbound parchment, 29 August 1343.

89. For the idea of honor accruing to the person who helps dower poor girls, see Taylor, "Gentile da Fabriano," 329. For a similar practice in Ragusa, see Stuard, "Slavery in Medieval Ragusa," 167-68.

Anthropologist Eric Wolf notes that the exchange of goods and services that is central to patron-client ties is often very unequal. While the client often receives tangible benefits, the patron tends to receive intangible ones, including demonstrations of esteem (honor). See Wolf, "Patron-Client Relations," 16-17.

90. In 1377 Biachino de Gaffa, a former slave, married Lucia de Rossia, also a former slave. Lucia had been the slave of nobleman Giacobello Querini; her dowry was sixty ducats. ASV, CI, Busta 93, notary Giuliano fu Nicolò, protocol, fol. 11r, 9 March 1377. Nobleman Nicoleto Trevisan left a bequest for his slave Calana to marry. The records of his estate show that she married a cobbler. ASV, PSM, de Ultra, Commissarie, Commissaria of Nicolò Trevisan da San Giacomo dall'Orio, Busta 275, notebook with testament, receipt dated 4 February 1342mv.

91. ASV, CI, Busta 186, notary Simeon, protocol B, fol. 8r, June 1361; ASV, NT, Busta 567, notary Bartolomeo fu Benvenuto, unbound testaments, 8 April 1394; 25 April 1367; 23 August 1378.

92. Diambra selected Dandolo as her sole executor. She also left the balance of her estate at Dandolo's discretion. ASV, NT, Busta 982, notary Andrea presbiter Santa Trinità, protocol, testament 45, 15 April 1320. Beatrice's other executors were her husband and her comother. Ibid., testament 62, 19 September 1327.

In her will Donina, wife of wealthy popolano Andrea Borsa, left sixteen ducats to increase the estate of a certain Armelina, who named Donina as her executor. Donina noted that Armelina "used to live in our houses" (habitabat in nostris domibus). ASV, NT, Busta 575, notary Giorgio de Gibellino, unbound testament 692, 29 July 1400.

93. Steno's will is published in Bernardi, *Antichi testamenti*, fasc. 6 (1887): 19–29. See, for example, the wills of Maddalena, widow of Bertuccio Malipiero, and Eufemia, wife of Giovanni da Mosto. ASV, CI, Busta 199, notary Pietro della Turre (Torre), unbound parchment, 3 June 1340 (?); Sebellico, *Felice de Merlis*, doc. 1116.

94. I analyzed 39 wills of patrician men and 61 wills of patrician women.

95. Of the 39 men's wills, 9 left bequests to the poor of the home parish; 16 left money to dower poor girls. Of the 61 women's wills, 8 left bequests to the poor of the parish; 4 left money to dower poor girls.

96. Of those naming non-nobles, women left, on average, bequests to 3.4 non-nobles; men left bequests to 3.1 non-nobles. The presence of Doge Steno's will may skew the figures somewhat. He left bequests to 18 non-nobles—8 more than the next highest testator, Engoldisa Falier. If his will is not included, the number of non-nobles named in patrician men's wills drops to an average of 2.4. Steno's generosity to non-nobles may have been in part because he felt obliged as doge to demonstrate largesse and in part because as the last of his family he had no immediate relatives to whom he could bequeath his estate. See da Mosto, *I dogi*, 153–54.

97. In his will, Giovanni Vallaresso left a bequest of clothes for poor persons, but he specifically stated that it was not to be given to anyone "per aliqua amicicia." See ASV, NT, Busta 982, notary Andrea presbiter, protocol, testament 92, 13 January 1337mv. Maria Orio included similar restrictions in her will. ASV, NT, Busta 819, notary Antonio Polo, protocol, fols 3v–4r, 11 October 1336.

98. da Mosto's will is published in Bernardi, *Antichi testamenti*, fasc. 1 (1882): 27–32. In her will, Richiolda Tiepolo entrusted her charitable bequests to her only female executor, her daughter Cecilia. The other executors were her brother, her nephew, and her son-in-law. See Sebellico, *Felice de Merlis*, doc. 1086.

99. Susan Stuard argues that the ties between former slaves and servants and noble families in Ragusa were strong and that these ties positively affected "the social life of the entire community." However, her contention that "working class families [in Ragusa] were substantially more heedful of noble preferences and purposes than working class families in other communities" needs further examination. See Stuard, "Slavery in Medieval Ragusa," 170.

100. Anthropologists posit a linear model of patronage development and transformation. They suggest that in traditional societies relations between patrons and clients are personal and the favors exchanged between them tangible. For example, the use of land will be exchanged for political support. But as societies modernize and a bureaucratic state structure emerges, patronage is transformed. The patron delivers fewer tangible benefits and becomes instead an intermediary between the client and the state. His role becomes less the distribution of favors and more the exercise of influence. The Venetian example suggests the two can operate simultaneously. See Wolf, "Patron-Client Relations," 17–18; and Weingrod, "Patrons," 381–85.

101. V. Lazzarini, "Aneddoti," 81–83; F. Zago, *Consiglio dei Dieci* 1, register 2, docs. 384, 385, 386, 449, 548.

SEVEN From Community to Hierarchy: The Transformation of Venetian Social Ties

1. Tamba, *Bernardo de Rodulfis*, doc. 378.
2. The estimo of 1379 contains a certain Pantalon, *partidor* from Santa Sofia, who had an assessment of 300 lire. This was almost certainly the same man. Luzzatto, *I prestiti*, doc. 165, p. 169.
3. Pantaleone refers to her as "mia fia d'anema." For the institution of *filia animae*, see Ruggiero, *Boundaries of Eros*, 41, 150–52, 197–98.
4. For Bedoloto, see ASV, Signori di Notte al Criminal, Processi, Register 9, fols. 80r–82v; for Bono, see ASV, Maggior Consiglio, Grazie, Register 9, fol. 17r.
5. ASV, Avogaria di Comun, Raspe, Register 3642 (section beginning 1354), fols. 227v–228r, 316v.
6. Ibid. (section beginning 1345), fol. 119v; (section beginning 1348), fols. 137r, 164r; (section beginning 1354), fols. 254r, 286r.
7. ASV, Signori di Notte al Criminal, Processi, Register 10, fols. 86r–86v.
8. Lazzarini, *Paolo de Bernardo*, 1. Lazzarini paraphrases him as saying, "Hai conosciuto la mia adolescenza vagabonda e discola mentre potevo esser con te, vagavo per le calli e i campielli, coi pescatori, i macellai, e «cum ambubiarum turba»."
9. For the *novi cives*, see Becker, "'Novi Cives' and Florentine Politics," 35–82; and Hyde, *Society and Politics*, 165–77.

For the nonviolence of this group, see Ruggiero, *Violence*, 120–21. There is not a complete congruence between Ruggiero's "important people" and the group I have termed the popolo grande.

10. L. Lazzarini, *Paolo de Bernardo*, 93. See also King, *Venetian Humanism*, 58–63.
11. Tassini, *Curiosità*, 98.
12. ASV, Signori di Notte al Criminal, Processi, Register 7, fols. 3v–4v.
13. The warning reads, "cave quod facias, quia posset essere filius alicuius nobilis, qui faceret tibi displacere."
14. Cited in Ruggiero, *Violence*, 129.
15. Waterbury, "Patrons and Clients," 334. See also Eisenstadt and Roniger, "Patron-Client Relations," 277. I would like to thank Ronald Weissman for these references.
16. Lane, *Venetian Ships*, 146–88; *Venice*, 271.
17. Lane, *Venice*, 12; and R. Zago, *I Nicolotti*.
18. Muir, *Civic Ritual*, 99–100.
19. Daniele di Chinazzo reports in his chronicle that the candidates were compared "l'un con l'altro e metando tuti ch'i haveva più voxe da una parte." See di Chinazzo, *Cronica de la guerra*, 206. See also BNM, Ital. VII, 601 (7950), *Miscellanea veneta*, fol. 45r. Telesforo Bini reports the direct competition of Regla and Paruta. See Bini, *I Lucchesi* 1:239.
20. For a *mattinata*, see ASV, Signori di Notte al Criminal, Processi, Register 10, fols. 92r–92v. For carnival in Venice, see Muir, *Civic Ritual*, 156–81.
21. An analysis of ninety wills of residents of the parish of Santa Trinità for the same period illustrates the same trend. In the period 1297–1347, 20 percent of parishioners left money to their poorer neighbors and 10 percent left

bequests to San Lazzaro; by the period 1382–1423, the figures were exactly reversed.

22. On the impact of the plague in Venice, see Brunetti, "Venezia durante la peste."

23. An example of the 'culture shock' encountered by immigrants is found in a letter of an immigrant from Lucca. In the letter he describes the different dotal customs in Venice. See Bini, *I Lucchesi* 2:377. Immigrants are very visible in the records of the criminal courts. This is perhaps an indication of the difficulties they encountered adapting to life in Venice. See Chojnacki, "Crime, Punishment," 202–18.

24. For the Pesaro sale, see Luzzatto, *I prestiti*, doc. 178 and discussion on p. clxxi; for Carlo, see Mueller, "Effetti," 36.

25. For Morosini, see Mueller, "Effetti," 37; for Regla, Luzzatto, *I prestiti*, doc. 173 and discussion on p. clxxi.

26. Mueller, "Effetti," 37–38; Finlay, *Politics in Renaissance Venice*, 92.

27. Peter Burke has suggested that in the early modern period increased demands of the state raised the political consciousness of the subordinate classes. It seems likely that in the precocious urban environment of Italy such a change occurred even earlier. See Burke, *Popular Culture*, 269.

28. D. Kent, *Rise of the Medici*.

29. Cited in Finlay, *Politics in Renaissance Venice*, 75. The state was geared to the protection of the constituent families. A good example of this was the position of the bowman of the quarterdeck. A post with few real responsibilities, it provided impoverished young noblemen with an opportunity to learn mercantile and maritime skills and to engage in trade. Such an appointment allowed fifteenth-century nobleman Andrea Barbarigo to begin rebuilding the family fortune. See Lane, *Andrea Barbarigo*, 14–15, 17–19, 43–44.

30. Molmenti, *La dogaressa di Venezia*, 141–42.

31. Chojnacki, "In Search," 82, n. 44.

32. Lane, "Enlargement of the Great Council," 241–42; Lane, *Venice*, 253.

33. Muir, *Civic Ritual*, 170; Venturi, "Le compagnie."

34. See Chojnacki, "Political Adulthood," 791–810.

35. Molmenti, *La storia di Venezia* 1:74–75; Lane, *Venice*, 266.

36. Mackenney, "Arti e stato," 140.

37. Martin, "Out of the Shadow."

38. Cracco, "*Relinquere laicis que laicorum sunt.*"

39. Prodi, "Church in Renaissance Venice," 411.

40. Pullan, *Rich and Poor*, 63–83.

41. Bouwsma, *Defense of Republican Liberty*, 60–61; Cessi, *Storia della Repubblica*, 365.

42. See Arslan, *Gothic Architecture*, 146, 154; and Wolters, *La scultura veneziana* 1:46–47, 178–79.

43. ASV, Maggior Consiglio, Deliberazioni, Register 21 (Leona), fol. 238v.

44. Martines, *Power and Imagination*, 139–40, 256, 298, 313–14.

45. Bouwsma, *Defense of Republican Liberty*, 61; Finlay, *Politics in Renaissance Venice*, 43.

Bibliography

Archival Sources
Archivio di Stato di Venezia
Archivio Notarile, Testamenti
  Busta
    54: Cechinus Albertus
    55: Bartolomeo de Arcangelis
    335: Bortolo da Venezia, Simeon
    364: Basilius Darvasio
    380: Nicolò Benedetto
    447: Victor, presbiter San Canciano, Petrus Foscolo, Ludovico Falcon
    467: Giacomo Cavalier
    545: Lorenzo Buscareno
    567: Bartolomeo fu Benvenuto
    568: Bartolomeo fu Benvenuto
    572: Giorgio de Gibellino
    573: Giorgio de Gibellino
    575: Giorgio de Gibellino
    645: Conte di Bertoldi
    819: Antonio Polo, Nicolaus Pelegrino
    827: Stefano Pianigo
    850: Nicolò Bon, Bartolomeo de Recovratis
    858: Marco Raphenellis
    915: Constantino de Cison
    921: Nicolò Saiabianca
    925: Lotus
    947: Henricus Salamon
    982: Nicolaus Verde, Andrea presbiter Santa Trinità
    1023: Ariano Passamonte
    1062: Lorenzo della Torre
    1063: Bertucius Pandin
    1115: Lucianus Zeno
    1226: Fantin Rizzo
Avogaria di Comun, Raspe
  Registers 3641–47
Cancelleria Inferiore, Miscellanea Testamenti
  Busta 22, Notai Diversi
Cancelleria Inferiore, Notai
  Busta
    14: Gregorio Bruno, Bertuccio Sant'Angelo
    16-I: Suriano Belli
    17: Antonio de Belanzinis, Giovanni Barbafella

20: Bartolomeo fu Benvenuto, Bartolomeo di Sant'Angelo
34: Giacomo Cavalier, Pietro de Compostellis
38: Francesco Cavazza
69: Damiano fu Cristoforo
70: Basilius Darvasio
79: Gasparino Favaccio, Ludovico Falcon
87: Nicolò Grimanis
93: Giovanni Gazo, Bartolomeus de Gilberto, Giuliano fu Nicolò
104: Tommaso Luciano fu Agostino
114: Marino San Tomà
119: Servodio Mazor
128: Nicolaus Sant'Angelo
130: Nicolò Nadal
140: Pietro Pino
141: Antonius Polo
143: Stefano Pianigo
156: Giovanni Rizzo
162: Francesco de Recovratis
166: Fantin Rizzo
180: Vivianus
185: Nicolò Staniero
186: Simeon
187: Nicolò Saiabianca
189: Antonio Spinello, Pietro Sagredo
190: Stefano, Enrico Salamon
199: Pietro della Turre (Torre)
201: Tommaso di Tommasi
210: Prospero de Tomasi
219: Vettore
241: Petrus Zane

Cinque Savi Alla Mercanzia
    Register 22 ter, Capitolare degli Estraordinari (formerly Miscellanea Codice 132)
Consiglio dei Dieci, Deliberazioni, Miste
    Register 10
Giudici del Piovego
    Busta 3, Codex Publicorum
Giudici di Petizion, Sentenze e Interdetti
    Register 3
Maggior Consiglio, Deliberazioni
    Register 8 (Magnus/Capricornus); 10 (Presbiter); 12 (Clericus/Civicus); 15 (Fronesis); 17 (Spiritus); 19 (Novella); 21 (Leona); 22 (Ursa)
Maggior Consiglio, Grazie
    Registers, 3–18
Procuratori di San Marco, de Ultra
    Commissarie
    Busta 19, 20, 32, 36, 117A, 211, 243, 275
Procuratori di San Marco, de Ultra, Miscellanea Testamenti
    Busta 1–2
Procuratori di San Marco, Misti
    Commissarie
    Busta 74A, 103A, 119, 179
Scuola Grande di San Giovanni Evangelista
    Tomes 3, 5, 6, 7
Scuola Grande di Santa Maria della Carità
    Tomes 233, 233 bis, 234
Scuola Grande di Santa Maria della Valverde
    Busta A, Mariegole 1, 2, 3

Scuole Piccole
  Busta 24, 57bis, 726
Senato, Deliberazioni Miste
  Registers 15–24, 36–40, 50–52
Signori di Notte al Criminal, Processi
  Registers 7–12

Biblioteca Nazionale Marciana

  Manuscripts
  Ital. VII 15–18 (8304–7), Girolamo Alessandro Capellari Vivaro, *Il campidoglio veneto.*
  Ital. VII 156 (8492), Marco Barbaro, *Libro di nozze patrizie.*
  Ital. VII 601 (7950), *Miscellanea veneta.*
  Ital. VII 925–28 (8594–97), Marco Barbaro, *Genealogie delle famiglie patrizie venete.*
  Ital. VII 2051 (8271), *Cronaca di Venezia dalle origini al 1396.*

Museo Civico Correr

  Manuscripts
  Codice Cicogna 3063, Fascicle 10. *Serie delli Guardiani Grandi della Scuola Grande di San Giovanni Evangelista.*
  Mariegola 17, *Veluderi.*

Printed Sources

Bernardi, J. *Antichi testamenti tratti dagli archivii della Congregazione di Carità di Venezia.* 12 fascicles. Venice: Tipografia della società di M. S. Fra Comp. Tip., 1882–93.
Bertanza, Enrico, ed. *Documenti per la storia della cultura in Venezia.* Vol. I, *Maestri, scuole e scolari in Venezia fino al 1500.* Monumenti Storici della R. Deputazione Veneta di Storia Patria, ser. I, vol. 12. Venice, 1907.
Bertanza, Enrico, and Lazzarini, Vittorio, eds. *Il dialetto veneziano fino alla morte di Dante Alighieri, 1321.* Reprint. Bologna: Forni Editore, 1969.
Cessi, Roberto, ed. *Deliberazioni del Maggior Consiglio di Venezia.* 3 vols. Reprint. Bologna: Forni Editore, 1970.
———. *Gli statuti veneziani di Jacopo Tiepolo del 1242 e le loro glosse.* Venice: Officine Grafiche Carlo Ferrari, 1938.
Cessi, R., and Sambin, P., eds. *Le deliberazioni del Consiglio dei Rogati (Senato): Serie "Mixtorum."* Vol. 1, *Libri I–XIV.* Monumenti Storici della Deputazione di Storia Patria per le Venezie, n.s., vol. 15. Venice: A Spese della Deputazione, 1960.
Cessi, R., and Brunetti, M., ed. *Le deliberazioni del Consiglio dei Rogati (Senato): Serie "Mixtorum."* Vol. 2, *Libri XV–XVI.* Monumenti Storici

della Deputazione di Storia Patria per le Venezie, n.s., vol. 16. Venice: A Spese della Deputazione, 1961.

da Canal, Martin. *Les Estoires de Venise: Cronaca veneziana in lingua francese dalle origini al 1275.* Edited by Alberto Limentani. Florence: Leo S. Olschki, 1972.

Danduli, Andreae. *Chronica per extensum descripta.* Edited by Ester Pastorello. Rerum Italicarum Scriptores, vol. 12, pt. 1. Bologna: Zanichelli, 1938.

de Monacis, Laurentii. *Chronicon de rebus venetis ab u.c. ad annum MCCCLIV.* Edited by Flaminius Cornelius. Venice: Typographia Remondiniana, 1758.

di Chinazzo, Daniele. *Cronica de la guerra da Veniciani a Zenovesi.* Edited by Vittorio Lazzarini. Monumenti Storici della Deputazione di Storia Patria per le Venezie, n.s., vol. 11. Venice: A Spese della Deputazione, 1958.

Dorini, Umberto, and Bertelè, Tommaso, eds. *Il libro dei conti di Giacomo Badoer (Costantinopoli, 1436-1440).* Rome: Istituto Poligraphico dello Stato, 1956.

Favaro, Elena, ed. *Cassiere della bolla ducale: Grazie—Novus Liber (1299-1305).* Fonti per la Storia de Venezia. Venice: Il Comitato Editore, 1962.

Lombardo, Antonino, ed. *Le deliberazioni del Consiglio del XL della Repubblica di Venezia.* 3 vols. Monumenti Storici della Deputazione di Storia Patria per le Venezie, n.s., vols. 9, 12, 20. Venice: A Spese della Deputazione, 1957-67.

———. *Nicola de Boateriis, notaio in Famagosta e Venezia (1355-1365).* Fonti per la Storia di Venezia. Venice: Il Comitato Editore, 1973.

Luzzatto, Gino. *I prestiti della Repubblica di Venezia (sec. XIII-XV).* Documenti finanziari della Repubblica di Venezia, ser. 3. Padua: A. Dragi, 1929.

Monticolo, G. *I capitolari delle arti veneziane sottoposte alla Giustizia Vecchia dalle origini al MCCCXXX.* 3 vols. Fonti per la Storia d'Italia. Rome: Istituto Storico Italiano, 1896-1914.

Morozzo della Rocca, Raimondo, ed. *Lettere di mercanti a Pignol Zucchello (1336-1350).* Fonti per la Storia di Venezia. Venice: Il Comitato Editore, 1957.

Morozzo della Rocca, R., and Lombardo, A., eds. *Documenti del commercio veneziano nei secoli XI-XIII.* 2 vols. Turin: Libraria Italiana, 1940.

Roberti, Melchiorre. *Le magistrature giudiziarie veneziane e i loro capitolari fino al 1300.* 3 vols. Monumenti Storici della R. Deputazione Veneta de Storia Patria. Venice: Tip. Emiliana, 1907-11.

Rosada, Maurizio, ed. *S. Maria Formosa.* Fonti per la Storia di Venezia. Venice: Il Comitato Editore, 1972.

Sansovino, Francesco. *Venetia città nobilissima et signolare.* 1663. Reprint. Farnborough: Gregg International Publishers Limited, 1968.

Sebellico, Andreina Bondi, ed. *Felice de Merlis, prete e notaio in Venezia ed Ayas (1315–1348).* Fonti per la Storia di Venezia. Venice: Il Comitato Editore, 1973–78.

Strina, Bianca Lanfranchi, ed. *Codex Publicorum (Codice del Piovego).* Vol. 1. Fonti per la Storia di Venezia. Venice: Comitato per la Pubblicazione, 1985.

Stussi, Alfredo, ed. *Testi veneziani del Duecento e dei primi del Trecento.* Pisa: Nistri-Lischi Editori, 1965.

Tamba, Giorgio, ed. *Bernardo de Rodulfis, notaio in Venezia (1392–1399).* Fonti per la Storia di Venezia. Venice: Il Comitato Editore, 1974.

Tiepolo, Maria Francesca, ed. *Domenico prete di S. Maurizio, notaio in Venezia (1309–1316).* Fonti per la Storia di Venezia. Venice: Il Comitato Editore, 1970.

Volumen statutorum, legum, ac iurium d. venetorum. Venice, 1564.

Zago, Ferruccio, ed. *Consiglio dei Dieci: Deliberazioni Miste.* Vol. 1. *Registri I–II (1310–1324).* Fonti per la Storia di Venezia. Venice: Il Comitato Editore, 1962.

——. *Consiglio dei Dieci: Deliberazioni Miste.* Vol. 2. *Registri III–IV (1325–1335).* Fonti per la Storia di Venezia. Venice: Il Comitato Editore, 1968.

Secondary Works

Arcangeli, A. "La commenda a Venezia specialmente nel secolo XIV." *Rivista italiana per le scienze giuridiche* 33 (1901): 107–64.

Archivio di Stato di Venezia. *Dalla Guerra di Chioggia alla Pace di Torino, 1377–1381.* Venice: Tip. Helvetia, 1981.

Arslan, Edoardo. *Gothic Architecture in Venice.* Translated by Anne Engel. London: Phaidon, 1972.

Becker, Marvin B. "An Essay on the 'Novi Cives' and Florentine Politics, 1343–1382." *Mediaeval Studies* 24 (1962): 35–82.

Bellavitis, Giorgio, and Romanelli, Giandomenico. *Venezia.* Rome: Editori Laterza, 1985.

Bellemo, V. "La vita e i tempi di Benintendi de' Ravagnani Cancelliere Grande della Veneta Repubblica." *Nuovo archivio veneto,* n.s., 23 (1912): 237–84; 24 (1912): 54–95.

Beloch, Karl Julius. *Bevölkerungsgeschichte Italiens.* 3 vols. Berlin: De Gruyter, 1937–61.

Beltrami, Daniele. *Storia della popolazione di Venezia dalla fine del secolo XVI alla caduta della Repubblica.* Padua: Cedam, 1954.

Betto, Bianca. "Linee di politica matrimoniale nella nobiltà veneziana fino al XV secolo. Alcune note genealogiche e l'esempio della famiglia Mocenigo." *Archivio storico italiano* 139 (1981): 3–64.

Bini, Telesforo. *I Lucchesi a Venezia: Alcuni studi sopra i secoli XIII e XIV.* 2 vols. Lucca: Felice Bertini, 1853–56.

Bishop, Morris, trans. *Letters from Petrarch*. Bloomington: Indiana University Press, 1966.
Borsari, Silvano. "Una famiglia veneziana del medioevo: Gli Ziani." *Archivio veneto*, 5th ser., 110 (1978): 27–72.
Botero, Giovanni. *The Reason of State*. Translated by P. J. and D. P. Waley. New Haven: Yale University Press, 1956.
Bouwsma, William J. *Venice and the Defense of Republican Liberty*. Berkeley: University of California Press, 1968.
Bowsky, William M. "The Impact of the Black Death upon Sienese Government and Society." *Speculum* 39 (1964): 1–34.
Brown, Judith C. "A Woman's Place Was in the Home: Women's Work in Renaissance Tuscany." In *Rewriting the Renaissance: The Discourses of Sexual Difference in Early Modern Europe*, edited by Margaret W. Ferguson, Maureen Quilligan, and Nancy J. Vickers, 206–24. Chicago: University of Chicago Press, 1986.
Brown, Peter. *The Cult of the Saints: Its Rise and Function in Latin Christianity*. Chicago: University of Chicago Press, 1981.
Brucker, Gene A. "The Ciompi Revolution." In *Florentine Studies: Politics and Society in Renaissance Florence*, edited by Nicolai Rubinstein, 314–56. London: Faber and Faber, 1968.
———. *Renaissance Florence*. Rev. ed. Berkeley: University of California Press, 1983.
Brunello, Franco. *Arti e mestieri a Venezia nel medioevo e nel rinascimento*. Vicenza: Neri Pozza Editore, 1980.
Brunetti, Mario. "Venezia durante la peste del 1348." *Ateneo veneto* 32 (1909): pt. 1, 289–311; pt. 2, 5–42.
Burke, Peter. *Popular Culture in Early Modern Europe*. New York: Harper and Row, 1978.
Cappelletti, Giuseppe. *Storia della Repubblica di Venezia*. 13 vols. Venice: Giuseppe Antonelli Editore, 1848–55.
Cecchetti, Bartolomeo. "La donna nel medioevo a Venezia." *Archivio veneto* 31 (1886): 33–69, 307–49.
———. "Funerali e sepolture dei Veneziani antichi." *Archivio veneto* 34 (1887): 265–84.
———. "Nomi di pittori e lapidici antichi." *Archivio veneto* 33 (1887): 43–65.
———. *La Republica di Venezia e la Corte di Roma nei rapporti della religione*. 2 vols. Venice: P. Naratovich, 1874.
———. *La vita dei Veneziani nel 1300*. Bologna: A. Forni Editore, 1980.
Cessi, Roberto. *La politica dei lavori pubblici della Repubblica Veneta*. Rome: Libreria dello Stato, 1925.
———. *Storia della Repubblica di Venezia*. Reprint in 1 vol. Florence: Giunti Martello, 1981.
Cessi, Roberto, and Alberti, Annibale. *Rialto: L'isola, il ponte, il mercato*. Bologna: N. Zanichelli, 1934.
Chojnacki, Stanley. "Crime, Punishment, and the Trecento Venetian

State." In *Violence and Civil Disorder in Italian Cities, 1200–1500*, edited by Lauro Martines, 184–228. Berkeley: University of California Press, 1972.

———. "Dowries and Kinsmen in Early Renaissance Venice." *Journal of Interdisciplinary History* 4 (1975): 571–600.

———. "In Search of the Venetian Patriciate: Families and Factions in the Fourteenth Century." In *Renaissance Venice*, edited by J. R. Hale, 47–90. London: Faber and Faber, 1974.

———. "Kinship Ties and Young Patricians in Fifteenth-Century Venice." *Renaissance Quarterly* 38 (1985): 240–70.

———. "Patrician Women in Early Renaissance Venice." *Studies in the Renaissance* 21 (1974): 176–203.

———. "Political Adulthood in Fifteenth-Century Venice." *American Historical Review* 91 (1986): 791–810.

Cohn, Samuel Kline, Jr. *The Laboring Classes in Renaissance Florence.* New York: Academic Press, 1980.

———. Review of *Violence in Early Renaissance Venice* by Guido Ruggiero. *Journal of Social History* 15 (1981): 298–301.

Comune di Venezia. *Arti e mestieri nella Repubblica di Venezia.* Verona: Editoriale Bortolazzi-Steri, 1980.

Contento, Aldo. "Il censimento della popolazione sotto la Repubblica Veneta." *Nuovo archivio veneto* 19 (1900): 5–42, 179–240; 20 (1900): 5–96, 171–235.

Cornelio [Cornaro], Flaminio. *Ecclesiae venetae antiquiis monumentis nunc etiam primum editis illustratae.* 13 vols. Venice: J. B. Pasquale, 1749.

———. *Notizie storiche delle chiese e monasteri di Venezia, e di Torcello tratte dalle chiese veneziane, e torcellane.* Padua: Stamperia del Seminario, 1758.

Cracco, Giorgio. "*Relinquere laicis que laicorum sunt:* Un intervento di Eugenio IV contro i preti-notai di Venezia." *Bolletino dell'Istituto di Storia della Società e dello Stato Veneziano* 3 (1961): 179–89.

———. *Società e stato nel medioevo veneziano (secoli XII–XIV).* Florence: Leo S. Olschki, 1967.

Craven, Paul, and Wellman, Barry. "The Network City." In *The Community: Approaches and Applications*, edited by Marcia Pelly Effrat, 57–88. New York: Free Press, 1974.

Crouzet-Pavan, Elisabeth. "Murano à la fin du Moyen Age: Spécificité ou intégration dans l'espace vénitien?" *Revue historique* 268 (1982): 45–92.

da Mosto, Andrea. *L'Archivio di Stato di Venezia.* 2 vols. Rome: Biblioteca d'arte editrice, 1937–41.

———. *I dogi di Venezia nella vita pubblica e privata.* Milan: A. Martello, 1960.

Davis, James C. *The Decline of the Venetian Nobility as a Ruling Class.* Baltimore: Johns Hopkins Press, 1962.

---. *A Venetian Family and Its Fortune, 1500–1900*. Philadelphia: American Philosophical Society, 1975.

Davis, Natalie Zemon. "The Sacred and the Body Social in Sixteenth-Century Lyon." *Past and Present* 90 (1981): 40–70.

Delort, R. "Un aspect du commerce vénitien au xve siècle: Andrea Barbarigo et le commerce des fourrures (1430–1440)." *Le Moyen Age* 71 (1965): 29–70, 247–73.

Demus, Otto. *The Mosaics of San Marco in Venice*. 2 pts. in 4 vols. Chicago: University of Chicago Press, 1984.

Effrat, Marcia Pelly. "Approaches to Community: Conflicts and Complementarities." In *The Community: Approaches and Applications*, edited by Marcia Pelly Effrat, 1–32. New York: Free Press, 1974.

Eisenstadt, S. N., and Roniger, Luis. "The Study of Patron-Client Relations and Recent Developments in Sociological Theory." In *Political Clientelism, Patronage and Development*, edited by S. N. Eisenstadt and René Lemarchand, 271–95. Beverly Hills, Calif.: Sage Publications, 1981.

Ell, Stephen R. "Citizenship and Immigration in Venice, 1305 to 1500." Ph.D. diss., University of Chicago, 1976.

Fano, N. "Ricerche sull'arte della lana a Venezia nell xiii e xiv secolo." *Archivio veneto*, 5th ser., 18 (1936): 73–213.

Fasoli, Gina. "Comune veneciarum." In *Venezia dalla Prima Crociata alla Conquista di Costantinopoli del 1204*, 71–102. Florence: Sansoni, 1965.

Ferro, Marco. *Dizionario del diritto comune e veneto*. 2d ed. in 2 vols. Venice: Andrea Santini e Figlio, 1845–47.

Finlay, Robert. *Politics in Renaissance Venice*. New Brunswick, N. J.: Rutgers University Press, 1980.

Francastel, Galienne. "Une peinture anti-hérétique à Venise?" *Annales E.S.C.* 20 (1965): 1–17.

Fulin, R. "Cinque testamenti di pittori ignoti del sec. xiv." *Archivio veneto* 12 (1876): 130–50.

Gallicciolli, Giovanni Battista. *Delle memorie venete antiche profane ed ecclesiastiche*. 8 vols. Venice: D. Fracasso, 1795.

Gallo, R. "Una famiglia patrizia: I Pisani ed i palazzi di S. Stefano e di Stra." *Archivio veneto*, 5th ser., 34–35 (1944): 65–228.

Geary, Patrick J. *Furta Sacra: Thefts of Relics in the Central Middle Ages*. Princeton: Princeton University Press, 1978.

Goffen, Rona. *Piety and Patronage in Renaissance Venice: Bellini, Titian, and the Franciscans*. New Haven: Yale University Press, 1986.

Goldthwaite, Richard A. *The Building of Renaissance Florence: An Economic and Social History*. Baltimore: Johns Hopkins University Press, 1980.

Grossi Bianchi, Luciano, and Poleggi, Ennio. *Una città portuale del medioevo: Genova nei secoli x–xvi*. Genoa: Sagep Editrice, 1979.

Hazlitt, W. Carew. *The Venetian Republic: Its Rise, Its Growth, and Its*

Fall: A.D. 409–1797. 2 vols. 1915 Reprint. New York: AMS Press Inc., 1966.
Heers, Jacques. *Family Clans in the Middle Ages*. Translated by Barry Herbert. New York: North-Holland Publishing Co., 1977.
―――. "Urbanisme et structure sociale à Gênes au Moyen-Age." In *Société et économie à Gênes (xive–xve siècles)*, 371–412. London: Variorum Reprints, 1979.
Herlihy, David. "Family and Property in Renaissance Florence." In *The Medieval City*, edited by Harry A. Miskimin, David Herlihy, and A. L. Udovitch, 3–24. New Haven: Yale University Press, 1977.
―――. "The Population of Verona in the First Century of Venetian Rule." In *Renaissance Venice*, edited by J. R. Hale, 91–120. London: Faber and Faber, 1974.
Herlihy, David, and Klapisch, Christiane. *Les Toscans et leur familles. Une étude du catasto florentin de 1427*. Paris: Editions de l'École des Hautes Études en Sciences Sociales, 1978.
Hillery, George A., Jr. "Definitions of Community: Areas of Agreement." *Rural Sociology* 20 (1955): 111–23.
Howard, Deborah. *Jacopo Sansovino: Architecture and Patronage in Renaissance Venice*. New Haven: Yale University Press, 1975.
Hufton, Olwen. "Women and the Family Economy in Eighteenth-Century France." *French Historical Studies* 9 (1975): 1–22.
Hughes, Diane Owen. "Domestic Ideals and Social Behavior: Evidence from Medieval Genoa." In *The Family in History*, edited by Charles E. Rosenberg, 115–45. Philadelphia: University of Pennsylvania Press, 1975.
―――. "Kinsmen and Neighbors in Medieval Genoa." In *The Medieval City*, edited by Harry A. Miskimin, David Herlihy, and A. L. Udovitch, 95–112. New York: Yale University Press, 1977.
―――. Review of *Violence in Early Renaissance Venice* by Guido Ruggiero. *Speculum* 58 (1983): 223–26.
―――. "Toward Historical Ethnography: Notarial Records and Family History in the Middle Ages." *Historical Methods Newsletter* 7 (1974): 61–71.
Hyde, J. K. *Society and Politics in Medieval Italy*. New York: St. Martin's Press, 1973.
Kedar, Benjamin Z. "The Genoese Notaries of 1382: The Anatomy of an Urban Occupational Group." In *The Medieval City*, edited by Harry A. Miskimin, David Herlihy, and A. L. Udovitch, 73–94. New Haven: Yale University Press, 1977.
―――. *Merchants in Crisis: Genoese and Venetian Men of Affairs and the Fourteenth-Century Depression*. New Haven: Yale University Press, 1976.
Kent, Dale. *The Rise of the Medici: Faction in Florence, 1426–1434*. Oxford: Oxford University Press, 1978.
Kent, D. V., and Kent, F. W. *Neighbors and Neighborhood in Renais-*

sance Florence: The District of the Red Lion in the Fifteenth Century. Locust Valley, N.Y.: J. J. Augustin, 1982.

———. "A Self-Disciplining Pact Made by the Peruzzi Family of Florence (June 1433)." *Renaissance Quarterly* 34 (1981): 337–55.

Kent, F. W. *Household and Lineage in Renaissance Florence: The Family Life of the Capponi, Ginori, and Rucellai.* Princeton: Princeton University Press, 1977.

———. "The Rucellai Family and Its Loggia." *Journal of the Warburg and Courtauld Institutes* 35 (1972): 397–401.

King, Margaret Leah. "Caldiera and the Barbaros on Marriage and the Family: Humanist Reflections on Venetian Realities." *Journal of Medieval and Renaissance Studies* 6 (1976): 19–50.

———. *Venetian Humanism in an Age of Patrician Dominance.* Princeton: Princeton University Press, 1986.

Kirshner, Julius. "Pursuing Honor While Avoiding Sin: The Monte delle doti of Florence." *Quaderni di "Studi senesi"* 41 (1978): 1–82.

Klapisch, Christiane. "'Parenti, amici e vicini': Il territorio urbano d'una famiglia mercantile nel xv secolo." *Quaderni storici* 33 (1976): 953–82.

Klapisch, Christiane, and Demonet, Michel. "'A uno pane e uno vino': La famille rurale toscane au debut du xve siècle." *Annales E.S.C.* 27 (1972): 873–901.

Kohl, Benjamin G., and Witt, Ronald G. *The Earthly Republic: Italian Humanists on Government and Society.* Philadelphia: University of Pennsylvania Press, 1978.

Kuehn, Thomas. *Emancipation in Late Medieval Florence.* New Brunswick, N.J.: Rutgers University Press, 1982.

Labalme, Patricia H. *Bernardo Giustiniani: A Venetian of the Quattrocento.* Rome: Edizioni di Storia e Letteratura, 1969.

Lane, Frederic C. *Andrea Barbarigo: Merchant of Venice, 1418–1449.* Baltimore: Johns Hopkins University Press, 1944.

———. "The Enlargement of the Great Council of Venice." In *Florilegium Historiale: Essays Presented to Wallace K. Ferguson,* edited by J. G. Rowe and W. H. Stockdale, 236–74. Toronto: University of Toronto Press, 1971.

———. "Family Partnerships and Joint Ventures." In *Venice and History: The Collected Papers of Frederic C. Lane,* 36–55. Baltimore: Johns Hopkins University Press, 1966.

———. "Investment and Usury." In *Venice and History: The Collected Papers of Frederic C. Lane,* 56–68. Baltimore: Johns Hopkins University Press, 1966.

———. *Venetian Ships and Shipbuilders of the Renaissance.* Baltimore: Johns Hopkins University Press, 1934.

———. *Venice: A Maritime Republic.* Baltimore: Johns Hopkins University Press, 1973.

Lanfranchi, L., and Zille, G. G. "Il territorio del ducato veneziano dall'

VIII al XII secolo." In *Storia di Venezia* 2: 3–65. Venice: Centro Internazionale delle Arti e del Costume, 1958.

Lazzarini, L. "Amici del Petrarca a Venezia e Treviso." *Archivio veneto*, 5th ser., 14 (1933): 1–14.

———. *Paolo de Bernardo e i primordi dell'umanesimo in Venezia*. Geneva: Leo S. Olschki, 1930.

Lazzarini, V. "Aneddoti della congiura Quirini-Tiepolo." *Nuovo archivio veneto* 10 (1895): 81–91.

———. *Marino Faliero*. Florence: G. C. Sansoni, 1963.

———. "Obbligo di assumere pubblici uffici nelle antiche leggi veneziane." *Archivio veneto*, 5th ser., 19 (1936): 184–98.

———. "Il testamento di Pantaleone Giustinian Patriarca di Costantinopoli (1282, luglio 1)." *Archivio veneto*, 5th ser., 27 (1940): 80–88.

LeRoy Ladurie, Emmanuel. *Montaillou: The Promised Land of Error*. Translated by Barbara Bray. New York: Vintage Books, 1979.

Loenertz, Raymond J. *Les Ghisi: Dynastes vénitiens dans l'Archipel, 1207–1390*. Florence: L. S. Olschki, 1975.

Lopez, Robert S., and Raymond, Irving W. *Medieval Trade in the Mediterranean World*. New York: Columbia University Press, 1955.

Lorenzetti, Giulio. *Venezia e il suo estuario: Guida storico-artistico*. Venice: Bestetti e Tumminelli, 1926.

Luzzatto, Gino. "La commenda nella vita economica dei secoli XIII e XIV con particolare riguardo a Venezia." In *Studi di storia economica veneziana*, 59–79. Padua: Cedam, 1954.

———. "Il costo della vita a Venezia nel Trecento." In *Studi di storia economica veneziana*, 285–297. Padua: Cedam, 1954.

———. *Storia economica de Venezia dall'XI al XVI secolo*. Venice: Centro Internazionale delle Arti e del Costume, 1961.

Lynch, Joseph H. *Godparents and Kinship in Early Medieval Europe*. Princeton: Princeton University Press, 1986.

Mackenney, Richard. "Arti e stato a Venezia tra tardo medio evo e '600." *Studi veneziani*, n.s., 5 (1981): 127–43.

———. "Devotional Confraternities in Renaissance Venice." In *Voluntary Religion*, edited by W. J. Shields and Diana Wood, 85–96. London: Basil Blackwell, 1986.

———. "'In Place of Strife': The Guilds and the Law in Renaissance Venice." *History Today* 34 (May 1984): 17–22.

———. *Tradesmen and Traders: The World of the Guilds in Venice and Europe, c.1250–c.1650*. Totowa, N. J.: Barnes and Noble, 1987.

Maranini, Giuseppe. *La costituzione di Venezia*. 2d ed. in 2 vols. Florence: La Nuova Italia, 1974.

Maretto, Paolo. *L'edilizia gotica veneziana*. Rome: Istituto Poligrafico dello Stato, 1961.

Martin, John. "Out of the Shadow: Heretical and Catholic Women in Renaissance Venice." *Journal of Family History* 10 (1985): 21–33.

Martines, Lauro. *Power and Imagination: City-States in Renaissance Italy.* New York: Vintage Books, 1980.

Mazzi, Giuliana. "Note per una definizione della funzione viaria a Venezia." *Archivio veneto,* 5th ser., 99 (1973): 5–31.

Molho, Anthony. "Cosimo de' Medici: *Pater Patriae* or *Padrino?*" *Stanford Italian Review* 1 (1979): 5–33.

Molmenti, Pompeo G. *La dogaressa di Venezia.* Turin: Roux e Favale, 1884.

———. *La storia di Venezia nella vita privata.* 7th ed. in 3 vols. Trieste: Edizioni LINT, 1973.

———. "Venezia e il clero." *Atti del Reale Istituto Veneto di Scienze, Lettere, ed Arti* 60 (1900–1901): 673–84.

Monticolo, G. *L'ufficio della Giustizia Vecchia a Venezia dalle origini sino al 1330.* Monumenti Storici della R. Deputazione Veneta di Storia Patria, 4th ser., vol. 12. Venice: R. Deputazione Veneta di Storia Patria, 1892.

Mueller, Reinhold C. "Catalogo: Dalla reazione alla prevenzione." In *Venezia e la peste, 1348/1797,* 77–92. Venice: Marsilio Editori, 1979.

———. "Effetti della Guerra di Chioggia (1378–1381) sulla vita economica e sociale di Venezia." *Ateneo veneto,* n.s., 19 (1981): 27–41.

———. "Peste e demografia: Medioevo e rinascimento." In *Venezia e la peste, 1348/1797,* 93–96. Venice: Marsilio Editori, 1979.

———. "The Procurators of San Marco in the Thirteenth and Fourteenth Centuries: A Study of the Office as a Financial and Trust Institution." *Studi veneziani* 13 (1971): 105–220.

Muir, Edward. *Civic Ritual in Renaissance Venice.* Princeton: Princeton University Press, 1981.

Mumford, Lewis. *The City in History: Its Origins, Its Transformations, and Its Prospects.* New York: Harcourt, Brace and World, 1961.

Muratori, Saverio. *Studi per una operante storia urbana di Venezia.* Rome: Istituto Poligrafico dello Stato, 1959.

Najemy, John. *Corporatism and Consensus in Florentine Electoral Politics, 1280–1400.* Chapel Hill: University of North Carolina Press, 1982.

———. Review of *A Medieval Italian Commune: Siena under the Nine, 1287–1355* by William M. Bowsky. *Speculum* 58 (1983): 1029–33.

Neff, Mary. "A Citizen in the Service of the Patrician State: The Career of Zaccaria de' Freschi." *Studi veneziani,* n.s., 5 (1981): 33–61.

Newett, M. Margaret. "The Sumptuary Laws of Venice in the Fourteenth and Fifteenth Centuries." In *Historical Essays,* edited by T. F. Tout and James Tait, 245–78. Manchester: Manchester University Press, 1907.

Origo, Iris. "The Domestic Enemy: The Eastern Slaves in Tuscany in the Fourteenth and Fifteenth Centuries." *Speculum* 30 (1955): 321–66.

———. *The World of San Bernardino.* New York: Harcourt, Brace and World, Inc., 1962.

Pavan, Elisabeth. "Recherches sur la nuit vénitienne à la fin du Moyen Age." *Journal of Medieval History* 7 (1981): 339–56.

Pillinini, G. "Marino Falier e la crisi economica e politica della metà del '300 a Venezia." *Archivio veneto,* 5th ser., 84 (1968): 45–71.
Pincus, Debra. *The Arco Foscari: The Building of a Triumphal Gateway in Fifteenth-Century Venice.* New York: Garland Publishing, Inc., 1976.
Piva, Vittorio. *Il Patriarcato di Venezia e le sue origini.* 2 vols. Venice: Tip. S. Marco and Studium Cattolico Veneziano, 1938–60.
Pozza, Marco. *I Badoer: Una famiglia veneziana dal x al xiii secolo.* Padua: Aldo Francisci Editore, 1982.
Prodi, Paolo. "The Structure and Organization of the Church in Renaissance Venice: Suggestions for Research." In *Renaissance Venice,* edited by J. R. Hale, 409–30. London: Faber and Faber, 1974.
Pullan, Brian. *Rich and Poor in Renaissance Venice.* Cambridge, Mass.: Harvard University Press, 1971.
———. "The Significance of Venice." *Bulletin of the John Rylands University Library of Manchester* 56 (1974): 443–62.
Queller, Donald E. "The Civic Irresponsibility of the Venetian Nobility." In *Economy, Society, and Government in Medieval Italy,* edited by David Herlihy, Robert S. Lopez, and Vsevolod Slessarev, 223–35. Kent, Ohio: Kent State University Press, 1969.
———. *The Venetian Patriciate: Reality versus Myth.* Urbana: University of Illinois Press, 1986.
Rapp, Richard Tilden. *Industry and Economic Decline in Seventeenth-Century Venice.* Cambridge, Mass.: Harvard University Press, 1976.
Robbert, Louise Buenger. "L'inventario di Graziano Gradenigo." *Studi veneziani,* n.s., 5 (1981): 283–310.
Roberti, M. "Di un *Liber Forbannitorum* della fine del Dugento. (Note intorno alla criminalità nel secolo xiii)." *Nuovo archivio veneto,* n.s., 19 (1910): 145–58.
Romanin, S. *Storia documentata di Venezia.* 3rd ed. in 10 vols. Venice: Libreria Filippi Editore, 1973.
Romano, Dennis. "Charity and Community in Early Renaissance Venice." *Journal of Urban History* 11 (1984): 63–82.
———. "*Quod sibi fiat gratia:* Adjustment of Penalties and the Exercise of Influence in Early Renaissance Venice." *Journal of Medieval and Renaissance Studies* 13 (1983): 251–68.
Rosand, David. *Painting in Cinquecento Venice: Titian, Veronese, Tintoretto.* New Haven: Yale University Press, 1982.
Ross, James Bruce. "The Middle-Class Child in Urban Italy, Fourteenth to Early Sixteenth Century." In *The History of Childhood,* edited by Lloyd deMause, 183–228. New York: The Psychohistory Press, 1974.
Ruggiero, Guido. *The Boundaries of Eros: Sex Crime and Sexuality in Renaissance Venice.* New York: Oxford University Press, 1985.
———. "Modernization and the Mythic State in Early Renaissance Venice: The Serrata Revisited." *Viator* 10 (1979): 245–56.
———. "Sexual Criminality in the Early Renaissance: Venice 1338–1358." *Journal of Social History* 8 (1975): 18–37.

———. "The Status of Physicians in Renaissance Venice." *Journal of the History of Medicine and Allied Sciences* 36 (1981): 168–84.
———. "The Ten: Control of Violence and Social Disorder in Trecento Venice." Ph.D. diss., University of California, Los Angeles, 1972.
———. *Violence in Early Renaissance Venice*. New Brunswick, N.J.: Rutgers University Press, 1980.
Sapegno, Natalino, ed. *Poeti minori del Trecento*. Milan: Riccardo Ricciardi Editore, 1952.
Sbriziolo, Lia. "Per la storia delle confraternite veneziane: Dalle Deliberazioni Miste (1310–1476) del Consiglio dei Dieci. *Scolai comunes*, artigiane e nazionali." *Atti dell'Istituto Veneto di Scienze, Lettere ed Arti* 126 (1967–68): 405–42.
Schulz, Juergen. "The Houses of Titian, Arentino, and Sansovino." In *Titian: His World and His Legacy*, edited by David Rosand. 73–118. New York: Columbia University Press, 1982.
———. "Wealth in Mediaeval Venice: The Houses of the Ziani." In *Interpretazioni veneziane: Studi di storia dell'arte in onore di Michelangelo Muraro*, edited by David Rosand, 29–37. Venice: Arsenale Editrice, 1984.
Sjoberg, Gideon. *The Preindustrial City, Past and Present*. New York: The Free Press, 1960.
Spada, Nicolò. "Leggi veneziane sulle industrie chimiche a tutela della salute pubblica dal secolo XIII al XVIII." *Archivio veneto*, 5th ser., 7 (1930): 126–56.
Stone, Lawrence. *The Family, Sex and Marriage in England 1500–1800*. Abridged ed. New York: Harper and Row, 1979.
Stuard, Susan Mosher. "Urban Domestic Slavery in Medieval Ragusa." *Journal of Medieval History* 9 (1983): 155–71.
Tassini, Giuseppe. *Curiosità veneziane*. 8th ed. Venice: Filippi Editore, 1970.
———. "D'una lapide mortuaria conservata nel Civico Museo." *Nuovo archivio veneto* 4 (1892): 389–90.
Taylor, Michael D. "Gentile da Fabriano, St. Nicholas, and an Iconography of Shame." *Journal of Family History* 7 (1982): 321–32.
Tenenti, Alberto. "The Sense of Space and Time in the Venetian World of the Fifteenth and Sixteenth Centuries." In *Renaissance Venice*, edited by J. R. Hale, 17–46. London: Faber and Faber, 1974.
Trebbi, Giuseppe. "La cancelleria veneta nei secoli XVI–XVII." *Annali della Fondazione Luigi Einaudi* 14 (1980): 65–125.
Trexler, Richard C. "Le célibat à la fin du Moyen Age: Les religieuses de Florence." *Annales E.S.C.* 27 (1972): 1329–50.
———. *Public Life in Renaissance Florence*. New York: Academic Press, 1980.
Trincanato, Egle. "Venezia nella storia urbanistica." *Urbanistica* 52 (1968): 7–69.
Turner, Victor, and Turner, Edith. *Image and Pilgrimage in Christian*

Culture: Anthropological Perspectives. New York: Columbia University Press, 1978.

Venturi, Lionello. "Le compagnie della calza (sec. xv–xvi)." *Nuovo archivio veneto* 16 (1908): 161–221; 17 (1909): 140–233.

Waley, Daniel. *The Italian City-Republics.* New York: McGraw-Hill, 1969.

Waterbury, John. "An Attempt to Put Patrons and Clients in Their Place." In *Patrons and Clients in Mediterranean Societies,* edited by Ernest Gellner and John Waterbury, 329–42. London: Duckworth, 1977.

Weingrod, Alex. "Patrons, Patronage, and Political Parties." *Comparative Studies in Society and History* 10 (1968): 377–400.

Weissman, Ronald F. E. *Ritual Brotherhood in Renaissance Florence.* New York: Academic Press, 1982.

Wirobisz, André. "L'attività edilizia a Venezia nel xiv e xv secolo." *Studi veneziani* 7 (1965): 307–43.

Wohl, Hellmut. *The Paintings of Domenico Veneziano, ca. 1410–1461: A Study in Florentine Art of the Early Renaissance.* New York: New York University Press, 1980.

Wolf, Eric R. "Kinship, Friendship, and Patron-Client Relations in Complex Societies." In *The Social Anthropology of Complex Societies,* edited by Michael Banton, 1–22. London: Tavistock Publications, 1966.

Wolters, Wolfgang. *La scultura veneziana gotica (1300–1460).* 2 vols. Venice: Alfieri, 1976.

Zago, Roberto. *I Nicolotti: Storia di una comunità di pescatori a Venezia nell'età moderna.* Padua: Francisci Editore, 1982.

Zordan, Giorgio. "I vari aspetti della comunione familiare di beni nella Venezia dei secoli xi–xii." *Studi veneziani* 8 (1966): 127–94.

Index

Alberghi, 120
Alexandria, 1
Arengo, 157
Arian, Antonio, 146–47
Arian, Marco, 37, 112–13
Arsenal, 13, 80
Arsenalotti, 150
Artisans: charitable contributions by, 81–82; distribution of guild sites, 80–81; hierarchy and stratification among, 156; parochial clergy, from artisan class, 93; popolo grande, 83–90, 181 n. 105; popolo minuto, 86–89; professional endogamy among, 77–78; residential distribution of, 78–81; social world of, 77–90; wills of, 57–58, 63, 81–82; women, from artisan class, in convents, 104, 185 n. 73; workplace distribution of, 78–81. *See also* Guilds
Augustinians, 104–6
Avogadori di comun, 88, 119–20, 140

Badoer family 41–45, 49, 115, 120–21
Bakers' guild, 79
Baptism, 96–97
Barbarigo, Andrea, 69, 197 n. 29
Barbaro, Francesco, 131, 134
Barbaro, Marco, 51
Barbers' guild, 73–74
Bedoloto family, 51–52, 126
Bell-founders' guild, 71, 75
Bellini, Gentile, 131
Belluno, 89
Benedictines, 13, 115
Bequests, 152–53, 196 n. 21; of artisans, 81–82; of patrician men, 138–39, 195 nn. 95–96; of patrician women, 135–39, 194 n. 87, 195 n. 96. *See also* Convents, endowments of; Monasteries, endowments of; Scuole, of guilds
Bernardino, Saint, 4
Black Death, 10–11, 36, 127, 153
Boatmen, 31, 35
Boccono, Marino, conspiracy of, 4
Bolladore, 70
Bologna, 86; household size in, 56
Bon, Nicolò, 99–101, 128–29, 144
Bonichi, Bindo, 179 n. 75
Boteghieri, 8
Botero, Giovanni, 6–7
Bridges, construction of, 17, 26
Brocha, Bartolomeo, 83–84, 126, 176 n. 24
Broglio, 130
Brown, Peter, 1
Building trades, 30, 67
Burial sites, 114–18

Ca' d'Oro, 30
Caldiera, Giovanni, 56
Canals, 6–7, 25–26
Candia, 129
Capi di contrate, 18–20
Capi di sestieri, 20
Capitulary Concerning the Bridges and Streets of Venice, 18
Capodistria, 124, 129
Carmelites, 104–5
Carpenters' guild, 71–72
Case nuove, 32, 166 n. 66
Case vecchie, 32, 166 n. 66
Castellani, 21
Castello, 14, 21

Catasto (of Florence), 32
Caulkers' guild, 71–72, 75, 80–81
Cessi, Roberto, 9
Chojnacki, Stanley, 8, 33, 49, 120, 134
Ciompi, 73
Cittadini, 7–8, 29, 32, 56, 145; hierarchy and stratification among, 156
Clergy, 29, 32; as social group, 91. See also Clergy, parochial; Convents; Monasteries; Scuole
Clergy, parochial: as investors, 101–2; legal functions of, 98–99; loans by, 99–100; location of, 93–94; as notaries, 98; number of, 165 n. 56; social backgrounds of, 91–95
Cobblers, 35; guild of, 20, 71, 75
Colleganze, 100–101
Commenda, 17
Community, ideal of, 2–4, 65–66, 90, 151–52
Compagnie delle calze, 155–56
Compari, 69
Consoli dei mercanti, 70, 73–74
Constantinople, 121
Contrata. See Parishes
Convents, 103–4, 106; endowments of, 104–6
Coopers' guild, 79
Cornaro, Flaminio, 91–92
Corner, Doge Marco, 155
Coron, 101, 125
Council, Ducal, 122, 155
Council, Great. See Great Council
Council of Forty: and appointments to office, 127–28; and grazie, 124, 129; and Marie, 48
Council of Ten, 9, 119–20, 140; and capi di contrate, 18; and capi di sestieri, 20; and compagnie delle calze, 156; and scuole, 107, 191 n. 43
Courtyards, 135, 193 n. 73
Cracco, Giorgio, 9
Crete, 10, 68
Custodes, 20

da Canal, Martino, 2, 65, 90, 157
Dalle Boccole family, 46–49, 148
da Mosto, Marco, 139
Dandolo, Doge Andrea, 32, 95, 141, 160 n. 9
Dandolo, Doge Giovanni, 2
Dante, 13
de Bernardo, Paolo, 146
de' Caresini, Raffaino, 32, 36
de' Freschi, Zaccaria, 8
Degani (of guilds), 69
Delort, Robert, 69
de Merlis, Felice, 39, 44, 93–94, 101, 127–29, 144
de Monacis, Lorenzo, 5
de Quarteriis, Marino, 119–20, 146
de' Ravagnani, Benintendi, 36, 51, 126
De re uxoria (Barbaro), 131, 134
Disenove family, 50–51
Doge: election of, 154, 157; and grazie, 123–24; power of, 16–17; restriction of power of, 123–24
Dominicans, 13, 104–5, 118
Doria family (of Genoa), 120
Dowries, 34–35, 77–78, 137
Drapers' guild, 70–75, 88
Duke. See Doge

Ecclesiae venetae antiquis monumentis (Cornaro), 91–92
Egypt, 13
Estimo (of 1379). See War of Chioggia, assessment in support of
Estoires de Venise, Les (da Canal), 2, 65
Eugenio IV, 156

Falier, Doge Marino, conspiracy of, 4–6, 122
Families: Badoer, 41–45, 49, 115, 120–21; Bedoloto, 51–52, 126; Dalle Boccole, 46–49, 148; Disenove, 50–51; Doria, 120; Ghisi, 42, 59; Gradenigo, 15–16; Michiel, 16; Orio, 15, 22; Participazi, 15; Peruzzi, 120; Regla, 52–54, 126, 144; Sagredo, 125
Family: in Florence, 155; among patricians, 41–50, 54–55, 59, 63–64, 120–22; among popolo grande, 50–56, 63; among popolo minuto, 56–64
Ferrara, 46, 61, 126
Ferry operators, 31
Finlay, Robert, 41
Florence, 6, 9–11; and Black Death, 36; concentration of industry in, 149;

family in, 155; gabella del vino in, 72; gonfalons in, 20, 130; guilds in, 8, 90, 182 n. 105; household size in, 56; marriage in, 57; neighborhoods in, 120-22, 130; patricians in, 45, 130
Fondaco dei Tedeschi, 13, 19, 26
Fondaco dei Turchi, 45, 122, 154
Food retailing, 67
Foscari, Doge Francesco, 11, 130-31, 157
Franciscans, 13, 104-5, 113, 118
Fraterna, 41-43
Funeral arrangements, 112-13
Funeral practices, 112-18
Fur industry, 67-69
Furriers' guilds, 5, 70, 79-80, 83-88
Furta sacra, 1
Fustagnarii, 69
Fustian guild, 71-72

Gafaro, Marco, 128-29
Garzoni, Bandino, 33, 36
Gastaldi (of guilds), 69-70, 73
Gemini, 14
Genoa, 6, 11, 126, 129; artisan districts in, 178 n. 69; marriage in, 57; neighborhoods in, 120-21
Gente nuova, 146
Ghezzo, Raffaele, 24
Ghisi family, 42, 59
Giudecca, 22, 79-80, 108
Giudici (of guilds), 69-70
Giudici del piovego, 2, 22-25
Giudici del proprio, 127-28
Giudici di petizion, 102
Giustiniani, Bernardo, 127
Giustizieri vecchi, 8, 66, 70-76, 148, 151
Glassmakers' guild, 71, 74, 79
Glassmaking, 67-69
Goldsmiths, 35; guild of, 88
Goldthwaite, Richard, 67
Gradenigo family, 15-16
Grado, 13
Grand chancellor, 29. See also de' Caresini, Raffaino; de' Ravagnani, Benintendi
Grave sites. See Burial sites
Grazie, 11, 123, 126-27, 130, 154; and patricians, 124-25, 127; and popolo grande, 126; and popolo minuto, 126, 128-29
Great Council: and appointment or election to office, 127-28; and capi di contrate, 18-19; and election of the doge, 157; and gastaldi (of guilds), 73; and giudici del piovego, 22, 25; and grazie, 124-27, 129; and Marie, 122-23; membership in, 28-29, 36, 155; and prohibition of armed retainers, 122; and public improvements, 26, 37-38; and public sanitation, 25-26; Serrata of the, 4, 10, 28, 38, 123, 155
Greece, 127
Guilds, 8; election procedures of, 73-75; in Florence, 90; number of, 165 n. 58; officers of, 69-70; organization of, as influenced by commodity production, 67-69; religious activities of, 65; scuole of, 65, 71, 80-82; solidarity within, 65-67, 71, 77-82; statutes of, 65; tensions within, 71-73, 76, 88-90
Guild sites, distribution of, 80-81

Heraclea, 14
Heresy, 5
Hierarchy, in Venetian society, 152, 155-57
Households, size of, in northern Italy, 56

Immigration, 73, 86, 153-54
Inquisitors (of drapers' guild), 70
Intermarriage, between patricians and popolo grande, 50-56, 88, 145
Istria, 125
Iuspatronatus, 15, 121, 162 n. 10

Jacketmakers' guild, 20, 71
Jesolo, 13
Jews, 99

Kinship networks. See Families; Family

Lane, Frederic, 7-8, 69, 155
Libro d'Argento, 156
Libro d'Oro, 28, 155-56

218 INDEX

Lido, 141, 146
Loans. See Clergy, parochial, loans by; Colleganze
Love feast (caritade), 4, 85, 143, 153
Lucca, 51, 197 n. 23
Luminaria, 71
Lunghi, 154
Luprio, 14
Luzzatto, Gino, 7, 33

Mackenney, Richard, 8
Mairano, Romano, 16
Malamocco, 14
Mallaza, Franco, 142, 147–48
Marie, festival of the, 19, 38, 48, 122–23, 152
Mark, Saint, 1–2, 12, 19
Marriage: in northern Italy, 57; among patricians, 40–42, 46, 49, 63–64; between patricians and popolo grande, 50–56, 88, 145; among popolo, 40; among popolo grande, 50, 63; among popolo minuto, 56, 59–64
Martines, Lauro, 7
Mazzorbo, 106
Medici, 11, 120, 155
Medici, Cosimo de', 72, 122
Merceria, 119–20
Michiel, Leonardo, 39–40
Michiel, Maddalena, 39–40
Michiel family, 16
Militia, 19, 122
Mocenigo, Doge Tommaso, 30, 157
Modon, 101, 125
Monasteries, 103, 106; endowments of, 104–6
Monte, 147–48
Monte di Pietà, 99
Monticolo, Giovanni, 8, 66, 76
Morosini, Doge Michele, 33, 154
Muir, Edward, 8
Murano, 13, 22, 30, 77, 79

Najemy, John, 9
Neighborhoods, 8, 120–23, 130; in northern Italy, 120; orientation away from, 152–53; women and, 131–39. See also Parishes
Networks, of patrician women, 133–38
Nicolotti, 20–21, 150

Nightwatch, Lords of the, 20, 28
Nobles. See Patricians
Notaries, 30, 98, 124, 127–28, 136, 142. See also de Merlis, Felice
Novi cives, 146

Olivolo. See Castello
Orders, religious. See Augustinians; Benedictines; Carmelites; Dominicans; Franciscans; Servites
Orio, Pietro, 15, 22
Orio, Tiso, 15, 22
Orio family, 15, 22

Padua, 11, 129, 143
Pantaleone, 113, 144; will of, 142–44, 146
Parin. See Patrinus
Parishes, 8, 18–19, 135; establishment of, 14–15. See also Neighborhoods
Participazi, Agnello, 15
Participazi family, 15
Paruta, Bartolomeo, 150–51
Patrician regime, attitudes toward, 141. See also Popolo grande, and patrician regime; Popolo minuto, and patrician regime
Patricians, 7–8, 28–29, 32, 36–37, 151–52; family among, 41–50, 54–55, 59, 63–64, 120–22; in Florence, 45; and grazie, 124–25, 127; hierarchy and stratification among, 155–56; intermarriage with popolo grande, 50–56, 88, 145; marriage among, 40–42, 46, 49, 63–64; men, 123–31; and neighborhoods, 120–23, 130; number of, 165 n. 55; parochial clergy, from patrician class, 92; and popolo, 8–10, 122; and popolo grande, 144–47; as procurators of parishes, 95–96; residences of, 120–21; and War of Chioggia, 154; wills of, 44–46, 48–49; women, 131, 133–40; women, from patrician class, in convents, 103–4. See also Case nuove; Case vecchie
Patriline. See Family, among patricians
Patrinus, 97–98
Patronage, 194 n. 89, 195 n. 100; of patrician men, 120, 123, 129–31, 140; of

patrician women, 120, 135–40. See also State patronage
Pepin, 14
Perleone, Pietro, 127
Peruzzi family (of Florence), 120
Petrarch, 4, 13, 95
Pietro Candiano III, 19
Pisa, 32; household size in, 56
Plebani. See Clergy, parochial
Popolani. See Popolo
Popolano grande. See Popolo grande
Popolano minuto. See Popolo minuto
Popolo, 4–5, 29–31, 67; marriage among, 40; occupational groups within, 30–31; and patricians, 8–10, 122
Popolo grande, 36–37, 167 n. 79; as artisans, 83–89; family among, 50–56, 63; and grazie, 126; hierarchy and stratification among, 156; intermarriage with patricians, 50–56, 88, 145; marriage among, 50, 63; parochial clergy, from popolo grande class, 93–95; and patrician regime, 144–47, 150–51; and patricians, 144–47; and popolo minuto, 10; as procurators of parishes, 96; and War of Chioggia, 154; women, from popolo grande class, in convents, 54–55, 103–4. See also Pantaleone
Popolo grasso, 167 n. 79
Popolo minuto, 4, 36–37; alienation of, 147–49; as artisans, 86–89; dispersal of, 148–49; family among, 56–64; and grazie, 126, 128–29; marriage among, 56, 59–64; parochial clergy, from popolo minuto class, 93; and patrician regime, 147–51; and popolo grande, 10; and War of Chioggia, 154; widowhood, attitudes toward, 62; wives of, 61–62. See also Malaza, Franco; Monte
Poveri del pevere, 128–29
Priuli, Girolamo, 155
Procurators: of drapers' guild, 70; of parish, 95–96; of San Marco, 21, 127, 130, 138
Prodi, Paolo, 102, 156–57
Provveditori di comun, 72–73
Pucci, Antonio, 40
Pullan, Brian, 7–8, 106

Querini, Elena, 24
Querini, Marco, conspiracy of, 4
Querini-Tiepolo conspiracy, 4, 6–7, 119, 121–22, 126

Rabia, Francesco, 88–89, 126
Ragusa, 195 n. 99
Rapp, Richard, 8
Regla family, 52–54, 126, 144
Relics, translations of, 1
Rialto, 19–20, 149; as center of male power, 119–20, 130–31, 140; as commercial center, 13, 21–22, 27, 38; market at, 16, 70, 78, 83; settlement of, 14; taverns at, 31, 87
Rivoalto. See Rialto
Rock crystal carvers' guild, 71
Rolandino of Padua, 4
Ropemakers' guild, 79
Rosso, Biancafiore, 39–40
Rosso, Nicoleto, 39–40
Ruga, 78
Ruggiero, Guido, 9
Russia, 13

Sagredo family, and grazie, 125
Salamon, Clara, 119–20
Salamon, Michele, 119
San Lazzaro, 143, 153
San Marco (basilica), 1–2
San Marco (piazza), 13–14, 19, 21, 26–27, 38, 149–50; as center of male power, 119–20, 130–31, 140; market at, 70, 80; taverns at, 87
Sanuto, Marino, 130
Sardinia, 124
Scuole, 5, 85–86, 103, 106, 112, 145; membership in, 107–11
Scuole, of guilds, 65, 71, 80–81; bequests to, 81–82
Scuole dei battuti, 106
Scuole grandi, 7–8, 107–9, 143–44; hierarchy and stratification in, 157
Scuole piccole, 109–12
Serrata. See Great Council, Serrata of the
Servants, 134–38. See also Wet nurses
Servites, 104–5
Sestieri, 19–20, 163 n. 26; distribution of scuole members by, 108–9

220 INDEX

Shipbuilding, 30, 67
Siena, 9, 11; and Black Death, 36; terzi in, 20
Signoria, 124
Signori di notte, 20, 88
Slaves, 31, 134–36, 138, 194 n. 90
Smiths' guild, 71, 75
Solicho, 115
Sovrastanti (of guilds), 69
Spinalunga, 14
State, orientation toward, 152–53. See also Patrician regime, attitudes toward; Popolo grande, and patrician regime; Popolo minuto, and patrician regime
State patronage: appointments to office, 127–28, 191 n. 43; grazie, 123–30
Steno, Doge Michele, 138, 195 n. 96
Stevano, Bertuccio, 5
Stonecutters' guild, 74
Stratification, in Venetian society, 28, 31–32, 37–38, 152, 155–58
Syria, 13

Tailoring, 67
Tailors' guild, 71
Tanners' guild, 79
Taverns, 31, 87, 126, 135
Tenenti, Alberto, 9
Terzi (in Siena), 20
Tiepolo, Baiamonte, 121; conspiracy of, 4
Tiepolo, Dogaressa Marchesina, 65, 121, 157
Tiepolo, Doge Lorenzo, 65, 121
Titian, 21
Tiziano (furrier), 84–85, 98, 104, 114, 181 n. 105
Tombs, 113
Torcello, 13, 49
Trevisan, Angelo, 119
Trevisan, Bartolomeo, 84–85
Treviso, 46, 62, 85, 115, 122
Tuscany, 36, 73, 153

Venice: administration of, 18–21; civic harmony in, 2, 4; conflict in, 4–6; description of, 12–13; distribution of wealth in, 32–36; economy of, 7; geography of, 6; household size in, 56; immigration to, 73, 86, 153–54; industrial organization of, 67–69; myth of, 4, 151; perception of, as city, 22–27; public improvements in, 26, 37–38; public sanitation in, 25–26; settlement of, 13–16; social groups in, 28–32, 36–38 (see also Artisans; Cittadini; Clergy; Patricians; Popolo; Popolo grande; Popolo minuto); specialization of districts within, 21–22; topography of, 6–7; twelfth- and thirteenth-century transformation of, 16–18
Venice, stability of: challenges to, 27; explanations for, 149–52; factors promoting, 139–40, 149–52; historical analysis of, 6–9
Venier, Doge Antonio, 133
Verona, 11; household size in, 56
Vicenza, 11
Villani, Giovanni, 12

War of Chioggia, 11, 19, 28, 128–29, 154–55; assessment in support of, 32–34
Waterbury, John, 149
Wet nurses, 134–36, 193 n. 70
Widowhood, attitudes toward, among popolo minuto, 62
Wills: of artisans, 57–58, 63, 81–82; of patricians, 44–46, 48–49; of popolo grande, 142–44, 146. See also Bequests; Convents, endowments of; Monasteries, endowments of
Wives, of popolo minuto, economic importance of, 61–62
Women, 31; and convents, 103–4; as officeholders in scuole, 112; patrician, relations among, 131–134; patrician, relations with popolano women, 134–38; in scuole, 109–10. See also Artisans; Bequests; Neighborhoods; Networks; Patricians; Patronage; Popolo grande; Popolo minuto; Widowhood; Wives
Wool industry, 30, 67, 69. See also Drapers' guild

Zane, Marco, 119
Ziani, Pietro, 16
Ziani, Sebastiano, 16
Zucchello, Pignol, 32, 36, 175 n. 11

Designed by Martha Farlow.
Composed by A. W. Bennett, Inc., in Trump Medieval.
Printed by the Maple Press Company on 50-lb. S. D. Warren's Sebago Eggshell Cream and bound in Joanna Kennett and James River Papan.